*King George VI*
*&*
*Queen Elizabeth*

# King George VI
## &
# Queen Elizabeth

## A PORTRAIT

by
### Christopher Warwick

**BEAUFORT BOOKS**
PUBLISHERS
NEW YORK

*For*
# Elizabeth Longford

**Library of Congress Cataloging in Publication Data**
Warwick, Christopher, 1949 –
King George VI and Queen Elizabeth.
Bibliography: p.
Includes Index.
1. George VI, King of Great Britain, 1895-1952.
2. Elizabeth, Queen, Consort of George VI, King of Great Britain, 1900-    . 3. Great Britain–Kings and Rulers–Biography.    4. Great Britain–Queens–Biography.
I. Title.
DA584.W37    1985    941.084'092'2    [B] 85-7436
ISBN 0-8253-0330-3

920    Published in the United States by
Beaufort Books Publishers, New York.

Originally published in Great Britain in 1985 by
Sidgwick & Jackson Limited

Printed in Great Britain    First American Edition

10   9   8   7   6   5   4   3   2   1

# Contents

# List of Plates

# Acknowledgments

In a book of this kind there are, inevitably, a large number of people to whom the author would like to extend his warmest and sincere thanks.

For assistance and encouragement in ways too diverse to specify, I have incurred many debts of gratitude, which I hope an acknowledgment here will help to discharge. Though in no particular order of precedence, I am very happy to offer my profound thanks to:

Theo Aronson, Dulcie M. Ashdown, the Earl and the Countess of Longford, the Lady Elizabeth Shakerley, Lady Donaldson, Laura Hayward, Robert Baldock, Valerie Garner, Hilary Close, Gwen Robyns, Wayne Swift, Hugo Vickers, James Lees-Milne, Michael Bloch, the Honourable Lady Mosley, Joanna Crawford, Violet F. Anderson, Carey Smith, Charlotte Balazs, Charles Bissett, Marlene Eilers and Herbert White.

My gratitude to several other people is no less deep, but they have each expressed a wish to remain known only to themselves and to me – a wish I must, of course, respect.

My agent Doreen Montgomery, and my good friend Brian Auld, counselled me wisely, especially when the end of my sometimes precarious work seemed nowhere in sight. I am particularly grateful to them for their patience and, indeed, understanding.

Finally I must thank Margaret Willes of Sidgwick & Jackson for asking me to write this book. I hope her confidence has been justified.

*Christopher Warwick*
*London, February 1985*

# A Sacred Trust

Lady Elizabeth Bowes Lyon was a most reluctant bride. Twice in two years Prince Albert, Duke of York, had proposed and twice he had been rejected. 'You'll be a lucky man if she accepts you,' his father King George V had said, but 'Bertie', as he was known to his family, pressed on undeterred. On 13 January 1923 he proposed again and Elizabeth Lyon, as she preferred to call herself, finally accepted.

In triumph the Prince cabled his mother at Sandringham House in Norfolk, 'All right. Bertie.' His economy of words, far from being a display of parsimony, was, in fact, a pre-arranged signal informing the King and Queen that at last his tenacity had paid off.

Two days later Prince Albert appeared at Sandringham in person. 'Bertie . . . arrived after tea and informed us that he was engaged to Elizabeth Bowes Lyon, to which we gladly gave our consent. . . .' George V noted in his diary that evening. 'We are delighted and he looks beaming,' confided Queen Mary to hers.

'You and papa were both so charming to me . . . about my engagement,' Bertie later wrote to the Queen. 'I am very very happy & I can only hope that Elizabeth feels the same as I do.'

Looking back over more than sixty years to a time when it still wasn't unknown for young women to put what was considered to be their duty before any real feelings of love, one might indeed wonder what Elizabeth Bowes Lyon's emotions were. Doubtless we shall never know. For, despite the longevity of her life, the future Queen Elizabeth – to the dismay of her family – has never at any time kept a diary. Nor are we ever likely to know what her innermost feelings were about marrying into so awe-inspiring a family.

To a girl of only twenty-two, whose own family had always gone out of its way to shun publicity, as well as the sometimes doubtful delights of 'high society', becoming a member of the royal family may not have been a thought that filled her with unreserved delight.

During the 1920s and 1930s the rules of royal protocol, far more stringent than they are today, were rigidly observed. Then as now the mystique of royal family life was jealously preserved by officers of the Household, some of whom appeared far grander and more autocratic than those they served, while a stiffly regimented army of servants, above as well as below stairs, helped keep the cogs and wheels of the monarchical machine ticking over with religious efficiency. Over all presided the formidable figures of George V and Queen Mary, supported by the King's mother, the seventy-nine-year-old Queen Alexandra, and a number of elderly princes and princesses, including the four surviving children of Queen Victoria.

It would not be unreasonable to assume, therefore, that while Elizabeth Bowes Lyon – though scarcely blind to her opportunities – finally yielded to Prince Albert's proposals, she did so without any precise notion of what would be expected of her once she had become Duchess of York.

In 1984, by which time very considerable, one might almost say revolutionary, changes had taken place within the royal family, Princess Michael of Kent – in conversation with the present author about her own life – commented, 'Everyone thinks that before you marry into the Family you know what you are doing and what you are getting into. There is *no* way that you know what it is going to be like.'

In January 1923 the future Duchess of York stood poised to embark on her own royal career when she and her parents, the Earl and Countess of Strathmore, arrived at Sandringham as guests of the King and Queen.

'Elizabeth is charming, so pretty & engaging & natural,' Queen Mary enthused. 'She is a pretty and charming girl,' echoed the King. 'Bertie is a lucky fellow.'

'Now know ye that we have consented . . . to the contracting of Matrimony between His Royal Highness Albert Frederick Arthur George, Duke of York, and the Lady Elizabeth Angela Marguerite Bowes Lyon, youngest daughter of the Right Honourable Claude George, Earl of Strathmore and Kinghorne.' So ran the King's proclamation at a meeting of his Privy Council, convened at Buckingham Palace to give formal approval to his son's marriage.

By the time the Sovereign's official assent had been given, it was already February and much of the royal programme of engagements for 1923 (including the state visit the King and Queen were to make to Italy that May) had been planned. Nevertheless a suitable date for the wedding of the King's second son had to be found and Thursday 26 April was soon decided upon as the most convenient for all concerned.

In the meantime the traditional tokens of betrothal had been given and received. The Duke of York gave his bride a sapphire ring, together with a necklace of diamonds and pearls, and in return Lady Elizabeth gave the Duke a dress watch-chain of platinum and pearls. Jointly the King and Queen gave the bride-to-be an ermine cape, while the Queen, of her own volition, dipped into her not inconsiderable collection of jewels, to select a few accessories befitting a royal duchess in the making. Thus Queen Mary garlanded Elizabeth Lyon with a tiara, a necklace and some hair ornaments of diamonds and pale Persian turquoises, a pendant of sapphires and diamonds, and a fan of old lace set on a mother-of-pearl frame. From the Countess of Strathmore the Duke of York received an especially fine miniature of her daughter, surrounded by diamonds and set in a leather and velvet case. This likeness of his bride was destined to preside over the Duke's desk until the day he died.

On a far wider scale, gifts, from the most opulent to the most humble, began to arrive in London almost from the moment the couple's betrothal was announced. They came not just from within the United Kingdom but, or so it seemed, from even the remotest reaches of the then British Empire. Unlike today, none but the privileged was given the opportunity of inspecting the wedding gifts sent to the Duke of York. Even then some who were fortunate enough to gaze upon the royal treasures were decidedly unimpressed.

H.H. Asquith (later 1st Earl of Oxford and Asquith) wrote:

I went in my knee breeches and medals after dinner to Buckingham Palace, where the rooms big as they are were very nearly crowded. There were huge glass cases like you see in the Bond St. shops, filled with jewels and every kind of gilt and silver ware: not a thing did I see that I would have cared to have or give. The poor little bride, everyone says, is full of charm and stood in a row with the King and Queen and the bridegroom, and was completely overshadowed.

If, to Mr Asquith, Elizabeth Bowes Lyon seemed not to have got off to an especially propitious start, the man-in-the-street and his wife were already enchanted. Some remembered Lady Elizabeth as a bridesmaid at the wedding, twelve months before, of the King's only daughter Princess Mary; others anticipated taking the bride of 1923 to their hearts in much the same spirit as they received Lady Diana Spencer half a century later.

What pleased the nation most was that Elizabeth Bowes Lyon was *British*. Not for centuries had a prince taken a British bride: Queen Mary had had a German father, Prince Francis, 1st Duke of Teck, and a half-English mother, Princess Mary Adelaide, daughter of Adolphus, Duke of Cambridge (seventh son of King George III) and Augusta, Princess of Hesse. Queen Alexandra had a Danish father, Christian of Schleswig-Holstein-Sonderburg-Glücksburg, afterwards King Christian IX of Denmark, and a German mother, Louise of Hesse-Cassel. Queen Victoria's mother had been Victoria of Saxe-Coburg-Saalfeld, Dowager Princess of Saxe-Leiningen, while her father's thoroughly English title, Prince Edward, Duke of Kent, belied his thoroughly German descent.

To find so much as a drop of foreign blood in Elizabeth Bowes Lyon's veins was to look back to the seventeenth century and her great-great-great-great-great-grandfather, Hans William Bentinck of The Netherlands, who, as Groom of the Stole to the Prince of Orange, later King William III, came to Britain in 1677 when the Prince married Mary, elder surviving daughter of James II.

A royal marriage may, according to the Victorian constitutional expert Walter Bagehot, 'rivet mankind', but the twentieth century has become much more riveted by such events. Victorian royal

4

bridal couples could never have found themselves central to the same kind of excessive interest that has grown up around royal weddings today.

Curiosity about Elizabeth Bowes Lyon resulted in the publication of almost every kind of detail likely to be of interest. For one shilling and sixpence (the equivalent of 7½ new pence), for example, *Vogue* magazine provided sketches of selected outfits from the bride's trousseau: hats from Zyrot et Cie, and day and evening wear from the salons of such designers as Jay, and W. Ujhely. There were, among other items, a 'long-line' jacket in white kid, and another in green flannel covered with 'Egyptian motifs' in black and silver. There was 'a charming country hat of straw, of which the cloche brim and the cockade of grey and green ribbon are bound with silver galon', teamed with 'a waistcoat blouse of yellow crêpe de Chine'. But most sumptuous of all was an evening cloak 'of tail-less ermine with corner panels of white broche let into it and further adorned by flowers made of the ermine . . .'.

Twenties' decorum, however, presumably precluded any mention of the camiknickers, slips, bed jackets and 'boudoir caps', all of 'hand embroidered pink georgette', that were supplied by Blanche d'Luzy. Forgotten names linked, in one way or another, with a half-forgotten event, but an event which ultimately proved to be the Crown's salvation in the years to come.

The marriage of the Duke of York and the Lady Elizabeth Bowes Lyon was solemnly celebrated at Westminster Abbey on 26 April, a spring morning not unlike a thousand spring mornings before and since. Rain had fallen steadily for most of the previous night and threatened to continue throughout the day of the royal wedding itself, disrupting completion of the street decorations which had to remain unfinished right up to the last possible moment.

For nearly four hours the Abbey bells had pealed out over Westminster. Huge crowds of onlookers, most of whom had begun to assemble outside Westminster Abbey, Buckingham Palace and along the processional route from the early hours, closely scrutinized the steady flow of cars and carriages bearing the wedding guests. Among the more immediately recognizable 'celebrities' were the Prime Minister, Bonar Law, Lloyd George,

Winston Churchill, Lady Diana Cooper, Mr and Mrs H.H. Asquith, Ramsay MacDonald, the Duchess of Rutland, and the Marchioness of Lansdowne, whose dress of 'pearl-grey embroidered with cut steel' and studded with the badges of five royal Orders and the riband – or sash – of yet another, won a special mention in *The Times* the following day.

Immediately preceding the arrival of the royal family came the bride's mother, the Countess of Strathmore, dressed in a long gown and cloak of black morocain and georgette, sprinkled with sequins and decorated with a collar of blue roses; a strange choice of colour for a wedding, but one that was no less dramatic in effect. Accompanying the Countess as she walked up the long blue-carpeted nave to her seat in the sacrarium, were members of her family, her kinsman the Duke of Portland, her daughter Lady Elphinstone, dressed in dove grey, and her daughter-in-law Lady Glamis, described by the *Illustrated London News* as wearing an outfit of 'almost liquid-looking silver'.

The arrival of the royal bridegroom, wearing the ceremonial uniform of a Group Captain of the RAF, closely followed that of members of his own family. Led by his sister Mary, in cream-lace and satin, the first royal procession was made up of individual royal family groups such as the Fifes and Argylls, Connaughts and Mountbattens. Then came the Duke's grandmother Queen Alexandra, clad in violet and gold, with her spinster daughter Princess Victoria. Finally there came the King and Queen Mary, His Majesty wearing the uniform of an Admiral of the Fleet, the Queen dressed in aquamarine and silver.

Moments later the eight bridesmaids, all dressed in white georgette and Nottingham lace, sashed with green tulle, arrived, and stood unobtrusively under the exterior awning to await the young bride. Occasionally looking into the church with its awe-inspiring congregation were Elizabeth's nieces, the young Cecilia Bowes Lyon and Elizabeth Elphinstone, who were to act as train-bearers. The adult attendants were all personal friends: Lady Mary Cambridge, later Duchess of Beaufort; Lady May Cambridge, daughter of Princess Alice and the Earl of Athlone; Lady Mary Thynne; Lady Katharine Hamilton (later Seymour) who was to become one of the bride's ladies-in-waiting; Miss Betty Cator who was shortly to marry the Honourable Michael Bowes Lyon, and the Honourable Diamond Hardinge.

With the Collegiate Church of St Peter in Westminster, as the Abbey is properly known, filled with the couple's relations and friends, politicians, members of the diplomatic corps, peers of the realm, and the near rent-a-crowd mêlée of innumerable unknown faces, the scene was set for the entrance of Lady Elizabeth Bowes Lyon.

According to King George V, 'It stopped raining at about 9.30 & the sun actually came out as the Bride entered the Abbey.' For a moment, while the strains of a fanfare heralding her arrival rang through the church, Lady Elizabeth stood with her father framed by the massive arch of the great west door. She was dressed in a simple short-sleeved, drop-waisted gown of ivory silk-crêpe banded with silver lamé, pearls and irridescent white beads – the work of Madame Handley-Seymour of New Bond Street – and, from a barely discernible chaplet of leaves, roses and sprigs of orange blossom, fell a veil of old *point de Flandres* lace, lent by Queen Mary.

Seconds before she started on her long walk to the high altar – the choir performing the processional hymn, 'Lead Us Heavenly Father, Lead Us' – Lady Elizabeth, presumably on impulse, stepped forward and laid her all-white bouquet of roses and heather on the Tomb of the Unknown Warrior, set in to the floor of the nave and dedicated little more than two years earlier, in November 1920.

At the steps of the sacrarium waited the Duke of York together with two of his brothers as his supporters, Edward, Prince of Wales (the future King Edward VIII, later Duke of Windsor, who was known to his family as 'David', the last of his seven Christian names) and Prince Henry (known as 'Harry', afterwards Duke of Gloucester).

The Archbishop of Canterbury, the Most Reverend Randall Davidson, Primate of All England, conducted the service, and the Archbishop of York (Dr Cosmo Gordon Lang, who in turn would be elected to the See of Canterbury) gave an address. In the course of it he told the bridal couple:

You have received from Him . . . a new life wherein your separate lives are now, till death, made one. With all our hearts we wish that it may be a happy one. But you cannot resolve that it shall be happy. You can and will resolve that it shall be noble. . . .

7

Will you take and keep this gift of wedded life as a sacred trust? Sacred it must be, for your love and God's love are within it. . . . You will have a great ambition to make this one life now given to you something rich, true and beautiful.

At the conclusion of the ceremony, which had not been broadcast to the nation, lest people should be listening in public houses or wearing hats, the Duke of York led his bride from the chapel of St Edward the Confessor – where they had signed the marriage registers – down the nave and out to the waiting Glass Coach in which, by newly established tradition, all royal brides were, if practicable, to travel in state on their wedding days. The couple's departure was closely followed by that of their imposing number of royal guests. Among the most important of them, and worthy of a distinctly separate note, was the Dowager Empress Marie Feodorovna of Russia. Younger sister of Queen Alexandra, the Dowager Empress was the mother of the last Russian Tsar, Nicholas II, who – or so history alleges – was murdered by the Bolsheviks, along with his wife and children, at Ekaterinburg in July 1918. Convinced to the day she herself died that her son and his family had not perished, Marie Feodorovna (or 'Minnie', as she was more intimately known) joined the British royal family in warmly congratulating her great-nephew and his bride when, via a circuitous processional route, they finally arrived at Buckingham Palace.

Of the bride's refreshingly informal demeanour – or, perhaps more to the point, because of it – one euphoric news item chirped:

She drove to the Abbey in the simplest possible manner. On her return all was changed. From a commoner she became as if by magic the fourth lady in the land, and she returned to the same spot which she had passed with such little ostentation an hour before, in the gorgeous . . . scarlet and gold coach and with an imposing escort of [the Household] Cavalry. The large crowds cheered them heartily. . . .

Early that afternoon 123 guests, more than 60 of them close relations of the bridal couple, sat down at circular tables, each decorated with pink and white tulips and lilac, to a magnificent eight-course wedding breakfast. On the menu were such specialities as *Consommé à la Windsor, Suprême de saumon Reine Mary, Côtelettes d'agneau Prince Albert, Chapons à la Strathmore, Salade Royale,* and *Fraises, Duchesse Elizabeth.* A little later the Duke and Duchess of York adjourned to the Green Drawing-Room to cut into their wedding cake. Decorated with the couple's armorial bearings, it stood nine feet tall and weighed 800 pounds. Then it was time for the guests to arm themselves with rose petal confetti in readiness for the departure of the bride and bridegroom.

From Buckingham Palace the Duke of York and his wife, soon popularly to be called 'the smiling Duchess', travelled in an open landau to Waterloo station, from where they entrained for Surrey and the home of the Honourable Mrs Ronald Greville.

A flamboyant society hostess of the Edwardian genre, not averse to singing her own praises, Maggie Greville (of whom 'Chips' Channon had written, 'There is no one on earth quite so skilfully malicious . . .') had delighted in putting her secluded and beautiful mansion, Polesden Lacey, at the disposal of the Duke and Duchess for the first two weeks of their honeymoon.

Amid all the pomp, pageantry, solemn rhetoric and high theatre of the royal wedding, the editor of *The Times,* naturally unaware of the significance of the event the nation had just witnessed, was of the opinion that there was one royal marriage to which the nation looked forward with still deeper interest. A marriage, he went on, that would give 'a wife to the Heir to the Throne and, in the course of nature, a future Queen to England and the British peoples'. How unobtrusively nature makes her plans.

From Polesden Lacey, the Duke and Duchess of York travelled north to Scotland, to spend twelve days at Glamis, the ancestral seat of the bride's family. It was there that the Duchess contracted whooping cough: 'So unromantic on your honeymoon,' as the Duke wrote home to Queen Mary.

Returning south once again on 19 May 1923, the couple concluded their honeymoon at Frogmore House, an elegant cream-painted mansion close to Windsor Castle. Once the retreat of Queen Charlotte, Consort of George III, and later the country home of Queen Victoria's mother, the house quietly dominates part of the private park known as Frogmore. The location is, however, more immediately associated with the two mausoleums enclosed within its boundaries. The larger of these, screening the

9

royal family's private burial ground, houses the remains of Queen Victoria and Albert, the Prince Consort, while the smaller contains the remains of Queen Victoria's mother, Victoria Mary, Duchess of Kent.

To have been absorbed into the royal family, particularly as it stood during the first thirty years or so of this century, must for Elizabeth Bowes Lyon have been like becoming partial custodian of an ancient feudal relic; not quite part of the real world, but still an indispensable focus for national emotions. Indeed, until she and her husband established for themselves a quiet niche of their very own, to which they could retreat in comparative privacy, the Duchess of York must surely have been reminded, at every turn, of the cloying traditions, customs and history of the ideals which surrounded her.

Before moving further, therefore, let us pause at this point to consider the two distinctly separate worlds into which the Duke of York and his Duchess were born.

## 2

# *Victorian Sunset*

At the time of the future King George VI's birth in 1895 his great-grandmother Queen Victoria had occupied the throne of Great Britain for fifty-eight years and that of India, the 'brightest jewel' in her Crown, since she was proclaimed Empress nearly twenty years earlier, in 1876.

The venerable Queen's heir, Albert Edward, by now aged fifty-four, had as Prince of Wales been king-in-waiting for longer than it pleased him to recall. 'It is one thing to pray to an Eternal Father,' he once remarked after attending church, 'but quite another to have an eternal mother.' His second and only surviving son was Prince George, Duke of York, who, upon the death in 1892 of his elder brother, Albert Victor, Duke of Clarence and Avondale, a young man of highly dubious character, had assumed the mantle of Heir Presumptive to his father's eventual inheritance.

On 6 July 1893, in the Chapel Royal, St James's Palace, 'Georgie' (as his mother, Alexandra, always called him) was married to his late brother's fiancée Victoria Mary of Teck, or Princess May as she was invariably known. Within the year the shy and reserved Princess had given her husband his first son and almost immediately was able to announce that a second child was on the way.

So it was that, on Saturday, 14 December 1895, at York Cottage on the Sandringham estate, an inadequate Victorian house with small, stuffy rooms, pervaded at meal times by the smell of cooking, and heavily laden with modern Maples furniture, the young Duchess of York gave birth to her second son, for whom the names Albert Frederick Arthur George were duly chosen.

Reaction to the birth of this second prince of York, however, could not have contrasted more sharply with that demonstrated eighteen months earlier, in June 1894, at the birth of his elder brother Prince Edward. On the former occasion, news of his first grandson's birth was received by the Prince of Wales during an Ascot-week ball he was hosting in the Fishing Temple, a royal folly on the edge of Virginia Water in Windsor Great Park. Stopping the music, the Prince joyfully announced to his guests, 'It is with the greatest pleasure that I am able to inform you of the birth of a son to the Duke and Duchess of York. I propose a toast to the young Prince.'

At Windsor Castle, a few miles away on the far side of the Great Park, Queen Victoria was no less delighted. Writing to her daughter Vicky, the widowed Empress Frederick of Germany, she declared, '. . . it seems that it has never happened in this Country that there shd. be three direct Heirs as well as the Sovereign alive'.

But in the winter of 1895 all was contrition. Family jubilation at the latest Prince's birth was nervously yet quite deliberately restrained, and for what appeared to be very good reason. The problem balanced purely on a point of bad timing. The fourteenth of December marked the death of the Queen's beloved Consort, Albert of Saxe-Coburg-Gotha in 1861, and, coincidentally, the tragic demise from diphtheria of their second daughter Alice, Grand Duchess of Hesse, in 1878. The fourteenth was therefore regarded as sacrosanct. It was the one specific day in the year on which Queen Victoria reverently mourned her dead, and expected the rest of the family – whether they had known the Prince Consort or not was academic – to do likewise. Victorian mourning was a very serious business.

Amid all the anxiety and the stream of messages apologizing for so unforgivable an intrusion upon the Queen's hour of supreme self-indulgence, there were the inevitable patriotic, even vaguely conciliatory, stirrings in the Press. The *Globe*, for example, ventured the opinion that the birth of a second son to the Duke and Duchess of York would 'be of significance as insuring to all appearances for many years to come the devolution of the Crown in the male line . . .'. The editorial went on, 'Henceforth it is permissible to hope that the august lady, in whose joys and sorrows the nation claims a right to share, may find in the felicitous event of December 14, 1895, a solace for the mournful memories of December 14, 1861, and December 14, 1878.'

In fact, the 'august lady' herself was not as much put out as her trembling family had reason to fear.

'I have a feeling it may be a blessing for the dear little boy and may be looked upon as a gift from God,' the Queen noted in her journal.

From the pompous and ultra-stiff court of the Kaiser at Berlin, the Empress Frederick wrote to her mother expressing similar thoughts. She exclaimed:

> I cannot say how much I rejoice! On the one hand I thought it rather to be regretted that the dear little Baby was born on a day of such inexpressibly sad memories to us, – but on the other – it is a gift from Heaven and a very precious one, – and there is something touching in the thought – that on this *darkest* day in your Life a ray of sunshine is sent in after years! and I like to look at it in this light!

Though she certainly accepted the Empress's 'ray of sunshine' (or more precisely, that unwittingly proffered by the Duchess of York) with equanimity, it is quite possible that Queen Victoria savoured to the full her family's discomfort with mild amusement. Nevertheless, proving herself truly magnanimous towards her latest great-grandson – and thus reassuring his 'erring' parents – the Queen exclaimed that she was, 'all impatience to see the *new* one'. She gladly accepted the Yorks' invitation to act as his godmother, naturally approved that he 'shd. have the dear name of *Albert* . . . which is the byeword for all that is great & good', and – gift of all gifts – she presented the infant with a bust of the Prince Consort!

Between the years 1894 and 1905 the Duchess of York bore her husband six children. The third child was the daughter the Duke had expressed a hope for during his wife's second pregnancy. Born in 1897, the year in which Queen Victoria celebrated her Diamond Jubilee, the Princess – like her elder brother – made her appearance at York Cottage. And like the young Prince Albert who had been named to gratify his great-grandmother, the little

Princess was diplomatically baptised 'Victoria' in tribute to the Queen.

As frequently happened in the royal family, however, neither child was known by its first name. Prince Albert was referred to by his family simply as 'Bertie', even after he had ascended the throne and had chosen to be known officially as George VI. His sister who in the fullness of time, was created Princess Royal, was always known as 'Mary', the last of her forenames.

Three more sons were to complete the York family group. Prince Henry was born in 1900, Prince George (later Duke of Kent) in 1902, and Prince John (an epileptic who, for the most part, spent his brief life of only fourteen years segregated from his family) was born in 1905.

Of these three Princes the Queen herself was only to meet – and indeed to have herself photographed with – the infant Prince Henry. Ten months after his birth, in the eighty-second year 'of her age' and the sixty-fourth year of her reign, Queen Victoria died peacefully at Osborne House on the Isle of Wight. On that day, 22 January 1901, Albert Edward, Prince of Wales, finally succeeded as King Edward VII. The Duke of York, soon to be created Prince of Wales in his father's stead, was now Heir Apparent, and his two eldest sons took one step closer to the throne that each in turn would occupy.

It was, of course, inconceivable for any but the very youngest of Queen Victoria's subjects to have remained oblivious to her passing. At home few had known any other sovereign. In 1837 at the age of eighteen, Princess Alexandrina Victoria of Kent had succeeded to the throne on the death of her uncle William IV, who had reigned for seven years as successor to his spectacular brother George IV, perhaps better known as the Prince Regent. Queen Victoria had gone on to preside – at least technically – over the powerful empire-building era that had adopted her name and, even during her own lifetime, had become a legend. The mother of nine children, eight of whom had married foreign princes and princesses, she was regarded as the 'Grandmother of Europe', a laudatory appellation bestowed on her by royal historians.

In even the most distant parts of the Empire, Queen Victoria represented very much more than a mere figurehead. To some she was the beneficent 'Great White Queen'; others saw her as a larger-than-life mother-figure. In Britain, attempts to rally support for the cause of republicanism during the latter half of the Queen's reign ultimately failed. Though she had, by this time, become a shadowy, reclusive figure, known as 'the Widow of Windsor' after Rudyard Kipling's poem, she nevertheless continued to command a kind of blind devotion among her subjects, hundreds of thousands of whom had never even seen her.

There was, however, among the youngest of the Queen's subjects one who was not only destined to join the ranks of the royal family, but who would one day by general consent find herself celebrated as the single most popular Queen Consort in British history. Born on 4 August 1900 the Honourable Elizabeth Bowes Lyon, ninth child and youngest daughter of the then Lord and Lady Glamis, was little more than five months old when Queen Victoria died.

Not until 1904 did the 'Hon' Elizabeth become the 'Lady' Elizabeth – an inconsequential fact that is all too easy to forget or overlook. Her elevation in status occurred when her father, the 22nd Lord Glamis, succeeded to the earldom of Strathmore and Kinghorne. As 14th Earl, Claude Bowes Lyon became head of one of Scotland's most ancient and aristocratic families. Its colourful and sometimes bloody history stretched back some six centuries to the time of independent Scotland's King Robert II (1316-90) who, because of his blood-shot eyes, became known as 'King Blearie'. It was through this quaintly nicknamed monarch that the Lyon family (the present surname 'Bowes Lyon' was not adopted until the nineteenth century) came into possession of the ancient royal lands of Glamis, lying between the Grampian mountains to the north and the Sidlaw Hills in the county of Angus. The family's ancestral seat was thus founded in 1376 when Sir John Lyon, Lord Chamberlain to Robert II, married the King's daughter Jean.

Glamis Castle itself has been described as 'everything a castle should be: many towers and battlements . . . several blood-curdling ghost stories, a secret room . . .' and has attracted numerous legends. William Shakespeare, who set his gruesome drama *Macbeth* at Glamis, wrote rather more romantically, 'This castle hath a pleasant seat; the air Nimbly and sweetly recommends itself Unto our gentle senses.' Two hundred years later, the 'senses' of Sir Walter Scott were less gently aroused when he stayed the night as a guest at the castle. 'After a very hospitable reception,' he noted in 1793, 'I was conducted to my apartments in a distant part of the building. I must own that when I heard door after door shut, after my conductor had retired, I began to consider myself too far from the living, and somewhat too near the dead.'

When the present 11th Duke of Grafton's grandmother, Constance Adeane, visited Glamis in 1861, she discovered a 'vast gloomy mass of building, with a still gloomier interior'. When she returned, almost fifty years later, the exterior looked much the same as before, but the atmosphere within had changed considerably. This was due entirely to the 14th Earl of Strathmore's wife, who had transformed the interior – in every sense – into a proper family home.

A warm-hearted, devout, down-to-earth woman of noble English birth, the Countess of Strathmore had little time for the excesses of high society and, despite her family connections, never aspired to social greatness. Through her late father, the Reverend Charles Cavendish-Bentinck, Lady Strathmore was a descendant of Robert Harley, Earl of Oxford, Lord High Treasurer to Queen Anne; of the 3rd Duke of Portland (who had twice held office as Prime Minister, first in 1783 and again in 1807-9); and of the 4th Duke of Devonshire.

Given away by her cousin, the 6th Duke of Portland, Nina Cecilia Cavendish-Bentinck was eighteen when she married the twenty-six-year-old Lord Glamis at Petersham in Surrey on 16 July 1881. The first of their ten children, a daughter – Violet Hyacinth (who was to die of diphtheria at the age of eleven) – was born the following year. A second daughter, Mary Frances, who was to marry the 16th Lord Elphinstone, was born in 1883, and a son, Patrick, who became the 15th Earl of Strathmore, was born in 1884.

Before the nineteenth century came to a close, Lady Strathmore had borne five more children: John Herbert (1886), Alexander Francis (1887), Fergus (1889), Rose Constance, who married the 4th Earl Granville (1890), and Michael Claude (1893).

Large families were not, of course, remotely unusual at any level during the Victorian and Edwardian eras. Yet, having provided her husband with eight children during the first eleven years of their marriage, Lady Strathmore perhaps welcomed the period between 1893 and 1900 in which she was free of all the paraphernalia of childbirth.

In an allusion to the biblical story of Joseph's favourite brother, the Countess of Strathmore was to refer to the last of her children as her 'two Benjamins'. Elizabeth, as we know, was born in August 1900 and her brother David in May 1902. It is, naturally, the birth of Elizabeth Bowes Lyon that concerns us here, not simply because her advent is of paramount significance to the pattern of modern royal history, but because of a mystery surrounding the precise location of her birth.

Until 1980, the year in which she celebrated her eightieth birthday, it had been generally accepted that the Strathmores' youngest daughter and penultimate sibling had been born at the family's Hertfordshire home, St Paul's Walden Bury. Indeed, to that effect a commemorative plaque was unveiled in the village church by the protagonist herself. Thus was perpetuated what might justifiably be called a 'royal myth', for the future Queen Elizabeth was, in fact, born in London. That neither she nor her advisers are prepared to say *where* in London; that contemporary history had, for so long, been quietly misled; that Queen Elizabeth herself approved the erroneous claim engraved on the church tablet, gives rise to many unanswered questions.

One theory put forward was that Lady Strathmore, then still Lady Glamis, gave birth to her daughter in the back of a London ambulance. Let's consider this possibility. Even though the London Ambulance Service as we know it today had yet to be founded, there were ambulances on the streets of the metropolis in 1900. The first such service had been formed in 1878 by the civil nursing body, St John of Jerusalem, followed in March 1889 by the establishment of the Bischoffsheim Ambulance Service, the brainchild of a certain Mr Thomas Ryan, Secretary of St Mary's Hospital in Paddington – a hospital which, coincidentally, has significant links with the present royal family. Among several other royal offspring, it was the birthplace of both Prince William and Prince Henry of Wales.

In the absence of more reliable information is it not just possible that an ambulance was summoned on that August day long ago, to transport Lady Glamis to St Mary's? Though hypothetical, the idea is not beyond the realm of feasibility. For the time being, however, we must simply accept the now-established fact that the future Queen Mother was born in London . . . precise whereabouts unknown.

Although divested of the signal distinction of having had a future queen born within its walls, St Paul's Walden Bury was nevertheless an especially favourite home of the young Elizabeth Bowes Lyon. There are those, including members of the Lyon family, who believe it ranks even higher in her affections than Glamis itself. 'The dear, friendly old house,' Queen Elizabeth has said of 'The Bury', as family and local people alike call it, 'we all loved it dearly.'

Built around 1730 of warm red brick, St Paul's Walden Bury is an exceptionally handsome, three-storey Georgian mansion, made yet more appealing by its formal garden. Laid out in the French style, it is reputedly the work of the 'Sun King' Louis XIV's 'gardener', the celebrated landscape artist Jean Le Nôtre.

The estate came into Strathmore possession through the Bowes family who, in turn, had inherited it from one of Lady Elizabeth's Hertfordshire forebears, Edward Gilbert. He and his wife had only one child, Mary, who married George Bowes, a wealthy Member of Parliament and the owner of Streatlam Castle in County Durham. Their daughter, Mary Eleanor, married John Lyon, 9th Earl of Strathmore in February 1767, and in due course St Paul's Walden became her inheritance.

Walden, mentioned in the Domesday Book, has a long history. For some time it had been known as Abbot's Walden and belonged to the suppressed St Albans Abbey, until King Henry VIII granted the parish to the Dean and Chapter of St Paul's Cathedral, whence the name of St Paul's was duly added.

Something of the joy Lady Elizabeth knew during the first fourteen years of her life spent at Walden can be gleaned from her own memories of childhood. Although often quoted, her words and the air of contentment they exude withstand the test of reiteration. In the third person she wrote, at the request of a friend:

At the bottom of the garden is The Wood – the haunt of fairies, with its anenomes and ponds and moss-grown statues, and the big oak under which she reads and where the two ring-doves contentedly coo in their wicker-work 'Ideal Home'. There are carpets of primroses to sit on and her small brother David is always with her. . . . Now it is time to go haymaking, which means getting very hot in a delicious smell. Very often she gets up wonderfully early – about six o'clock – to feed her chickens and make sure they are safe after the dangers of the night. . . .

Besides hens there are bantams, whose eggs-for-tea are so good.

Later still, Lady Elizabeth recalled yet more delights, 'a friendly still room', and 'the attic of a tumbledown brewhouse to play truant in'. In this hide-away, which was called 'The Flea House', and where there were to be found any number of kittens, the child Elizabeth and her brother David – her inseparable companion – hid from their nurse or laid in stores, all quite safe since the only means of access was by way of a rotting wooden staircase, which could support a child but not the weight of an adult.

At St Paul's Walden Bury, Lady Elizabeth went on, were all the things that children could desire, 'dogs and tortoises, Persian kittens and 'Bobs' the Shetland pony [who would follow his young mistress in and out of the house, even up and down stairs], bullfinches to tame, fields to roam, flowers to love, ripe apples to drop . . . and on wet days the books that are best read on the floor in front of the fire. . . .' There were family picnics too, by the statues of Diana or the Discus Thrower (nicknamed by the children 'The Bounding Butler'). What she might have added to this idyllic, enviably simple picture of Edwardian youth was a vignette or two not simply about the love of her parents, but of their presence.

In the upper echelons of society, family life tended to follow a rigidly distinct pattern of behaviour and ritual, a pattern in which children were normally 'presented' to their parents at a specified time of day, frequently during the early evening. Dressed up for the occasion, upper-class progeny would spend perhaps an hour in their parents' company before they were returned to their nurseries and the control of their nannies. The Strathmore household did not operate in such a fashion. No unquestioned distance existed between the Earl and Countess and their sons and daughters, and in this respect it might be said that Lord and Lady Strathmore were streets ahead of their time.

The Earl himself may have been a quiet, somewhat reserved man, and of his kind uncharacteristically modest, but he was always an attentive, affectionate – and to his youngest, an indulgent – parent. It was true that he liked the convivial society of his contemporaries, but at heart he was a country-loving squire. When in Scotland he was happy enough watching the Forfar football team play on a Saturday afternoon. He enjoyed his daily hour of exercise chopping wood and took satisfaction in visiting his farms or settling down to his civic and business commitments. A judicious magistrate, he was always the most sympathetic of men, and as a Lord-Lieutenant (of Forfarshire, an office to which he was appointed shortly after he succeeded to his father's title), none undertook the attendant responsibilities more dutifully.

The Countess of Strathmore's, on the other hand, was a much more ebullient, out-going personality. A woman of distinguished mind and character, freer by far than many of her contemporaries, she exerted the direct yet persuasive kind of authority that would, before long, become clearly recognizable in her youngest daughter. Within the family she wielded a kindly but nevertheless dominant influence. Never bossy nor remotely bombastic, her strength lay in her supremely unruffled approach to her obligations and, indeed, to life generally. 'I never heard her say a harsh word, but we had to obey her,' recalled her second daughter, Lady Elphinstone.

Governesses inevitably featured in the early lives of the Bowes Lyon children but, particularly where her daughters were concerned, Lady Strathmore took care of what she considered to be their educational requirements herself. Well-read, artistically and musically talented, possessing a knowledge from her own 'schooldays' of French and Latin, together with some German and Italian, Cecilia Strathmore taught all her children to read, instructed them in the Bible and, so far as her 'two Benjamins' were concerned, also provided them with their first lessons in music, dancing and drawing.

Said to have been an admirer of Froebel's precepts of teaching by play, Lady Strathmore with her progressive attitudes clearly did much to establish and foster the self-confidence of her offspring. The idea, so prevalent earlier this century, that 'children should be seen, but not heard', was not one to which she subscribed. An amusing example of the Strathmore children's freedom of speech is given in a story concerning the prospects of a wealthy but unpersonable young man. Unaware that Lady Elizabeth was quietly occupying herself in the same room, one visitor ventured to say, 'How sad to think that the poor man will be married only for his position and money', whereupon, from behind a sofa, a young voice piped up, 'Perhaps someone will marry him 'cos she loves him.'

Elizabeth Bowes Lyon would appear to have been an endearingly angelic – if slightly precocious – child. Such, at least, is the cumulative impression left by many who knew her. Yet even allowing for the variable moods of human nature, the influence of her parents and the undeniable warmth of the environment in which she was raised may well have made her unique among children. But if the surviving memories of her come down to us today as so many rosy platitudes, the sincerity behind them is rather more difficult to dispute. We may assume for instance, that, for the most part, such memories as are nowadays on record were chronicled before Lady Elizabeth's apotheosis, and are therefore free of the taint of sycophancy that is so often a part of people's recollections of royalty.

At the age of about six, while her mother was temporarily absent, Lady Elizabeth is said to have warmly greeted a guest of Lady Strathmore, rung for tea, poured it with great aplomb, then asked, 'Shall us sit and talk now?' At the same age she admonished her soul-mate, brother David, not to bother another of her parents' visitors, Lord Gorrell. 'The unconcealed object being to bother me herself,' he later wrote. At seven or eight, Lady Elizabeth – during her holiday visits to Glamis – was already eager to acquaint visitors with the castle's history. 'What a glorious place,' one guest reported. 'Little Lady Elizabeth Lyon showed me over.'

By the testimony of one governess, Fräulein Kathie Keübler, Elizabeth was at thirteen, 'far more mature and understanding than her years warranted'. In later life Sir David Bowes Lyon remembered his adored sister's 'great sweetness and sense of fun' and a certain roguish quality. 'The personality which I see now was there already.'

Comfortable and easy-going though life was within the Bowes Lyon family, one upper-class tradition, invariably closely observed, was the annual progress from house to house as dictated by society's seasons. Home, as we have clearly seen – and as Lady

Elizabeth herself averred – was St Paul's Walden Bury. Then there was her parents' London town house at 20 St James's Square, Pall Mall. Streatlam Castle in County Durham was there for visits, while Glamis represented family holidays.

Given this familiar unchanging pattern, it is perhaps time to demolish the curiously widespread belief that Elizabeth Bowes Lyon is something of a thoroughbred Scot. There is, of course, no doubt whatsoever that Scottish blood flows through her veins, but no more forcefully than the English blood of her mother and that of a succession of aristocratic English forebears.

English home life and the unsurpassed delights of Hertfordshire were to be interrupted for four long years, beginning on Lady Elizabeth's fourteenth birthday, 4 August 1914. At midnight on that day, Britain's ultimatum to Germany expired and the Great War was about to begin. Presently Glamis Castle was turned into a hospital for wounded soldiers under the supervision of Lady Strathmore. Her sons Patrick, John and Fergus went away to serve with the Black Watch, Michael enlisted with the Royal Scots, while her daughter, Lady Rose, enrolled for nursing training.

At a time of such intense activity, it was perhaps just as well that Elizabeth Lyon was 'far more mature and understanding than her years warranted', as her governess had described her only twelve months before. To all intents and purposes her childhood had come to a sudden end, and now responsibilities loomed high before her.

In later years, particularly as a wife and mother, as Duchess of York and as Queen, Lady Elizabeth would recall the warm days of her childhood with an understandable contentment. In contrast the childhood of the future King George VI could scarcely have been colder.

# ∝ 3 ∝

# *A Prince called Bertie*

'Now that you are five years old, I hope you will always try and be obedient and do what you are told, as you will find it will come much easier to you the sooner you begin. I always tried to do this when I was your age and found it made me much happier.' This stultifying message from his father, Prince George, Duke of York, rather than a rousing chorus of 'Happy Birthday, dear Bertie', awaited the little Prince Albert on the morning of 14 December 1900.

Virtually from birth the Prince found himself at several disadvantages – not one of them of his own making. First, he was the child of undemonstrative and strangely unworldly parents which, in any walk of life, is very likely to have a marked effect on a child's psychological development. The incapability of one parent to show emotion is not, perhaps, too unnatural. But in Prince Albert's case, both mother and father were painfully deficient in this all-important area. At times it was almost as if they were scarcely human. Yet these royal parents were themselves victims of disadvantage in a world which ostensibly offered everything.

Both as a prince and later as king, George of York was no intellectual and in most respects he was singularly uncultured. The son of parents who were representatives – if not quite pioneers – of everything fashionable, he was, to quote his most recent biographer Kenneth Rose, 'handicapped by an ingrained conservatism'. Coupled with 'only the limited education of a nineteenth-century naval officer', the Prince's shortcomings were betrayed, as much in the changeless cut of his clothes as in the immutable routine of his daily life. On the eve of his forty-fifth birthday, his horizons did not stretch beyond the duties and pastimes of a Norfolk squire. He was indifferent to science and politics, to history and the arts; he spoke scarcely a word of any foreign language. [One of his most famous remarks as George V is surely, 'I don't like abroad. I've been there'.] Public ceremonial affected his nerves and entertainment his digestion.

Yet perhaps Prince George's conservatism wasn't his only handicap. The suffocating, possessive affection of his mother, ever called 'Motherdear' by her children, cannot have helped matters. Though very far from foppish, the Prince – even at the age of twenty-one, and a serving officer aboard HMS *Dreadnought* – wasn't, in spirit, so very far from his mother's apron strings. Bemoaning a missed reunion with Princess Alexandra at Sandringham, he wrote, 'How I wish I was going to be there too, it almost makes me cry when I think of it. I wonder who will have that sweet little room of mine, you must go and see it sometimes and imagine that your little Georgie dear is living in it.'

If since boyhood Prince George had never chafed beneath the wing his mother was unable to remove from his shoulders, his wife, not surprisingly, found her mother-in-law trying in the extreme. Coincidentally, Princess May, Duchess of York, was herself a victim of maternal eclipse.

A popular, if today somewhat obscure, royal figure, Princess May's mother, Mary Adelaide, Duchess of Teck, was a jovial woman who not only appreciated but determinedly enjoyed the good things in life. Most often resembling a ship in full sail, she was tactfully described as 'a personage of unusual girth', or more mildly as 'rotund'. To the Victorian public she was bluntly, but ever affectionately, 'Fat Mary'.

Princess Mary Adelaide's extravagant ways repeatedly landed her in debt to the extent that, in 1883, the Teck family, Fat Mary, her husband Francis, Duke of Teck, their sixteen-year-old daughter May, and their three sons, Adolphus (known as 'Dolly'), Francis ('Frank') and Alexander-George ('Alge'), travelling as the family 'Hohenstein', made a rather necessary exit to Florence in an attempt to live more modestly. It was a faint hope and one that was echoed by the incorrigible Princess Mary Adelaide's first cousin Queen Victoria. 'It was with much regret that I heard you were gone to Florence,' the Queen wrote to the 'Countess Hohenstein', 'for living in a town full of attractions & temptations to expense, made me very anxious. Some quieter & more retired spot would surely have been better.'

The Tecks' financial situation did not improve, but at least their enforced sojourn did much to nurture Princess May's nascent appreciation of the arts.

Two years later Princess Mary Adelaide, Prince Francis and their daughter were back in London, returning on May's eighteenth birthday. When she left England the young Princess had been woefully shy, frequently embarrassed by her parents and overshadowed by her mother's personality. Upon her return she was certainly no less shy, but she had learned to conceal it beneath a poised and even determined exterior.

To be sure, Princess May as Duchess of York needed all the confidence she could muster, not quite so much to meet the demands of the elevated part she was expected to play, but to help her to cope with the attitudes of her in-laws. By her claims to Prince George's affections, she incurred the waspish jealousy of his mother and the stinging remarks of his favourite sister, the less-than-scintillating Princess Victoria. On one occasion, sparked as always by her own inadequacies, the Princess – one of 'The Three Hags', as she and her sisters Louise and Maud were sometimes called – told a fellow guest at Windsor, 'Now do try to talk to May at dinner, though one knows she is deadly dull.' Even in Germany the unfortunate Princess May had failed to make a particularly favourable impression on Prince George's Aunt Vicky, the Empress Frederick. There was in Princess May's manner, she observed, 'something very cold and stiff – and distant . . . each time one sees her . . . one has to break the ice afresh'.

Totally devoted to each other though Prince George and Princess May were through more than forty years of marriage, it was nevertheless doubtful if either was capable of a spontaneous gesture of affection. Even as late as 1930, by which time 'Georgie dear' was celebrating the twentieth anniversary of his accession to the throne as King George V, he could only tell his wife something of his feelings for her by letter. 'I can never sufficiently express my deep gratitude to you, darling May,' he wrote, 'for the way you have helped and stood by me. . . . This is not sentimental rubbish, but what I really feel.'

Bluff, hearty sailors were not given to outward displays of emotion or, indeed, of sentimentality. Equally shy princesses remained aloof and cool at times of personal joy or grief. The partnership of a couple so disposed, although harmonious as in the case of Prince George and Princess May, cannot – indeed did not – lend itself easily to parenthood.

In January 1919, following an epileptic attack at Wood Farm on the Sandringham estate, the death of her sixth and youngest child Prince John was recorded by his mother (by now Queen Mary) with characteristic detachment: 'The news gave me a great shock,' she wrote, 'tho' for the poor little boy's restless soul, death came as a great release.'

A decade or so later, apropos his tense relationship with his surviving sons, George V found himself unexpectely assailed by the intrepid Princess Alice, Countess of Athlone.

'George,' she asked, 'don't you love your children?'

'Of course I do,' the Sovereign replied gruffly.

'Then why don't you *show* it?!' Princess Alice snapped back.

Most of the disadvantages suffered by the future King George VI and their long-term consequences were, as may be supposed, interrelated. The second of them concerned his unsatisfactory state of health as a child, caused largely by the rank negligence of his nurse.

The first starch-fronted 'custodian' of the nursery at York Cottage had found herself dismissed for insolence; the second (whose influence, or the lack of it, had such a disastrous effect on the young Prince 'Bertie') was given her marching orders for incompetence. Unnamed, as servants so frequently are, this pathetic creature soon developed an obsessive preference for the Yorks' eldest child Prince Edward, to the detriment of her younger charge.

To quote Sir John Wheeler-Bennett:

So completely did she disregard [Prince Albert's] wants and comforts that he was frequently given his afternoon bottle while driving in a C-sprung victoria, a process not dissimilar to a rough Channel crossing – and with corresponding results. It is not surprising that the baby developed chronic stomach trouble, which may well have laid the foundation for the gastric complaint from which he was later to suffer so acutely.

'Lala' Bill, under-nurse to both of her predecessors, was soon in control of the nursery and an orderly routine was fast established.

Prince Albert's third disadvantage during his early years came about as a result of his position within the family. Like piggy-in-the-middle, he found himself sandwiched between his elder brother, the blond, blue-eyed Prince Edward, and his younger sister, the beguiling Princess Mary. The attractive qualities of his siblings meant that Bertie, an affectionate child – though already revealing himself to be shy, nervous, 'easily frightened and somewhat prone to tears' – caught little of the limelight. On one occasion, indeed, his presence was not even recorded by his great-grandmother Queen Victoria, whom he had just visited. In her journal she had written, 'The dear little York children came, looking very well. David [Prince Edward] is a delightful child, so intelligent, nice and friendly. The baby [Princess Mary] is a sweet pretty little thing.'

Outside the nursery the young Prince Albert found much of the love and affection he craved in his grandparents, the Prince and Princess of Wales (so shortly to become King Edward VII and Queen Alexandra). At Marlborough House, their official residence in London, and at Sandringham House (the 'Big House', as it was always known), the children were spoilt and indulged mercilessly, not only to *their* great delight, but to the even greater delight of their grandmother. As Princess of Wales and as Queen, the youthful Alexandra found untold happiness in the company of her grandchildren, who were a compensation for all the heartache her husband's infidelities caused her.

Attentive and kind though Alexandra was to each of her children's offspring, Prince Edward was once again especially favoured, more perhaps because he was her eldest grandson. The Prince of Wales, on the other hand, appears to have favoured Prince Albert, and when not enjoying his company frequently sent him affectionate notes.

When judged by today's standards the early years of family life for these royal children, even though they are said to have known a great deal of happiness together, appear to have been at best soulless. Much the same could be said of the routine in most upper-class households, however, which is precisely why the unity and comparative informality of the Bowes Lyon family seems to us so unique.

As he grew older, Prince Albert's personal circumstances cannot be said to have improved noticeably. By the age of seven he had developed the stutter that would plague him for the rest of his life. As an adult he learned, under the guidance of Lionel Logue – and with the inestimable support of his wife – to control the stutter by a laborious process of proper breathing and taking time over what he had to say – not always an easy matter. There was, however, no miracle cure in store, and it has even been said that the Prince's achievements in this direction were often exaggerated.

This debilitating handicap was not Prince Albert's only concern: his knock-knees were straightened by an excruciating method of tying his legs to splints, and a natural proclivity to write with his left hand was summarily dealt with by forcing him to use his right.

Spring 1902 saw the implementation of change in the lives of Prince Albert and his elder brother in that they graduated from the York Cottage nursery to the York Cottage 'schoolroom'. From the supervision of 'Lala' Bill and the sometimes disruptive influence of Princess Mary, they passed into the masculine world of Frederick Finch who, we are told, was 'a handsome, stalwart and muscular' thirty-year-old footman. 'Naturally respectful but without a trace of servility', he was to be all things to the two Princes: nurse, valet, confidant, confessor, referee, hero. In a sense, his was the role of surrogate father.

Into this milieu was introduced the virtually humourless Henry Peter Hansell. A graduate of Magdalen College, Oxford – with a second-class honours degree in history – he had been employed by the Duke of Connaught (third son of Queen Victoria) to educate his heir, Prince Arthur, in preparation for his admittance to Eton. Yet while Hansell succeeded in directing a minor princeling towards a broader education, his suitability as tutor to England's future kings is open to serious doubt. Certainly the boys' father – by now Prince of Wales – cannot have given the matter very much thought, for we know that he approved Hansell's appointment very largely because of his Norfolk origins and his prowess as a yachtsman. Few teachers can ever have assumed so responsible a position on flimsier references.

To his credit, however, Hansell had advised the Prince of Wales that in his opinion his royal charges would have fared far better at a proper school than under his tutelage. That the Prince did not share his views not only indicated his intense dislike of change, but more particularly harked back to the happy days of his own childhood, with its memories of the education he and his dissipated elder brother Albert Victor received from the Reverend John Neale Dalton.

By and by Mr Hansell was joined at York Cottage by three more teachers to assist him in his work: Monsieur Hua, who had attempted to teach the Prince of Wales French, would fulfil the same function for his sons; Professor Oswald was engaged to teach German; and Martin David of Tonbridge School was set the task of instructing the Princes in mathematics – a subject which would always confound the young Prince Albert.

Each of these masters, following Mr Hansell's lead, commented on their pupils' work and conduct in what was called the 'Report Book', presented daily to the Prince of Wales for his scrutiny. Though the idea of presenting the Prince with reports of his sons' progress was fair enough, the sense behind what amounted to a running commentary is surely open to question. Certainly Hansell and his colleagues appeared to expect more of their charges than they were able to give and each in turn seems to have been as insensitive as the Prince of Wales himself, making scant allowance for the shortcomings of youth and presumably none at all for the vagaries of a boy's day-to-day conduct. Small wonder, therefore, that Prince Albert especially dreaded the frequent summonses to his father's study and the ensuing admonitions for inattentiveness or indolence. These early audiences with his father often reduced the nervous and tongue-tied Prince 'Bertie' to tears. His frustration and subsequent fits of anger are all too easy to imagine, especially when, for example, Mr Hansell's Report Book callously advised the Prince of Wales that his son was, 'backward in oral work and disinclined to take part in French and German conversations'.

In his memoirs, *A King's Story*, Prince Edward, by now Duke of Windsor, discussed his schooldays at some length. Of his tutor, he wrote:

I used to wonder whether Mr Hansell did not have a secret yearning for some other kind of life and whether he ever regretted having dedicated himself to the care and education of unwilling and ungrateful little boys . . . looking back over those . . . curiously ineffectual years under him, I am appalled to discover how little I really learned.

If he harboured strong views about anything, he was careful to conceal them. . . . I am . . . unable to recall anything brilliant or original that he ever said.

Totally unacceptable though his attitudes and ideas would be nowadays, it would be unjust to allow his schoolroom methods to paint a picture of Hansell as some kind of ogre in a mortar-board. For if, as Sir John Wheeler-Bennett put it, he was not 'a born teacher', the Princes were by no means born scholars.

Five years later, in the spring of 1907, Prince Edward put the York Cottage schoolroom behind him and entered the Royal Naval College, Osborne, as a cadet. Eighteen months later, Prince Albert stood before the same examining board and, after a shaky start, acquitted himself in the oral examination, 'brightly and well'. A few weeks later his written examination papers – in English, history and French – were adjudged in his favour and, perhaps even to his own astonishment, he succeeded in passing the oral French examination.

In part Henry Hansell's final progress report to the Prince of Wales on his twelve-year-old son 'Bertie', advised '. . . I can state as a fact that he has reached a good standard all round, but we must remember that he is at present a "scatter-brain" and it is perfectly impossible to say how he will fare . . . at Osborne under the influence of all the excitement attendant on the new life. . . .'

# 4

# *Mr Johnson at Sea*

Prince Albert was no stranger to the Osborne estate of his great-grandmother Queen Victoria. With the exception of Balmoral, it was the most popular of her residences and, as with her 'Scotch-Baronial' castle in the Highlands, it was not only the scene of a great many family gatherings, but served as a permanent memorial to the manifold talents of the Prince Consort.

It was he who conceived Osborne House – the very height of modernity – near Cowes on the Isle of Wight, as an Italianate villa, complete with campanile, because he thought the view across the Solent like that across the Bay of Naples. Later, after the Queen had been proclaimed Empress of India, an 'Eastern' wing, the incongruously finished Durbar Room, was added to house the Queen-Empress's imperial trophies. Upon her death, Edward VII gave Osborne to the nation. Part of the house itself was designated a convalescent home for officers, while the Royal Naval College was established in the grounds – where it existed until 1921.

Along with more than seventy boys of the same age, Cadet His Royal Highness Prince Albert of Wales entered the Royal Naval College on 15 January 1909 as a member of the Grenville Term. He was to be treated, instructed his father, in exactly the same way as all the other cadets; any show of favouritism was strictly forbidden. The royal command was but a reiteration of that issued when Prince Edward joined the college as part of the Exmouth Term two years earlier. But now there were, perhaps, those who appreciated Mr Hansell's view that the Princes would have been

*31*

better equipped for the pace and rigours of Osborne had they first experienced life at a preparatory school.

Here came into its own yet another of the disadvantages that tended to make Prince Albert's formative years rather more heavy going than might otherwise have been the case. The Prince had entered an establishment that was totally new and bewildering to him. He had never known the company of boys *en masse*, yet here the place was swarming with young and competitive fellows who all had the singular advantage of proper schools behind them. Moreover their healthy disregard for royal rank – and to the majority Prince Albert was just another boy – meant that he came in for the inevitable ragging and bullying from which none was exempt. His stutter was aped mercilessly and, once again, his reticence in class because of it was sometimes misinterpreted as an irritating, extreme case of diffidence or quite simply as stupidity.

To reassure his parents that all was well he wrote letters telling them that he had settled in, but in truth, it took the best part of his first year at Osborne before he had mastered his feelings of homesickness and had become acclimatized to his surroundings.

As he found his feet, so his confidence grew, his personality started to become more noticeable and his popularity rose. Despite his basic shyness he made a handful of close friends who admired his 'sense of fun and mischief, his complete lack of 'side' and his 'integrity and courage'. Before long the captain of the college said enthusiastically of the Prince, 'He shows the grit and "never say I'm beaten" spirit which is strong in him.'

It was also at this time that Prince Albert met and befriended a man who was to play quite a large part in his life, Osborne's assistant medical officer, Surgeon-Lieutenant Louis Greig. At twenty-nine he was fifteen years older than the Prince. The friendship which began in the summer of 1909 when Prince Albert was admitted to the sick-bay suffering from whooping cough was, against all likelihood, to survive well beyond the Royal Naval College. Indeed Greig himself could scarcely have conceived that he would in time officially attend his young patient, first as equerry and later as comptroller. Nor for that matter could Greig have envisaged partnering the Prince at Wimbledon in championship tennis tournaments. But, for the moment, all that lay in the future. So for that matter did the death of Prince Albert's beloved grandfather, King Edward VII.

The King's 'Dearest little Bertie' and his brother Prince Edward were nearing the end of their Easter leave in May 1910 when disturbing news of the King's health postponed their return to college. Edward VII died at Buckingham Palace shortly before midnight on 6 May. It was, lamented his son and successor, 'A terrible day for us all'. To his diary the new King George V confided, 'I have lost my best friend and the best of fathers. . . . I am heartbroken and overwhelmed with grief, but God will help me in my great responsibilities. . . . '

At the moment of their grandfather's death, 'David' and 'Bertie' were asleep in the room they shared at Marlborough House. The following morning neither needed to be told of the significant change that had occurred within their family – and in their own lives.

Recalling that day some forty years later, the Duke of Windsor wrote:

> . . . I was awakened by a cry from my brother Bertie. From the window of our room he cried, 'Look, the royal standard is at half-mast!' I jumped out of bed to see for myself. Across the Mall, Buckingham Palace stood grey and silent, and on the roof in the bright morning sunlight the standard hung limply on the mast.

Not long afterwards the faithful Frederick Finch told the young Princes that their father wished to see them. For once, at least, neither boy anticipated a dressing-down for some misdeed. 'My father's face was grey with fatigue, and he cried as he told us that Grandpapa was dead,' the Duke of Windsor wrote. 'I answered sadly that we had already seen the Royal Standard at half-mast. My father seemed not to hear. . . . Then he asked sharply, "What did you say about the Standard?"

' "It is flying at half-mast over the Palace," I answered.

'My father frowned and muttered, "But that's all wrong," and repeating as if to himself . . . "The King is dead. Long live the King!" he sent for his equerry. . . . An hour later the Royal Standard was broken and flying "close up" over the house . . .'.

In the midst of his grief, the new King, though devoted to his late father, did not forget who he was or the outward trappings of the exalted office he had now assumed. The royal standard had erroneously been lowered, perhaps by a palace servant as a mark of respect, ignorant of the fact that it is the one flag that, even upon the death of a sovereign, is never flown at half-mast.

At the start of their careers as naval cadets, the then Prince of Wales had instructed that his sons were to be treated as equals among their young colleagues. The word 'equality' would now assume a different meaning, at least in the minds of the college personnel, if not to the rest of the boys. For the Princes Edward (who had by this time moved on to Dartmouth Royal Naval College) and Albert were no longer the grandsons of a king, but respectively Heirs Apparent and Presumptive to the reigning Sovereign.

If a shadow had been fleetingly cast over the royal family by the death of King Edward VII, another hovered over Prince Albert's return to Osborne. The complaints which had been voiced at York Cottage were aired afresh at the Royal Naval College. The Prince simply wasn't up to scratch in his work and there was serious doubt that he would prove himself capable of following in the footsteps of his father and elder brother to the senior Naval College at Dartmouth.

Since he entered Osborne Prince Albert had shown consistency in one thing – ranking, scholastically, among the last six of his term. More often than not, to his father's angry dismay, he occupied last or next-to-last place. The Captain of the college had reported, 'He is always very penitent with me, assures me that he is doing his best & so on. I am sure the boy has determination & grit in him but he finds it difficult to apply it to his work, tho' with games it comes out strongly.' His tutor, Mr James Watt, noted, 'With Prince Albert's mercurial temperament all things are possible. . . . I don't think he regards a rebuke any more seriously than his work.'

If King George V's dealings with his eldest sons as small boys had seemed insensitive, his exasperation with Prince Albert at this juncture is more readily understood. Yet even in the face of paternal cajoling, and any number of well-earned warnings to pull his socks up, the results of his final examinations at Osborne in December 1910 still placed 'Bertie' sixty-eighth out of sixty-eight. His tutor noted with evident disappointment, 'I am afraid there is no disguising . . . the fact that P.A. has gone a mucker.'

It may be said that, for any other boy, the opportunity of progressing to Dartmouth Royal Naval College would almost certainly have been lost for ever. Yet in spite of his record, Prince Albert packed his trunks and, in January 1911, set out on his journey to Kingswear to join his Grenville contemporaries on the banks of the River Dart. There the process of turning boys into men was to be continued with increased momentum. Engineer-Lieutenant Start was to give the Prince extra tuition in maths and engineering, while Lieutenant Henry Spencer-Cooper set himself the task of bringing the sportsman out in the King's son; riding, cross-country running and tennis were among the pursuits he actively encouraged.

Yet while there is no doubt that 'Bertie' was jolly good company, an impeccably well-mannered, charming and exuberant youth, who, like his chums, found himself punished for such things as 'Skylarking in the Gallery outside the Quarter Deck (with eight others)', 'Talking before Grace' and 'Talking outside Study', his record as a student did not much improve. In fact, he achieved no more than a shift from sixty-eighth place to sixty-seventh.

At Balmoral the King took his son aside and later wrote to him at college, 'I trust you will take to heart all I told you . . . & remember yr. position & that it is for you to set an example to the others & you must really work hard & try your best . . . as it really does look so bad that you are practically last in your term. . . .' By the end of the year things were looking up, and Prince Albert was congratulated for coming in sixty-*third*!

As the year 1912 drew to a close, Prince Albert left Dartmouth to join his family at Sandringham for Christmas. Ahead of him, during the first part of the new year, lay the final phase of training before the cadets were awarded their dirks and patches as midshipmen. Cruising aboard a battleship, this last experiment was when theory became practice; when all the cadets in turn became stokers, fuelling the furnaces with coal, stood watch in the shadow of their officers, and put to the test the fruits of their technical instruction.

From Devonport on 18 January 1913, Prince Albert put to sea aboard the 9,800-ton cruiser *Cumberland*, under the command of Captain Aubrey Smith. Also aboard, as part of the ship's company, were the familiar figures of Lieutenant–Commander Henry Spencer-Cooper, to whose charge Prince Albert was detailed, and Lieutenant Louis Greig, who was to act as ship's surgeon during the *Cumberland*'s six-months' training voyage to the Canary Islands, the West Indies and Canada.

Prince Albert proved to be a bad sailor, but he would doubtless have preferred prolonged sea-sickness to the strain of finding himself the cynosure of all eyes whenever the *Cumberland* docked. In Teneriffe he was required to drive round the town to be seen and applauded. Later on in the West Indies, where he was received with yet more enthusiasm, he was expected to open an extension of the Kingston Yacht Club and, to his even greater consternation, discovered that he had to make a speech. This he did, but badly. His nerves – hence his speech impediment – were greatly exacerbated by the nearness of the crowd of uninhibited young Jamaican women, all intent on touching the 'White Prince' – ankles, calves and thighs.

At times such as these George V's edict concerning his son's equal standing as a cadet was again turned upside down, and while those about him may have enjoyed basking in the warm light of reflected glory, Prince Albert squirmed with embarrassment. Canada's contrasting climate and scenic delights may have provided something of a change in tempo, but the Prince's curiosity value was no less diminished.

'I was hunted all the time by photographers and also by the Americans who had no manners at all . . . ' he opened the diary entry describing his and the cadets' visits to Niagara Falls, the Ontario Power Station and 'shooting the rapids' of Long Sault and Lachine.

The *Cumberland* finally sailed in to her home port of Plymouth in early July, permitting the cadets one week's leave before resuming this final phase of training. Prince Albert joined the King and Queen at Knowsley Hall near Liverpool, where they were staying privately as the guests of their old friend Lord Derby. Later on, at the conclusion of his son's training, and much gratified by his appearance and self-assurance, the King commended those responsible with the words, 'Thank you. I am pleased with my boy.'

Cadet HRH The Prince Albert ascended to the second rung of the naval ladder on 15 September 1913 with his appointment to the rank of midshipman; his sights firmly set – as were those of his companions – on the ultimate rank of a captain commanding his own man o'war. For the present, however, 'Mr Johnson', as the Prince was now known, worked as all 'snotties' worked. Subjected to the rigid discipline imposed by his superiors, he tackled the menial yet strenuous tasks of the 'apprentice', his rank considered 'the lowest form of marine life'.

Prince Albert had been serving aboard the 19,250-ton battleship HMS *Collingwood* for less than a year when the First World War broke out. Precipitated by the assassination at Sarajevo on 28 June 1914, of the Hapsburg heir-presumptive Archduke Franz Ferdinand and his morganatic wife Sophie, Duchess of Hohenberg, Austro-Hungary declared war on Serbia and menacing shadows swooped ominously low over Europe. Having interpreted all the portents, Winston Churchill as First Lord of the Admiralty one month later ordered the British Fleet to proceed, 'with all speed and secrecy', to its war station at Scapa Flow, the isolated, strategically crucial Royal Naval Base in the Orkneys, north of the Scottish mainland.

Prince Albert recounted that day's events in his diary, part of which read: 'The Captain gave us our war stations before lunch. . . . We started war routine at 1.0 p.m. We were all in 3 watches. The watchkeepers, control officers, searchlight officers, etc. I kept the afternoon watch alone, as I was one of the 3 midshipmen of the watch.'

Four days later Germany was at war with Russia. At midnight on 4 August, Britain was at war with Germany. 'Please God it may soon be over & that he will protect dear Bertie's life,' were the sentiments of the King.

More generally, but with no less sincerity, King George V issued a message from Buckingham Palace to the departing troops. Dated 9 August 1914, it read:

You are leaving home to fight for the safety and honour of my Empire.

Belgium, whose country we are pledged to defend, has been attacked and France is about to be invaded by the same powerful foe.

I have implicit confidence in you my soldiers. Duty is your watchword, and I know your duty will be nobly done.

I shall follow your every movement with deepest interest and mark with eager satisfaction your daily progress; indeed your welfare will never be absent from my thoughts.

I pray God to bless you and guard you and bring you back victorious.

Barely three weeks after the declaration of war, Prince Albert was taken ill with appendicitis and consequently missed the Royal Navy's first formal victory, the Battle of Heligoland Bight. In this engagement part of the Fleet, spearheaded by Sir John Jellicoe aboard the *Iron Duke*, vanquished and sank three German cruisers and two destroyers.

From now on, Prince Albert to his chagrin was to find himself plagued by a series of gastric illnesses, the legacy of childhood negligence. On this first occasion the Prince was out of action for six months – from August 1914 to February 1915 – during which time he missed a good deal more excitement and greatly resented the long period of inactive convalescence forced upon him by his father's surgeon Sir Frederick Treves. Above all Prince Albert missed being a part of HMS *Collingwood*. He missed not being able to man his post and, not unnaturally, he missed the comradeship of his friends.

In an effort to dissipate his son's growing despondency, King George V arranged for Prince Albert to take up a short-term posting in Whitehall, working in the Admiralty's War Room. It was a job which entrusted to him the classified task of plotting the movements of every British warship. The post temporarily eased the Prince's conscience, but before long the frustrating sense of restlessness returned with a vengeance. 'It seems such a waste of time to go [to the Admiralty] every day and do nothing,' he frequently complained.

At length Prince Albert was allowed to rejoin the *Collingwood*, despite the personal feelings of Sir Frederick Treves that, because of his health, he should never go to sea again.

Upon his return to his ship the Prince discovered a new defence system in operation, in that units now spent three consecutive days out in the North Sea and ten days at Scapa Flow. The midshipmen's duties were varied accordingly, which meant that Prince Albert, already a senior midshipman, instead of keeping watch at sea, alternated between controlling searchlights at night and taking charge of the submarine lookouts by day.

Throughout the war Prince Albert not only kept very much abreast of naval manoeuvres but, in a frequent exchange of letters with his father, discussed battles on land. In March 1915 and again in April, for example, the campaigns of Neuve-Chapelle and the second battle at Ypres, in which British losses totalled approximately 73,000, came under review. A few weeks later the King and Prince Albert expressed mutual horror at the sinking of the *Lusitania*, a commercial passenger liner torpedoed off the south-west coast of Ireland on 7 May with the loss of over a thousand lives. It was, thundered the King, 'a dastardly outrage & a great crime against civilisation'.

That same month, having only returned to duty some twelve weeks earlier, Prince Albert was again trying to cope with the agonies of what he put down to 'infernal indigestion'. Physical discomfort and loss of weight began to undermine the Prince's confidence and, in due course, the Fleet surgeon called in Sir Watson Cheyne (acting as temporary consultant to the Fleet), who took the immediate precaution of having the Prince transferred to the hospital ship *Drina* for observation. King George V approved this arrangement but not before promising his son that, should the Fleet put to sea, he would be returned to the *Collingwood*.

To Prince Albert, who had proven himself both keen and alert, his naval career was everything. Indeed at this point there was no reason to doubt that the Navy would remain central to his existence. To that end, he was assured that somebody from his ship would come across every day so that his studies for the late-summer examinations could continue without interruption. Such an assurance was vital to the Prince, since good results would mean his promotion to the rank of acting sub-lieutenant.

Prince Albert's 'infernal indigestion' was diagnosed as a weakening of the stomach's muscular wall, further aggravated by a 'catarrhal condition'. The remedy not only consisted of 'the artificial evacuation of the residuum from the stomach at night', but careful dieting and peace and quiet. This time the combined processes of treatment and recuperation kept Prince Albert away from his ship for almost ten months, from July 1915 to early May 1916. Greatly agitated though he was by the cumulative physical and psychological effects, the Prince appreciated the wisdom of his father's counselling: 'You can't expect to get well in a minute, anything to do with the stomach must take a little time to get right.'

In the meantime, however, the King again considered the possible consequences of the promise he had made to his son that, in the event of enemy action, Prince Albert would not be left behind when the *Collingwood* set sail. From the battleship itself, Captain James Ley, in consultation with the Prince's doctors, had advised the King that in his present condition – even though the overall signs were certainly favourable – Prince Albert could not be considered fit for active service and the promise, though made and endorsed in all good faith, would have to be broken.

Putting himself in his son's position, the King's reply accurately anticipated Prince Albert's own feelings. While there was, 'no reason to expect any early naval engagement', Captain Ley was informed by the Sovereign's Private Secretary Lord Stamford-ham,' . . . were the unexpected to happen and the Fleet were ordered to sea the day after you receive this letter, the King would prefer to run the risk of Prince Albert's health suffering than that he should endure the bitter and lasting disappointment of not being in his ship in the battle line.'


Successful in his examinations and restored to health – save for the uncomfortable effects of having indulged too heartily in a dish of soused mackerel, which had put him flat on his back – Sub-Lieutenant 'Johnson' leapt out of the sick-bay and into his turret when on 30 May 1916 the *Collingwood*, as part of the First Battle Squadron, set out to aid British cruisers under attack by the German High Seas Fleet, forty miles off the Danish coast. The Battle of Jutland was for Prince Albert all too brief. Nevertheless he had played his part well and had been exhilarated by the experience:

> We opened fire at 5.37 p.m. on some German light cruisers. The 'Collingwood's' second salvo hit one of them which set her on fire, and sank after two more salvoes were fired into her. We then shifted on to another light cruiser, we think the 'Derrflinger' ['Derfflinger'] . . . and one of the 'Collingwood's' salvoes hit her abaft the after turret, which burst into a fierce flame. After this she turned away from us and disappeared into the mist.

Prince Albert's next prolonged period of ill-health began in late August when doctors diagnosed a duodenal ulcer and once again prescribed that he should rest. His service aboard HMS *Collingwood* was now over. Towards the end of the year, however, the Prince reported for desk-duty at Portsmouth on the staff of the Commander-in-Chief, Sir Stanley Colville. It was not something that pleased the Prince in the least, but it was, he agreed, infinitely better than wasting his time at Windsor Castle doing nothing. Throughout the next six months Prince Albert maintained a determined campaign of agitation directed towards the King, Sir Stanley and the Admiralty for permission to return to sea. At last his efforts paid the yearned-for dividends and the Prince – as acting lieutenant – was enrolled as part of the company aboard the 27,500-ton battleship *Malaya*. It was now that the twenty-one-year-old Prince Albert re-established his friendship with Louis Greig who, to his delight, had been appointed to the post of the *Malaya*'s second surgeon.

If there had been even the slightest hope that a change of ship might augur well for a change in the Prince's health, disappointment was an early visitor. It had become abundantly clear that the career Prince Albert loved imposed a strain his constitution could not support. Distressed though he was, the Prince looked reality in the face. 'Personally I feel that I am not fit for service at sea,' he concluded and added, 'I don't think I can get any better without an operation [to remove the offending ulcer] and I should like to get it over and done with.' While the King did not disagree with his son's decision to quit the Navy, he and Queen Mary were doubtful about the Prince's request for surgery. On 28 November 1917, however, with Prince Albert lying prostrate in continual pain, the King and Queen gave their assent and the operation took place the following morning.

With his recovery Prince Albert was about to embark on a new phase of activity. At his own suggestion and with his father's full approval, he left the Navy for the naval wing of the Air Force, officially designated the Royal Air Force in February 1918. Thus, his appointment to the Royal Naval Air Service Station at Cranwell was formally gazetted in November 1917.

# 5

# Years of Change

The advent of the Great War seared the royal family's long and historic bonds with the royal families of Germany – ties which had not only furnished the British throne with kings and queens since the accession of George I in 1714, but had also supplied a large number of princes and princesses with acceptable spouses. Indeed George V himself hadn't far to look for the heavy Teutonic influences in his own small world.

Nevertheless, his outrage at German methods of warfare was second to none. Lord Stamfordham declared on his behalf, 'The King yields to no-one in abominating the general conduct of the Germans throughout the war,' but added that His Majesty, '. . . deprecates the idea of reprisals and retaliation; he has always hoped that at the end of the war we shall . . . stand before the world as having conducted it as far as possible with humanity and like gentlemen.'

It is not for angels to heed the call to arms and nothing is more unreal to mortal men than the distant rhetoric of princes and politicians. Not even the King, therefore, could prevent an understandable feeling of xenophobia from sweeping through the country. British emotions were perhaps best summed up in a poem published in the *Daily Express* of 26 August 1914. Entitled *The Day*, it was written by a certain Henry Chappell, then a railway porter at Bath.

> *You boasted the Day, and you toasted the Day,*
> *And now the Day has come,*

*Blasphemer, braggart, and coward all,*
*Little you reck of the numbing ball,*
*The blasting shell, or the 'white arm's' fall,*
 *As they speed poor humans home.*

*You spied for the day, you lied for the Day,*
 *And woke the Day's red spleen.*
*Monster, who asked God's aid Divine,*
*Then strewed His seas with ghastly mine;*
*Not all the waters of the Rhine*
 *Can wash thy foul hands clean.*

*You have wronged for the Day, you have longed*
 *for the Day,*
 *That lit the awful flame,*
*'Tis nothing to you that hill and plain*
*Yield sheaves of dead men amid the grain;*
*That widows mourn their loved ones slain,*
 *And mothers curse thy name.*

*But after the Day there's a price to pay*
 *For the sleepers under the sod,*
*And He you have mocked for many a day –*
*Listen, and hear what He has to say:*
*'Vengeance is mine, I will repay.'*
 *What can you say to God?*

When the nation looked inwards, the ancestry of its royal family was not forgotten. Lloyd George, for example, when summoned to see the King at Buckingham Palace, remarked, 'I wonder what my little German friend has got to say to me'; and in response to H.G. Wells' denouncement of Britain's 'alien and uninspiring Court', George V – who considered himself *thoroughly* British – replied, 'I may be uninspiring, but I'll be damned if I'm an alien.'

All the same the 'Court' was littered with royalties whose titles were inescapably Germanic: Battenberg, Teck, Schleswig-Holstein; descendants of the Houses of Hanover and Saxe-Coburg-Gotha; family trees spattered with the names of Brandenburg-Anspach, Brunswick-Wölfenbuttel, Mecklenburg-Strelitz, Saxe-Meiningen and Mecklenburg-Schwerin, Prussia, Hesse-and-by-the-Rhine, Waldeck-Pyrmont, and any number of and principalities which, in isolation, or when lumped all together, named the aggressor.

Thus, in 1917, it was decided to change the name of the British royal house and the King's Private Secretary suggested that 'Windsor' might be an appropriate alternative. So it was that, on 17 July, by royal proclamation, George V became the first Sovereign of the House and Family of Windsor. Those who were now deprived of their former titles, but who were not to bear the royal name, were compensated – at least to some extent – by finding themselves elevated to the English peerage.

Prince Louis of Battenberg took the anglicized surname Mountbatten, together with the title Marquess of Milford Haven. His sons, the Princes George and Louis became respectively, the Earl of Medina and Lord Louis (later Viscount and subsequently Earl) Mountbatten (of Burma). Their cousin Prince Alexander of Battenberg, eldest son of Queen Victoria's youngest child Princess Beatrice, was created Marquess of Carisbrooke. His surviving brother Prince Leopold assumed the title Lord Leopold Mountbatten. Their younger brother, Maurice, had died in the retreat from Mons in October 1914, while serving with the 60th Rifles.

Queen Mary's two surviving brothers, Prince 'Dolly' and Prince 'Alge' (Prince 'Frank' had died of pleurisy in 1910), became Marquess of Cambridge and Earl of Athlone respectively.

In Berlin at this time, King George V's megalomaniac cousin the Kaiser Wilhelm II – whose Garter banner had recently been removed from above his stall in St George's Chapel, Windsor Castle – scoffed at the royal proclamation, saying that he would enjoy hearing the famous opera *The Merry Wives of Saxe-Coburg-Gotha*.

Throughout the four years of war, men and women at home were galvanized by events in Europe. At the start, Field-Marshal Lord Kitchener called for an additional 700,000 men, 'who have the safety of our Empire at heart' to enlist forthwith. Within a month 438,000 men had signed up and, in what was hailed by the newspapers as, 'A Magnificent offer from The Indian Princes', a further 70,000 troops were sailing westward from the subcontinent. The Press Bureau announced that, 'The Expeditionary Force, detailed for foreign service', had been landed on French soil, 'without a single casualty', while from Whitehall was released an official warning to the public, not to place 'The slightest reliance on rumours regarding victories or defeats . . .'.

Invigorated by a keen sense of patriotism, one young trooper wrote home from the Front, 'It's a great war, whatever. Isn't it luck for me to have been born so as I'd be just the right age and just in the right place?'

On a more sober note, the poet Rupert Brooke, who was once described as 'the handsomest man in England', and who died shortly before his twenty-eighth birthday in April 1915 while serving as an officer in the Royal Naval Division of the Dardanelles Force, made a lasting contribution to the imagery of war in his poem *The Soldier*. It began,

> *If I should die, think only this of me:*
> *That there's some corner of a foreign field*
> *That is for ever England . . .*

Far away at Glamis Castle, Elizabeth Bowes Lyon formed her own impressions of war in a myriad different ways. The family read, and Elizabeth answered, the letters her brothers wrote home; soldiers being nursed back to health dictated letters to their own families and Lady Elizabeth wrote down their words. Indeed she helped out with so much correspondence during the war years that, had she but seen it, she may well have longed to recruit the services of a young woman who placed the following advertisement in the Personal Columns of *The Times*: 'Girl eager to do something, would be delighted to write letters to anyone going to the Front, who perhaps will not get many.'

There were, of course, other duties to occupy Lady Elizabeth's time. There were 'comforts' to be knitted – socks, mufflers, mittens, vests, scarves – shirts to be made for the men of the 5th Battalion, the Black Watch; tissue paper to be crumpled, 'until it was so soft that it no longer crackled, to put into the linings of sleeping-bags'.

The needs of the Glamis patients were, naturally, a paramount consideration, and in administering to them Elizabeth Lyon displayed an apparently limitless amount of patience, tempered by a wealth of genuine kindness. As 'guests' of the Strathmores, the numbers of soldiers who passed through were repeatedly enjoined to make Glamis their 'home'. For so many, who returned to the

*45*

trenches once fit, it was to be their last home. Such thoughts, however, were but fleetingly entertained in an atmosphere of warm intimacy, where the onerous responsibilities of warfare seemed light years away. For the time being at any rate, the emphasis was placed squarely on recuperation and the enjoyment such respite afforded.

Frequently the ancient walls of Glamis Castle would echo to the sounds of the men's voices singing such popular songs as 'Hello, Hello! Who's Your Lady Friend'; 'It's a Long Way to Tipperary'; 'Keep the Home Fires Burning', and perhaps a tamer version of 'Mademoiselle from Armentières . . . Parlez-vous?', a normally ribald number, of which it was said there were more than two thousand variants.

The grief of personal bereavement visited Glamis during the late summer of 1915 with the death of Fergus Bowes Lyon, the Strathmore's fourth son. Married to Lady Christian Dawson-Damer a year earlier, he had only just returned to France from Scotland, having seen his eight-week-old daughter for the first and last time. Not two years later came the equally grievous news that Michael Bowes Lyon, Fergus' younger brother, was missing – presumed dead. Lord and Lady Strathmore clung to one another in their desolation when a War Office telegram arrived confirming the 'death' of their fifth son and eighth child. It was a bitter blow, but one which Lady Elizabeth and her brother David refused to believe was true.

According to the spiritualist belief, which is taken infinitely more seriously today by ever-increasing numbers, every living creature possesses psychic gifts to varying degrees. In the Bowes Lyon family, 'second sight' was, in fact, called the 'giftie'. Mediumistic 'talents', though naturally evident in adults, are also apparent in young people and children, before scepticism, religious dogma, or a need to find a logical explanation for seemingly illogical 'happenings', mar their vision. Thus the fifteen-year-old David Bowes Lyon insisted, 'Michael is not dead! I have seen him twice. He is in a big house surrounded by fir trees. I think he is very ill. I don't care what the War Office says, I *know* he's alive.'

So adamant was the Strathmores' youngest child that he flatly refused to put on his black mourning tie. Three months later, Michael Bowes Lyon was indeed back 'from the dead'. It was discovered that, true to all young David had declared, Michael was in a house surrounded by fir trees. Moreover, having been shot in the head, and been taken prisoner by the Germans, he was, indeed, 'very ill' – so ill, in fact, that his captors wanted to send him home to Glamis. In the event he decided to stay where he was, returning to Scotland at the war's end, but offered his place to another wounded soldier.

In the light of David Bowes Lyon's experience, it is perhaps worth adding at this point that, following the death of King George VI in 1952, Queen Elizabeth rekindled her early links with the field of psychic phenomena, and drew comfort and encouragement from the private sittings she had with the medium Lilian Bailey. The Queen Mother was not the only member of a royal family – British or European, past or present – to receive evidence of life after death. George VI himself had said, 'My family are no strangers to Spiritualism.' Queen Victoria, for instance, was known to have been interested in the movement. It is believed that John Brown, the Queen's 'Highland servant', not only acted as her ghillie, but also as her personal medium – the channel through which the Prince Consort communicated with the Queen. Benjamin Disraeli was one 'intimate' who knew of Queen Victoria's interest in the subject and it is said that, as he lay dying, he was asked whether he would like a visit from the Queen – in itself a signal honour. His wry reply, though it may have been apocryphal, was, 'How kind of Her Majesty, but no thank you. I expect she only wants me to give a message to Albert.'

At Cranwell in Lincolnshire, the Prince Albert of this story found the rigid discipline of the naval wing of the soon-to-be-established Royal Air Force no different to all he had known before. It was, in fact, like serving aboard a vast land-locked ship. Even the ground on which he stood, when he reported for duty in February 1918, was knows as HMS *Daedalus*.

In his official life of King George VI, Sir John Wheeler-Bennett tells us, 'There was nothing about *Daedalus* in . . . 1918 to suggest the dignity and magnificence of the Royal Air Force Cadet College which was destined to replace it in later years.' When he joined, Prince Albert had his own reservations, too. It was, nevertheless, a life he came to enjoy and, furthermore, this was his first proper 'command'. As Officer Commanding No. 4 Squadron, Boy Wing, the King's son revealed himself to be a strict disciplinarian and told his father, 'With a little persuasion I hope to make them understand what I want.'

That April George V and Queen Mary visited Cranwell and the King saw for himself the results of Flight-Lieutenant Prince Albert's endeavours. Neither King nor Prince were to be disappointed by the Prince's 2,500-strong boys' parade. In his diary King George recorded, 'We motored to Cranwell which has now become the largest aerodrome in the world. Inspected the boys whom Bertie is in charge of, visited the sheds & saw all the different kinds of machines, also the classes at instruction & we saw the airships in their hangars, unfortunately it was misty & foggy so we could not see any flying.'

This change of direction in Prince Albert's life was wholly advantageous. 'I never trouble my head about myself now,' he was able to write to Queen Mary, 'as I feel a different person.' To make life even happier, he lived at South Rauceby, a few miles from Cranwell, sharing a cottage with Louis Greig and his wife. Doctor Greig had originally been seconded to the same service by special arrangement with the Admiralty to keep a watchful eye on the Prince's health. It was the kind of cosy, domestic set-up that 'Bertie' had never known before, and it suited him down to the ground.

Later that year Prince Albert progressed from Cranwell to RAF Headquarters at St Leonard's in Sussex. There he found himself appointed to No. 5 RAF Cadet Wing, undertook a two-weeks' course at the Cadet School and was then appointed to the command of the 5th Squadron. 'I certainly think you are in a better place than at Cranwell,' commented the King after he had visited St Leonard's, 'the whole spirit of the place is different.'

Even in Sussex, to where they, too, had moved, Prince Albert remained a permanent feature in the lives of Doctor and Mrs Greig. For an informal impression of the Prince 'off-duty', I am indebted to Mrs Violet Anderson who wrote,

> . . . as children, my brother and I used to watch the Prince with his squadron as they did their physical exercises on the beach as part of their training. Sometime later, when the Greigs were letting their house, called 'The Knoll', in the village of Hollington, about three miles from Hastings, my father was very interested in taking on the

tenancy. One day, therefore, my parents and brother were invited to view. While the Greigs were conducting my mother and father over the house, my brother – who had been left in the hall – noticed a large screen around the living-room fire. His curiosity aroused, he decided to take a peep. Also curious and taking a peep from the other side of the screen was Prince Albert, and they came face-to-face, almost bumping their heads together. Like the Prince, my brother also stammered badly, and in the shock of surprise, both found themselves stammering more than ever, as they endeavoured to apologise to one another.

In her letter, Mrs Anderson also recalled the night on which her aunt attended a private dance given by the Barrington family at their house near Hastings. It was a fancy-dress ball and, 'Prince Albert and some of his friends were present. The Prince was dressed as a baby in a frilly white dress with a large blue bow.

By now the Great War had entered its final stages and the German armies were being pushed into retreat by the Allied forces. Yet although the Air Force had claimed supremacy of the skies, Prince Albert had yet to participate and yearned to be posted to France before the enemy finally capitulated. In October his wish was granted and, together with Louis Greig, he flew across the Channel to General Trenchard's Headquarters at Autigny. Of the General, the Prince wrote home to the King, 'He knows a great deal more about what a squadron should have than the squadron commander. He fairly keeps everybody up to their work.'

A month later, on 11 November, a jubilant George V wrote to his son, 'The great day has come & we have won the war. It has been a long time coming, but I was sure if we stuck to it, we should win. . . .'

The following morning, *The Times* declared:

There were no scenes yesterday more remarkable than those which occurred outside Buckingham Palace. 'Empires and Kingdoms and Kings and Crowns are falling like withered leaves before a gale,' Mr Lloyd George said at Guildhall . . . but the Prime Minister spoke of the countries and monarchs that made the war. The Kaiser, the Austrian Emperor, and Tsar Ferdinand [of Bulgaria] are fugitives. King George, the Constitutional Sovereign of Great Britain, who is not clad in 'shining armour', and has never rattled a never sought war, and who has looked for no personal aggrandisement through the sword, was acclaimed by his people in the hour of victory. The first thought of thousands, as soon as the news of the signing of the armistice became known, was for the King, and in dense streams they made their way to the Palace to cheer and if possible to get a glimpse of their Sovereign.

While George V celebrated the end of the war at home with his people, Prince Albert – deputed by his father to act as his personal representative for the first time – witnessed equally jubilant scenes in Belgium, the country Britain had pledged to defend. In recognition of a promise honoured, the King of the Belgians had invited the King of England to send a royal representative to accompany him when he made his 'official entry' into Brussels.

On 22 November, King Albert, riding with his Queen and the British Prince Albert, returned to his capital. It was an understandably emotional reunion between a valiant monarch and an even more valiant nation. The Prince, in reporting back to his father, noted, 'The entry into Brussels went off very well. . . . The King told me how delighted he was that you had sent me to represent you. . . .' The Belgian King's delight at Prince Albert's presence, however, was as nothing when compared to George V's pleasure in his son. Indeed the Great War had provided something of a turning point in the King's relationship with the Prince, whose life – particularly in later years – was, to quote the Duke of Windsor, 'so much like that which [our] father led . . .'.

# ≈ 6 ≈

# *A Duke and His Duchess*

The question of university education for the sons of sovereigns seems always to have given rise to a certain amount of public debate. Today, especially in this more egalitarian society, the argument has tended to follow the line that princes are afforded places at Britain's most renowned universities simply because of who they are. Given the lives our princes are expected to lead, however, the argument of privilege *v.* merit is instantly invalidated by the practical advantages of putting royal figures in touch with as broad a cross-section of people as possible.

The prototype of such a plan was originally laid down well over a hundred years ago by the Prince Consort, who was resolved to have each of his children raised 'for its position' in life. Thus to his Private Secretary, Baron Stockmar, the Prince extolled the virtues of 'a good, moral, religious, but *not bigoted* or narrow-minded' education, but asked 'where to find exactly what one wants.' In short it is doubtful that the Prince Consort found a system which agreed with his criteria. Certainly where his eldest son, the then Prince of Wales, was concerned, he was to be bitterly disappointed.

As Chancellor of Cambridge, he nevertheless took the decision to send his heir to university and, in the event, the future Edward VII attended no fewer than three – Edinburgh, Oxford and Cambridge – all in as many years. The outcome, summed up by William Gladstone, was that the Prince knew everything, 'except what was in books'.

If this first experiment failed, a second Prince of Wales, the future Edward VIII, fared no better at Oxford. 'Bookish he will never be,' declared Sir Herbert Warren, President of Magdalen College. Undeterred by his eldest son's experiences, King George V decided that his second and third sons, the Princes Albert and Henry, should spend a year at Trinity College, Cambridge. If, once again, Prince Albert seemed anxious to do well, the unfortunately bovine Prince Henry was most decidedly not university material.

On the subject of his sons' accommodation at Cambridge, George V proved himself as immoveable as the Prince Consort, more than half a century earlier. The Princes would not – despite remonstrations by their tutors – have rooms in college, he decreed, but would live outside. To that end, the King leased a small house a mile or so from Trinity College, known as 'Southacre', and in the now time-honoured tradition Prince Albert and his brother cycled to and from their studies.

Wing-Commander Louis Greig had, by this time, been officially appointed equerry to 'P.A.' and he and his wife joined the royal undergraduates at 'Southacre' when they went up in October 1919. Of this period spent with Prince Albert, Greig later said, 'My principal contribution was to put steel into him.' What he meant was that he had tackled the remaining traces of immaturity still apparent in the twenty-four-year-old, helping him to overcome moodiness and depression when he encountered 'minor difficulties', and occasionally reprimanding him for outbursts of temper when things were not going his way.

A fine golfer (he was reputed to have a handicap of six), a man who loved the thrill of hunting, and an ardent tennis player, the Prince could still, on occasion, prove unsporting in the face of defeat, and was even known to abandon a game through frustration or if his chances of victory looked despairingly slim.

Greig's self-imposed task, therefore, cannot be said to have been an unqualified success. Prince Albert's alarming temper, for example, was a characteristic none could erase, and his irritability was another trait that was to stay with him throughout his comparatively short life. All the same Greig's influence was of enormous benefit to the Prince and, if nothing else, served to strengthen the bond of friendship between them.

During his year at Trinity, Prince Albert read history, economics and civics, but what absorbed him most was the British

Constitution as expounded by Dicey and Bagehot. In retrospect few subjects could have been more appropriate for the Prince to have studied.

As a twenty-first birthday gift in 1916, Prince Albert had been invested with the Most Noble Order of the Garter by his father and had been reminded by him that it is '. . . the oldest Order of Chivalry in the world'. Four years later, on 3 June 1920, as a sign of his personal approbation, as well as a reward for endeavour, King George V created his son Duke of York, Earl of Inverness and Baron Killarney; 'the same titles that I had', the Sovereign noted in his diary with evident nostalgia. Profoundly moved, Prince Albert thanked his father, 'ever so very much', and received the King's reply, 'I feel that this splendid old title will be safe in your hands & that you will never do anything which could in any way tarnish it.'

There was much to occupy the new Duke of York's time during the summer and autumn months of 1920, not least the ceremonial of his introduction to the House of Lords on 23 June, when he formally 'took his seat' as a peer of the realm. Then followed the excitement and the even greater sense of achievement, when he and Louis Greig fought and won the finals match in the RAF Doubles Competition at Wimbledon.

In a singles match between the Duke and Greig, the Equerry emerged victorious, 'which I knew he was sure to do', the Duke wrote. Later there was to occur a more significant defeat of the York-Greig partnership when they met Roper-Barratt and Gore on one of the side courts at the All England Lawn Tennis Club.

In those days at Wimbledon, the crowds of spectators were allowed to press more closely around the perimeter of the courts than they are today, and Lord Longford well remembers the Duke of York's 'painful nervousness' that afternoon. Almost from the start his game faltered and failed to recover. Presently, in what was meant to be an expression of loyal encouragement, one man called out to the Duke – who, interestingly enough, remained a left-handed sportsman – 'Try the other hand, Sir.' The crowd's sympathetic embarrassment not only for the young Duke but at his performance was almost tangible and, at the end of the first set, it slowly melted away, unable to watch.

That year also saw the start of an altogether different kind of game for the Duke of York – the equally unpredictable game of love. Although he and Lady Elizabeth Bowes Lyon are known to have met at a children's party very early this century – when the young Elizabeth is reputed to have given the Prince 'the cherries off the top of her cake' – their paths did not cross again until the Duke visited Glamis during the autumn of 1920. At the time his sister, Princess Mary, was staying at Cortachy Castle a few miles away, as a guest of Mabell, Countess of Airlie, who was not only a lady-in-waiting to the Queen, but a particularly close friend.

Princess Mary's own friendship with Lady Airlie's neighbour Elizabeth Lyon had developed through their mutual involvement in the Girl Guide movement, and it was perfectly natural that, while staying nearby, the Princess should drive over to visit her brother and the Strathmores. Within weeks 'Bertie' was already dropping hints to his mother about his growing fondness for the Lady Elizabeth. 'She seems a charming girl,' Queen Mary remarked to Mabell Airlie, 'but I don't know her very well.'

The Duke of York was not alone in his feelings for Elizabeth Lyon. She wasn't exactly what could be described as a 'social butterfly', even though she did the usual rounds of parties and soirées, and she was anything but a clone. No carbon copy 'flapper' with bobbed hair and short skirts, she was almost old-fashioned in the way she dressed. All the same, Lady Elizabeth possessed one particular asset that was absent in a great many of her contemporaries. She was, as the Queen had already remarked, simply and naturally charming. This was, perhaps, her greatest gift, one which generated 'an indefinable atmosphere' wherever she went, and which won her a number of would-be suitors and admirers, including – or so we are assured – the future King Edward VIII himself.

It was, however, the Duke of York who proposed in the spring of 1921 and was rejected. While Queen Mary was by now of the opinion that Elizabeth Lyon was, 'the only girl who could make Bertie happy', the Countess of Strathmore confided to a friend, 'I like him so much and he is a man who will be made or marred by his wife.' As we know, Lady Elizabeth Bowes Lyon finally accepted the Duke of York's third proposal and, in the antiquated language of royal proclamations, their 'betrothal' was made public in the Court Circular, issued from Buckingham Palace on 15 January 1923.

There were, in fact, several newsworthy royal items on which the nation seemed happy to feast during the first few months of that year. On 7 February, for instance, the King and Queen became grandparents for the first time, with the birth of a son, the present Earl of Harewood, to Princess Mary and Viscount Lascelles, her husband of little less than a year. A month later, in a message broadcast on 7 March, the Dowager Queen Alexandra – 'The Sea King's Daughter' of Tennyson's ode – sent her 'affectionate greetings to the British people' upon the sixtieth anniversary of her arrival in England as the bride of Albert Edward, Prince of Wales, in 1863. And on 26 April, the marriage of the Duke of York and Lady Elizabeth Bowes Lyon took place at Westminster Abbey.

'The better I know and the more I see of your dear little wife, the more charming I think she is & everyone falls in love with her. . . .' Thus wrote King George V to Prince 'Bertie', shortly after his wedding. Perhaps the ageing Sovereign himself was even a little in love with his first daughter-in-law? He certainly made allowances for her that were ever denied his own children. Indeed the Prince of Wales was known to tear strips off his car tyres in his manic drives to Windsor in order not to appear late for dinner with his parents; while on similar occasions, the sheepish arrival of Prince Henry would be greeted with a stern, 'Late again, Harry!' Elizabeth, Duchess of York, was forgiven such minor transgressions. When she arrived two minutes late for dinner, the King responded to her apologies, 'You are not late, my dear. I think we must have sat down two minutes too early'; and again, in reply to a courtier's bold remark about the Duchess's timekeeping, George V said, '. . . if she weren't late, she would be perfect, and how horrible that would be.'

To the public at large the Duchess of York was 'perfect', and they responded to her accordingly – gathering to catch a glimpse of her when she began fulfilling official engagements, and singling her out at ceremonial functions attended by the royal family *en masse*.

The Duchess's emergence into the strange new world of public appearances began two months after she and the Duke were married. First, however, came the more sober introduction to the ritual of royal mourning following the death on 9 June of Princess

Helena, George V's 'Aunt Lenchen'. Better known as Princess Christian, she was the fifth child and third daughter of Queen Victoria, who in 1866 had married Prince Christian of Schleswig-Holstein. Of their five children – three sons and two daughters – the eldest, Prince Christian Victor, had been killed in Pretoria in 1900 during the Boer War; Prince Frederick had lived for only eight days in May 1876; while the youngest, Princess Marie Louise, married to the brutal Prince Aribert of Anhalt, was the first member of the British royal family to have her unhappy marriage dissolved – with the blessing of Queen Victoria.

Princess Christian was the most philanthropic of women and at her death, a fortnight after her seventy-seventh birthday, spontaneous tributes were paid to her in the House of Commons. Among those who spoke was the socialist J.R. Clynes, who was to hold the office of Home Secretary at the time of Princess Margaret's birth in 1930. He said: 'She was devoted to humanitarian and to womanly duties and never wearied in well-doing, and for one so elevated in station and social position, she has left a memory of acts of benevolence and kindly social services.'

It was as Princess Christian's successor that the young Duchess of York assumed some of her earliest presidencies and patronages, and events connected with them helped to ease her into the excessively public role she has played ever since.

In the words of the Duke of Windsor, Elizabeth Bowes Lyon 'brought into the family a lively and refreshing spirit'. On a broader scale she achieved even more than that, for she invested the remote, even stern, public face of monarchy, with recognizably 'human' features. In a sense, though there is an assured irony in the realization, the Duchess of York – once she became established – fully complemented the sterling work undertaken by the Duke of Windsor as Prince of Wales during his lengthy public relations tours abroad. By virtue of their youth and comparative informality, both did much to revitalize the popular concept of monarchy.

There can be no doubt that to some extent the people's devotion to the royal family depends on a kind of 'personality cult'. We see it clearly today with the public's response to Diana, Princess of Wales, while during the 1950s it was evidenced by the widespread adoration of Princess Margaret. During the 1920s the future Duke of Windsor brought to life the public dream of a handsome and effervescent 'Prince Charming'; while his sister-in-law, the petite and utterly feminine Elizabeth of York, provided a welcome change to the general image of royal womenfolk as regally staid, unsmiling matrons.

The Duchess of York's public persona was not simply an extension of the charmed innocence of her youth, however, but rather a carefully conceived act, consciously developed in much the same way that a character actress might develop a particular role. In time the public performance was to consume the private until the two became indivisible.

When the question of a first married home for the Duke and Duchess of York was raised, Queen Mary suggested that George V might put at their disposal the handsome White Lodge in Richmond Park, 'to keep it in the family'. It was, alas, to pass from 'the family' in 1955, when it became the home of the Royal Ballet School, founded by Dame Ninette de Valois. During the past thirty years royal visitors to White Lodge have been few in number, but its connections with the Crown span two centuries. Standing solidly four-square, the three-storeyed Palladian-style mansion was built of white Portland stone for King George II and Caroline of Anspach in 1727-9. It was later to become an occasional residence of their daughter Princess Amelia after she was appointed Ranger of Richmond Park in 1751.

Later still, in 1858, Queen Victoria and the Prince Consort decided upon White Lodge as a suitable residence for their eldest son Albert Edward, Prince of Wales. There, decreed the Prince Consort, the boy would be allowed only 'to associate with those who are good and pure'. Not surprisingly, Albert Edward professed himself 'bored to death' with life at White Lodge, surrounded as he was by a household made up of middle-aged men, and deliberately segregated from people of his own generation. A decade later Queen Victoria gave the house to her colourful cousin Mary Adelaide, Duchess of Teck and her family, and it was there, on 23 June 1894, that her daughter May gave birth to the future Edward VIII.

The Duke and Duchess of York took up residence in June 1923 and the following month entertained the King and Queen to luncheon. Since the house had been specially decorated and arranged to her instructions, Queen Mary was naturally curious to see how her daughter-in-law had settled in and, given the Queen's reputation, to see if the Duchess had introduced any changes of her own.

Yet despite the manifold attractions of the location and the undeniable charm of Richmond itself, White Lodge soon proved inconvenient as the Yorks' official workload increased. A London home was thus considered essential and, until the Duke and Duchess acquired No. 145 Piccadilly, they lived a stone's throw from the garden of Buckingham Palace at Chesterfield House, lent to them by Princess Mary and Lord Lascelles.

As a young man, one of the Duke of York's keenest and most active appointments was centred around the Boys' Welfare Association – shortly to become known as the Industrial Welfare Society – which had been established by a former civil servant, Robert Hyde. The overall aim of the association was to entice industry to become more actively conscious of the need to better working conditions for employees, to establish health centres and factory canteens, and to provide recreation facilities. At the time such an objective was no easy matter and Mr Hyde encountered formidable opposition to his plans. He nevertheless succeeded and turned to the King with a request for royal patronage, *active* royal patronage. The ideal candidate, George V decided, was his second son, Prince Albert. When the idea was put to the Prince, he declared, 'I'll do it, provided there's no damned red carpet about it.'

For the Duke of York the Industrial Welfare Society came as something of a godsend, adding a new dimension to his formal life and affording a diversion from the frequently tiresome and repetitive obligations of royalty. In fact, comparing past and present, the Duke's enthusiasm could easily be paralleled with that of his granddaughter, Princess Anne, in her work as President of the Save the Children Fund. Like the Princess today, the Duke of York was at his happiest when visiting those he was trying to help, those who lived in the industrial regions of Great Britain.

Seeing for himself how working people survived, and spending time talking to them, was, for the Duke, like setting foot on foreign territory, far removed from anything he had known before. Through his constant sorties in to the midst of the less fortunate, he learned more about life as it was lived by tens of thousands than through anything his tutors could have devised. Never was there so much as a trace of the despised 'red carpet' to upset the desired informality of the Duke's visits, and rarely was he to be more relaxed, more self-assured in his work.

From his activities as President of the Industrial Welfare Society stemmed another scheme, this time of the Duke's own making. Known as 'The Duke of York's Camp', the scheme was conceived as an experiment in bringing together upper- and working-class boys, in what was hoped would be a friendly and mutually beneficial atmosphere of understanding. As an idea it was virtually revolutionary. In practice these annual camps, always held in the Duke's presence, were enormously successful, and in later years – and in various parts of the world – some of the boys who had joined the Duke in singing the 'Camps'' song, 'Under the Spreading Chestnut Tree', were to be instantly recognized by their royal President.

King George V regarded his son's work with pride and approval, not only because it heightened the Duke of York's personal popularity, but because royal benevolence of any kind clearly redounded to the monarchy's ultimate credit.

Nor indeed was the Duke's involvement in the sphere of industrial relations regarded as a five-minute wonder. He had become involved with the original Boys' Welfare Association as early as 1919 and until his accession to the throne, nearly twenty years later, he was still cultivating new links and strengthening old. As his official biographer put it, 'Captains of industry and Trade Union leaders became regular callers . . . and the Duke's influence made itself felt throughout the industrial life of Britain.' So absorbed was the Duke in this direction, that his brother nicknamed him 'The Foreman'.

During the 1920s the Duke of York consolidated the happiness and contentment he had always searched for. In his official capacity he was being loudly applauded as a man of his time. In private his improved relationship with his father put him on a more comfortable footing, while at home his wife created a loving and supportive atmosphere in which he flourished.

Something in which the Duchess – along with thousands of others – was unable to flourish was the damp, foggy British winter. Having 'whooped' her way through part of her honeymoon in the spring of 1923, she 'hacked' her way through the following winter, suffering from a severe bout of bronchitis. Thus the following year the Duke, with the King's permission, took his wife on safari to Kenya, a popular, even fashionable pursuit at that time. Unlike similar winter sojourns enjoyed by their closest contemporaries, however, the Yorks' trip wasn't undertaken purely for pleasure or, indeed, purely to spare the Duchess further ill-health. For some time the Duke had wanted to broaden his horizons still further and get to know the Empire a little better.

Kenya therefore provided an opportunity to combine public royal duties and private relaxation. On 5 December 1924, the Duke and Duchess of York, attended by Captain Basil Brooke, RN, (who succeeded the now-retired Louis Greig as Comptroller), Lieutenant Colin Buist (a newly appointed equerry) and Lady Annaly (acting as lady-in-waiting to the Duchess), sailed from Marseilles aboard the P&O liner *Mulbera*, which reached Mombasa seventeen days later on the twenty-second. Cheered to the echo by a crowd of thousands as they stepped ashore at Kilindini, the royal party's arrival was celebrated by a dance festival in which no fewer than five thousand participated, drawn from the tribes of Kenya, Uganda, Tanganyika, Nyasaland and the Belgian Congo.

From Mombasa the party travelled by train to Nairobi, where Christmas was spent at Government House as the guests of the Governor, Sir Robert Coryndon. A few days later the Yorks' first safari began to the north, taking them to both sides of Mount Kenya, on to the Uaso Nyero River to Archer's Post, thence into Masai – and lion – territory.

In February the Duke and Duchess spent a few days with Lord and Lady Francis Scott on their farm at Rongai, 250 miles from Nairobi, before the sudden death of the Governor introduced an unexpected note of sombre formality, and the Duke returned to Nairobi to attend Sir Robert's funeral. From Kenya the British VIP travellers moved on to Entebbe, via the Kavirondo Gulf and the northern waters of Lake Victoria. In Kampala formality again tempered the happy-go-lucky atmosphere, as the Duke and Duchess undertook two days of official engagements. Then the casual attire of bush-shirts, loose trousers and floppy hats reappeared as the party embarked on its Ugandan safari, during which the Duke and Duchess hunted elephants.

It is said that the tusks of one elephant brought down by the Duke were eventually mounted and shipped back to London, where they were displayed in the hall of the Yorks' house. Towards the end of their sixteen-week trip, the Duke and Duchess sailed down the Blue Nile to Khartoum, where they visited the battlefield of Omdurman, and formally laid the foundation stone of the Makwar Dam.

Finally, from Port Sudan on the Red Sea, the Duke and Duchess reluctantly set sail aboard the *Maloja*, another vessel owned by the famous P&O line, en route for Marseilles at the end of what had been a spectacular journey. Twelve days later on 19 April, the royal couple, having travelled from France aboard a special boat-train, arrived at Victoria Station to the rousing cheers of a crowd of onlookers.

The wonders and excitement of this African 'tour' were to linger in the Duke of York's mind long after his return to England; his enthusiasm was enriched by his recent appointment to the presidency of the second British Empire Exhibition, which he opened at Wembley Stadium on 10 May 1925.

Yet if most of that year had, in so many ways, been one of stimulation and happiness, a note of sadness was to be introduced before its close. At Sandringham House on 19 November, the Duke's grandmother, Queen Alexandra, had a sudden and severe heart-attack. George V and Queen Mary were already at 'the Big House', but by the time the Duke of York and his elder brother arrived the following afternoon from Leicestershire, where they had been hunting, the King's 'poor old blind and deaf old loving Motherdear' was dead. She was eighty-one.

Despite the shock at the old Queen's death and the usual formality of royal mourning, 1925 went out on an undiminished wave of personal joy for the Yorks. Two or three months earlier the Duchess had been able to tell her husband that she was expecting their first child at about the time of their third wedding anniversary the following spring.

# 7

# *The Yorks of Piccadilly*

In making plans for the royal *accouchement*, the Earl and Countess of Strathmore invited the Duke and Duchess of York to move in to their own town house at 17 Bruton Street, W1, a fashionable thoroughfare linking Berkeley Square with Bond Street in London's West End. It was a timely offer which neither could refuse, especially since White Lodge, Richmond – still the Yorks' official residence, but by now something of a white elephant in their lives – provided the only other alternative.

The young couple duly took up residence at No.17 upon their return from Sandringham at the end of January 1926. Three months later, at 2.40 on the morning of Wednesday 21 April, in the words of the formal announcement, 'Her Royal Highness the Duchess of York was safely delivered of a Princess. . . .' In other circumstances the delivery might not have been quite so safe, for the child, who was one day to reign as Queen Elizabeth II, was a breech baby and consequently came into this world by caesarian section.

'Such a relief and joy,' noted Queen Mary in her diary. Twelve hours later, both the King and Queen arrived from Windsor to inspect their first granddaughter, and the Queen pronounced her to be, 'a little darling with a lovely complexion & pretty fair hair'. In the curious way that royalties had of communicating with one another, the Duke of York later expressed his own feelings of delight in a letter to his mother:

You don't know what a tremendous joy it is to Elizabeth and me to have our little girl. We always wanted a child to make our happiness complete, and now that it has happened, it seems so wonderful and strange. I am so proud of Elizabeth at this moment after all she has gone through during the last few days, and I am so thankful that everything has happened as it should and so successfully. I do hope you and Papa are as delighted as we are. . . .

Later still the Duke was writing to his father asking him to sanction the choice of forenames for the infant Princess. 'I have heard from Bertie,' he told Queen Mary; 'he mentions Elizabeth Alexandra Mary. I quite approve & will tell him so. . . .'

The christening ceremony, performed in the private chapel of Buckingham Palace on 29 May by the Archbishop of York, was essentially a quiet family affair attended by parents, grandparents and godparents. The latter were King George V and Queen Mary, the Princess Mary, the Duke of Connaught, Lord Strathmore and Lady Elphinstone. The little Princess herself was dressed in the cream satin robe overlaid with Honiton lace that had been worn by nearly all of Queen Victoria's children, and her head was sprinkled with water from the River Jordan, contained in the magnificent silver-gilt font festooned with tiny water-lilies, which the Prince Consort, with his genius for design, had commissioned for the christening of his eldest child, the Princess Victoria, in 1841.

Long since gone were the days when a royal christening almost assumed the air of a state occasion. Certainly against the background of the twentieth century – and more specifically in the wake of the General Strike that had gripped the country between 4 and 12 May 1926 – a repeat of the kind of lavish celebration that followed the baptism of the future Edward VII might well have damaged the popular standing of the monarchy. On that occasion, in 1842, Queen Victoria has spent a colossal £200,000 celebrating her heir's 'union' with Christ, and the christening cake alone – which occupied the centre of a vast candlelit banqueting table in the Waterloo Chamber at Windsor Castle – was over eight feet in circumference.

Newly employed by the Duke and Duchess of York to look after their daughter was the familiar figure of Mrs Clara Knight, otherwise known as 'Allah' (pronounced 'Ah-la'). Once nanny to the Duchess herself, Mrs Knight had subsequently taken charge of Lady Elphinstone's children. Now she found herself starting all over again in a new, but this time 'royal', nursery.

Scarcely had the Duke and Duchess started to get to know their daughter, to say nothing of the pleasures of parenthood, than the King decided to despatch them on an official tour of Australia and New Zealand that would separate them from Princess Elizabeth for six months. 'We are not supposed to be human,' said the Duchess when she was told. Sixty years later the Duchess of York might have followed the example of the present Princess of Wales who, before undertaking a tour of the Antipodes with Prince Charles, made it perfectly clear that unless the young Prince William accompanied them she had no intention of leaving Britain. The Princess's gumption can only be admired, but in the 1920s the idea of a royal baby being hauled halfway round the world was unthinkable.

To some, the Duke of York's presence in Australia's new federal capital, Canberra, for the opening of the recently finished legislative buildings was unthinkable. Mr Stanley Bruce, the Commonwealth Premier, was frankly appalled at the prospect of the Duke stumbling awkwardly through an event of such significance in his country's history. To be fair, King George V had not reached his decision to send the Duke of York to Canberra swiftly or lightly. He, too, had taken his son's speech impediment into account, and nobody needed to remind him that the Yorks had yet to take on a full-length official royal tour as the Sovereign's representatives.

It was at this point, incidentally, that Lionel Logue entered the Duke's life in order to help him overcome the first hurdle. Of their first meeting, the speech therapist wrote, 'He entered my consulting room at three o'clock in the afternoon, a slim, quiet man, with tired eyes and all the outward symptoms of the man upon whom habitual speech defect had begun to set the sign. When he left at five o'clock, you could see that there was hope once more in his heart.'

A month later the Duke wrote to his father telling him that he had already noticed, 'a great improvement in my talking & also in making speeches. . . . I wish I could have found him [Logue] before, as now that I know the right way to breathe my fear of talking will vanish.'

At length the day of the Yorks' departure turned the corner. For them both the six months that lay ahead – from 6 January to 27 June 1927 – hung like an eternity over their heads, and the Duchess especially needed all the surface composure she could muster as she kissed her nine-month-old daughter farewell. In private it was a very different matter, and the Duke no doubt tried to console his tearful wife that, once under way, the tour would seem to be over in a flash.

The Duchess of York not only carried with her the tremendous disappointment at being apart from her child, but the natural anxieties a wife feels for a husband facing a considerable ordeal. Then there was her own very keen nervousness to combat at the prospect of occupying a very prominent, very public position for some twenty-odd weeks.

It has often been said that as Duchess of York and subsequently as Queen, George VI's beloved Consort never knew what it was to be nervous before a public function. This is not so. As Queen Mother she was to confide, 'I always had to steel myself before engagements because I was so dreadfully nervous. I used to think that would change when I became Queen, but it never did.'

The major part of the royal tour in 1927 began in New Zealand, much to the chagrin of all those in Australia who felt the Yorks should have visited them first. On that theme the King's Private Secretary, Lord Stamfordham, wrote to General Sir Charles Ferguson, Governor-General of New Zealand, 'The question of the Duke and Duchess of York's visit to New Zealand and its place in Their Royal Highnesses' itinerary has upset the equanimity of the Commonwealth Government.' Despite such nit-picking, the couple's plans were not altered to placate carping officialdom.

The first stop on the couple's voyage out was at Las Palmas, followed by visits to Jamaica, Colón, Panama, the Marquesas Islands and Fiji, before their arrival in Auckland on 22 February. Royal tours inevitably tend to follow a set formula – in most cases nothing too spectacular or even particularly inspiring. In New Zealand, and indeed in Australia, the Duke and Duchess attended formal dinners, garden parties, balls and civic receptions. Guards-of-honour were inspected, those in presentation lines had their hands shaken; visitors books were signed and framed photographs, duly autographed in advance by the royal visitors, were distributed as mementoes. The Duke and Duchess wore their most appealing faces, smiled their most alluring smiles, and the Duke delivered the diplomatically worded, if irksome, speeches that had been prepared and approved in London beforehand.

On the morning of their arrival, as the Duke of York wrote home to his mother from Rotorua, 'I had to make 3 speeches. . . . The last one . . . quite a long one, & I can tell you that I was really pleased with the way I made it. . . . Logue's teaching is still working well, but of course, if I get tired [the stammer] still worries me.'

To the King, the Governor-General reported, 'It is quite unnecessary to say that they both made themselves adored by everyone. This I know sounds like a newspaper expression but it is no more than the truth.'

Ten days before the royal couple's month-long tour of New Zealand ended, however, the Duke of York was left to cope with official engagements without the vital support of the Duchess, who had fallen victim to an attack of tonsillitis. To the Duke his wife's illness was a grievous blow and at first he was tempted to cancel the remaining part of their schedule. It was a fleeting moment of panic, one in which his confidence faltered partly because the Duchess's vivacity and strength of personality amply made up for his own more diffident nature, and partly because he had convinced himself that the New Zealanders wanted to look at her more than they wanted to see him.

In the event the Duke realized that it was his duty as the King's representative to carry on, and by so doing he learned that people *did* want to greet him for himself and not as the husband of the popular Duchess of York. By the time he had been received with great enthusiasm by crowds of loyal onlookers in Christchurch, Dunedin, Ashburton, Timaru, Waitaki and Oamaru, his confidence in himself had not only been restored, but had grown immeasurably.

On 26 March the *Renown*, bearing the Duke of York and his now fully recovered Duchess, entered Sydney Harbour on what Lord Stonehaven, the Australian Governor-General, described as, 'a perfect autumn morning – brilliant sunshine & just enough breeze to blow the flags out'.

The success of the Duke and Duchess's tour of Australia certainly equalled that of the New Zealand visit. To quote Sir John

Wheeler-Bennett once more, 'The enthusiasm of the welcome at Sydney struck the note for the whole Australian tour. In the ensuing two months the Duke and Duchess of York passed from State to State of the Commonwealth in a blaze of eager ecstasy . . .'.

The high point, and the chief purpose of the Duke of York's presence in Australia, was reached on 9 May with the formal royal opening of the new Parliament building in Canberra. In front of a crowd that has been variously estimated as being somewhere between twenty and fifty thousand, the Duke, dressed in naval uniform, accompanied by the Duchess wearing dove grey chiffon, ceremonially unlocked the huge doors, then turned to address the crowd. The idea of slipping in an additional speech, despite the Duke's understandable dislike of public speaking, had been his own. He said:

> We are gathered here this morning to open this first meeting of the Parliament of the Commonwealth of Australia in a new capital city, and I should like, if I may, to give expression to some of the thoughts that come to me at this historic moment.
>
> It is impossible not to be moved by the significance of today's events as a great landmark in the story of Australia. I say this not only because this day sees the opening of a new Parliament House and marks the inauguration of a new Capital City – but more because one feels the stirrings of a new birth, of quickened national activity, of a fuller consciousness of your destiny as one of the great self-governing units of the British Empire.
>
> Today marks the end of an epoch and the beginning of another, and one's thoughts turn instinctively to what the future may have in store. One's own life would hardly be worth living without its dreams of better things, and the life of a nation without such dreams of a better and larger future would be poor indeed.

From the throne inside the new building, the Duke of York delivered the 'official' speech on behalf of the Sovereign. In part he said,

> The British Empire has advanced to a new conception of autonomy and freedom, to the idea of a system of British nations, each freely ordering its own individual life, but bound together in unity by allegiance to one Crown. . . .

67

It is the King's earnest prayer, in which I fervently join, that under Divine Providence the future years may see the same advance in the development and prosperity of the Empire . . . the same spirit of mutual understanding and sympathy, and the same determination to support one another to the utmost, should need come.

As the notes of the national anthem sung by Dame Nellie Melba faded away, and the city clocks chimed noon, a trumpet fanfare rang out against the background thud of a twenty-one gun salute, and the ceremonial opening of Australia's Parliament had reached its conclusion. For the Duke of York – as for the Duchess, who sat quietly smiling her encouragement at her husband as he spoke – the great ordeal was at last over.

Two weeks later the entire tour was over and the Duke and Duchess were on their way home. The battleship *Renown* slipped anchor at Fremantle on 23 May. The return voyage was not all plain sailing, however, for only three days later as the vessel crossed the Indian Ocean, what was quite literally a potentially explosive situation occurred when fire broke out aboard, caused by leaking oil in one of the boiler-rooms. The place was soon an inferno. Contingency plans to flood the ammunition and, if need be, to abandon ship, were in hand as messages – understating the danger – were relayed to the Duke and Duchess. For some ten hours sailors of the fire party fought the blaze until it was at last extinguished.

Later when the Captain asked the Duchess if she had realized how bad the situation had been, her now famous reply was, 'Yes I did. Every hour someone came and told me there was nothing to worry about, so I knew there was real trouble.'

With the exception of a refuelling stop at the volcanic Great Hanish Islands, the Yorks' homeward journey was interrupted only three times when they visited the islands of Mauritius, Malta and Gibraltar.

At Portsmouth on 27 June, the Duke and Duchess of York were greeted by the Prince of Wales, Prince Henry and Prince George, while at Victoria Station later on, they were welcomed home by the King and Queen who had driven across from Buckingham Palace. 'We will not embrace at the station before so many people,' George V had already instructed his son, then added,

'When you kiss Mama take yr. hat off.'

Throughout the Duke and Duchess's protracted absence on the other side of the world, Queen Mary had kept her promise and despatched regular letters telling them of their baby daughter's progress. The biggest hugs and fondest kisses were therefore reserved for the little Princess Elizabeth upon her parents' return. Indeed her first appearance on the balcony of Buckingham Palace, at the age of thirteen months, took place that very afternoon. Shielded by one of Queen Mary's famous parasols, the child was carried out in her beaming mother's arms, to the acclaim of the crowds waiting below.

The royal family's reunion may, perhaps, have been tinged with that vague sense of shyness experienced by many long-distance travellers when they come home. If the Yorks felt at all 'strange' on that June day in 1927, then the sensation may conceivably have been exacerbated as they drove from Buckingham Palace to their new home. Number 145 Piccadilly, four doors away from Apsley House, the 'Iron' Duke of Wellington's mansion, a mere hop from Hyde Park, had been refurbished for the Duke and Duchess while they were away. Until the lease of the house had been acquired for the Duke, No. 145 had stood empty for several years. For some unknown reason it had proven impossible to let, and at one stage the Crown Estate Commissioners had even considered a proposal that it should be converted into several flats.

As a complete residence it had been up for letting since the autumn of 1921, when it was advertised as an 'important mansion . . . at Hyde Park Corner containing entrance hall, principal staircase hall, a secondary staircase with electric passenger lift, drawing-room, dining-room, ballroom, study, library, about 25 bedrooms, conservatory, etc. . . . '

That so well-appointed (and enviably proportioned) a house should have remained untenanted for so long seems a mystery. But there it was. Built in about 1795 from designs by the Adam brothers, No. 145 was a tall, four-storeyed building faced with grey stone. For some thirty years it had been the home of Sir John Smith-Burges, a director of the East India Company. On the demise of his widow the house was acquired by the 1st Marquess of Northampton, whose descendants made it their London home for several generations. It was, in fact, known at one time as Northampton House. Subsequent tenants included Sir William

Bass and Albert von Goldschmidt-Rothschild, son-in-law of Baron Edmond Rothschild.

During the Second World War, the house met an ignoble end when, on 7 October 1940, it received a direct hit from the Luftwaffe's bombs. For nineteen years it scarred Hyde Park Corner, a derelict reminder of times gone by. It was not demolished until 1959, and today, the frantically busy highway that is Park Lane runs over its foundations.

In 1927, however, 145 Piccadilly became an official royal residence and completely replaced White Lodge in the lives of the Duke and Duchess of York.

At the beginning of 1930, the Duchess of York was able to tell her delighted husband that she was again pregnant and expected to present him with their second child at about the time of her thirtieth birthday that August. Such news quite naturally seemed to complete their happiness. They were, of course, already well established in the nation's affections as public figures, and their home life could hardly have been more harmonious.

Lady Donaldson has said, 'It was thought very delightful that the Yorks were so happy together and succeeded in living a full private life.' It was this jealously guarded private life that meant so much to the Duke and Duchess, for through it the Duke not only felt secure, but whole. His home life was now as different as could possibly be from all he had known as a child and as a very young man. The credit for the Duke's happiness belonged indisputably to his wife and, indeed, as he changed and was strengthened so there occurred, slowly and imperceptibly, a change in the nature of his relationship with the Duchess. To begin with he had relied totally on her. Now in 1930, as they looked back over the first seven years of marriage, the Duchess could begin to draw strength and confidence from her husband.

One who knew the couple well has been quoted as saying, 'That was the measure of her greatness as a woman. She drew him out, and made him a man so strong that she could lean upon him.'

Princess Margaret, the Yorks' second and youngest child, was not born as early as had originally been anticipated. In fact, far from arriving early in the month, the birth did not take place until precisely 9.22 on the evening of 21 August. Whether that day had been chosen by nature or specifically by her mother, for this baby was also delivered by caesarian section, is immaterial. What is of interest is that Princess Margaret's birth was an event of particular distinction in the annals of Scottish history.

Born at Glamis Castle, the Princess was the first senior-ranking member of the royal family to have first seen the light of day north of the border since King Charles I, who had been born the son of James VI (James I of England) at Dunfermline on 19 November 1600.

The birth of Princess Margaret was formally announced to the nation by way of a blandly worded statement on 22 August, which read: 'Her Royal Highness The Duchess of York was safely delivered of a Princess at Glamis Castle. His Royal Highness The Duke of York and the Countess of Strathmore and Kinghorne were present. . . . Her Royal Highness and the infant Princess are doing well.'

'Got the news that Elizabeth had a little girl . . .' noted King George V in his diary. Later that same day he and the Queen, together with Prince George, left Sandringham for Scotland. The Duchess was looking very well, thought Queen Mary, 'and the baby a darling'.

In October the infant received the names Margaret Rose at her christening by the Archbisop of Canterbury at Buckingham Palace. The first was a name the King particularly liked, and 'Rose' had been chosen in preference to 'Ann' (a name the King did not like at all), as a compliment to the Duchess of York's sister, Countess Granville.

Now the dependable 'Allah' had two young charges in the nurseries at the top of 145 Piccadilly and, within the year, a new member of staff had arrived with whom there was to be fierce competition over the children. In 1931 a tall, slim Scotswoman with somewhat pointed, though pleasant features, was engaged by the Duchess of York to act as governess. She was Miss Marion Crawford, or 'Crawfie' as she was soon to be nicknamed by Princess Elizabeth. At twenty-two Queen Mary considered her far too young for so responsible a position, but the Duchess stood firm. Indeed she wanted the atmosphere surrounding her daughters to be one of cheerful youthfulness. 'Crawfie' had, moreover, already proven herself perfectly competent, for she had come to the York household highly recommended by the Duchess's sister

Rose, whose own daughter Mary she had taught.

Of her royal appointment 'Crawfie', who had originally intended to become a teacher rather than a governess in private service, wrote much later, 'It seemed to me then that this was just a pleasant interlude, a temporary arrangement to fill in the time between one course of study and the next.' Little could she have known that she would remain a part of royal family life for well over a decade and, at the end of the day, find the kind of fame few servants ever enjoy. As the author of a number of books and articles about the Princesses, 'Crawfie' incurred the displeasure of her employers, by then King George and Queen Elizabeth, and the expression 'Doing a Crawfie' duly entered the royal vocabulary to describe all those who, at least in the minds of the royal family, betray positions of trust.

In 1931, however, such things lay in the distant future and, for the time being, there was little to threaten the comfortable pattern of the Yorks' daily life.

At 145 Piccadilly the Duke and Duchess, while monitoring the way in which their establishment was run, left its supervision to a household staff far bigger than most members of the royal family could afford to employ today. Quite apart from their office staff and those connected with the royal nursery – 'Allah' the treasured nanny, Margaret MacDonald, the nursery maid (nicknamed 'Bobo' – who today holds sway as dresser to the Queen), and 'Crawfie' the governess – there was a butler, an under-butler, a housekeeper, two footmen, a cook and three kitchen maids, a valet for the Duke and a dresser for the Duchess, an RAF orderly, an odd-job-man, a night-watchman, a telephonist and a chauffeur, most of whom 'lived in'.

Though the royal way of life is scarcely fraught with the everyday cares and worries that beset most people, it is a mistake to imagine that it is one of constant glamour and excitement. While it is of course true that all kinds of material benefits, the perks of office, are there more or less for the asking, routine is as much a part of royalty's existence as any other. Clearing official as well as private paperwork, conferences with Private Secretaries, audiences and the like, were invariably morning tasks for the Duke and Duchess of York, but work was not begun until after a visit from their children. Public engagements, where possible, were reserved for later in the day, though naturally there were those that were inescapably *ante meridiem.*

Though the Duchess was profoundly happy loving and mothering her husband, ever her first priority throughout her marriage, it was never entirely to the exclusion of a rewarding and mentally stimulating social life.

Their friends, not unexpectedly, were drawn largely from the aristocratic families with whom they had always associated. Thus names like Airlie, Abercorn, Buccleuch, Leicester, Adeane, Salisbury, Devonshire, Spencer, Pembroke, Nevill and so on were warmly familiar to them. There were royal friends too. The Duchess of York had been close to her sister-in-law, the Princess Royal, for some years, and she was especially fond of Prince Paul of Yugoslavia, who spent much of his time in London, despite his Eastern European connections.

Yet if the hand of intimate royal friendship was rarely extended beyond these traditional circles, the Yorks nevertheless counted amongst their acquaintances many men and women from the world of the arts. Among them, for instance, were included Harold Nicolson and his wife, the novelist Vita Sackville-West, Woodrow Wyatt, Cecil Beaton, Edith Sitwell and her fellow poet John Betjeman, Hugh Casson, Benjamin Britten, Frederick Ashton, John Piper, Edward Seago, the actor Noël Coward and the actress Celia Johnson. Another who came to know the couple well, though more particularly after they had become King and Queen, was Kenneth Clark. As Surveyor of the King's Pictures, a post he held from 1934 to 1944, he came to appreciate Queen Elizabeth not only as a woman of good taste, but as a willing student of contemporary art who was anxious to start her own modern collection and who naturally wanted to understand what she was looking at.

During the late 1930s, therefore, Clark was a frequent guest and he invariably engaged the Queen in long conversations, sometimes during their walks together through the gardens at Windsor. The empathy between his Consort and his Surveyor (who delighted in his new role as royal mentor), however, gave rise to what Clark regarded as unreasonable jealousy on the King's part which, on two occasions, led to angry scenes. Yet if Kenneth Clark (who considered George VI to be as ignorant about art as he was complacent about the awe-inspiring Royal Collections) was bewitched by Queen Elizabeth, he was by no means alone. As we have already seen, any number of his contemporaries had been held hopelessly spellbound by the Queen's charm and overall manner, which has been repeatedly described as 'flirtatious', though 'in a very proper, romantic old-fashioned Valentine sort of way'.

As Lady Elizabeth Bowes Lyon the Duchess of York had of course enjoyed a number of close friendships with members of both sexes; friendships she had no wish to abandon once she married into the royal family. But what had not been envisaged was the psychological barrier which tended to impede the flow of uninhibited communication between the Duchess and those to whom she was particularly attached. To her dismay she soon realized that her royal position made her real friends hold back, while others of her acquaintance had no compunction at pushing themselves forward, in vain attempts to force a royal friendship.

Though almost imperceptibly, there also occurred a change in the attitudes of the Duchess's own family — as if from being an adored daughter, sister, aunt and cousin, she was now one step above them all. A particularly apt example of this new deference arose early in 1923, when the Countess of Strathmore summoned her family to announce that, henceforth, all family nicknames for the new Duchess of York should be dropped as a mark of respect. All such names were, in fact, forgotten with the exception of one. To this day Queen Elizabeth is still affectionately, if curiously, known to her Elphinstone nephews and nieces as 'Peter'. The precise origins of this particular nickname are now lost. Some members of the family have suggested that it was a child's first attempt at pronouncing 'Elizabeth', though it should be said that they hardly believe it themselves. However it came about, the name started with the young Elizabeth, daughter of 'May' Lady Elphinstone, who had attended the York wedding as a train-bearer. That the nickname has survived is due entirely, so the author was told, to the absence of the Elphinstone family from the 'clan' conference of 1923.

During the 1920s members of the royal family enjoyed a luxury that they find today in very small measure, that of privacy. The Yorks, however, were particularly vulnerable to public curiosity because, unlike most royal residences, No.145 Piccadilly was not screened by high walls or long private drives, but opened directly on to the street, so that their comings and goings attracted rather more attention than would otherwise have been so. 'Bloody people', the Duke of York once snapped in an off moment, as he and the Duchess stepped out of their front door to be met by the usual scene of gawping faces pressed against the railings. The little Princesses, indisputably one of the main attractions, fared no better.

In those days, when royal offspring were educated privately – there was never any suggestion that they might attend proper schools – a period of recreation was naturally part and parcel of their well-ordered days. During that hour the Princesses Elizabeth and Margaret enthusiastically entered into the spirit of such games as hide-and-seek and cowboys and indians. But once again the vigilant attention of strangers proved an irksome drawback, if only because best behaviour was demanded of two boisterous little girls, even when at play. This was another disadvantage of No. 145's location, for it had no private garden of its own but shared with its neighbours a communal area of lawn and bushes known as Hamilton Gardens. Here the Princesses played their games, sometimes joined by their father, who was as much an expert at hop-scotch as they, but ever watched at a distance by members of the public. Their silent presence, said Princess Margaret, was never something she or her sister got used to. On wet days or in winter the Princesses enjoyed the welcome respite of playing indoors when the game of 'horses' – probably their most favourite activity of all – well and truly came into its own. Beneath the glass-domed roof at the top of the house were 'stabled' the Princesses' collection of rocking-horses, which required 'exercise', 'grooming' and 'feeding' 'all day' as Princess Margaret recalled.

## ～ 8 ～

# *Year of the Three Kings*

In the upper echelons of British society, one of the outward symbols of wealth and position has always been the country house, as distinct from the essential town residence. Today it would appear that the business of maintaining two houses confounds many of those whose families have been accustomed to enjoying more than one home for generations. In consequence a large number of 'ancestral piles' have reluctantly passed into the care of the National Trust, or have fallen beneath the auctioneer's hammer in the interests of economy.

Members of the royal family have, for obvious reasons, fared infinitely better and, almost without exception, retain country estates. The Prince and Princess of Wales, Princess Anne, and Prince and Princess Michael of Kent, privately own Highgrove, Gatcombe Park and Nether Lypiatt Manor, respectively, all of them located in Gloucestershire. The Duke and Duchess of Kent have Anmer Hall near Sandringham, while the Duke and Duchess of Gloucester spend much of their free time at Barnwell Manor in Northamptonshire, a 2,500-acre estate acquired by the Duke's late father, Prince Henry, in 1938. Only Princess Margaret (who owns a comparatively modest, four-bedroomed property on the Caribbean island of Mustique) and Princess Alexandra do not have country houses in England.

At the beginning of the 1930s, the future George VI and Queen Elizabeth had only one home, their official residence at Hyde Park Corner. King George V technically owned Windsor Castle and any number of 'grace and favour' properties in England and

76

Scotland, ranging from palaces to cottages, and also claimed private possession of both Sandringham and Balmoral, as the Sovereign does today.

Edward, Prince of Wales, officially ensconced at York House, St James's Palace, privately owned a 4,000-acre ranch in Alberta, and had, since April 1930, enjoyed a retreat in Windsor Great Park known as Fort Belvedere, 'a castellated conglomeration', as he described it.

In turn the thoughts of the Duke and Duchess of York moved towards trying to find a country house for themselves and in 1931 they were offered the Royal Lodge. Like Fort Belvedere, which George V declared to be 'a queer old place', Royal Lodge is also situated in Windsor Great Park. Not far from the broad sweep of Smiths Lawn, where the present Prince of Wales regularly plays polo, the pink-washed, two-storey house is approached by a long winding drive wending its way through immaculate grounds to the far side of the royal chapel of All Saints. Securely fenced in and hidden from the view of those using the public paths by a thick barricade of trees, hedges and rhododendron bushes, the garden front (or rear) of Royal Lodge commands a magnificent vista across the Great Park.

During the eighteenth century there existed on the site a red-brick house known as the Lower Lodge, occupied by Thomas Sandby, Deputy Ranger of Windsor Great Park and the brother of Paul Sandby whose exquisite watercolours form a part of the royal collection. Later on, the Prince Regent decided to demolish the Lodge and, with his love of the outrageous and grandiose (the Royal Pavilion at Brighton survives as a clear testimonial), set about building a 'Royal Lodge' on a far more flamboyant scale. Existing plans show the Prince Regent's house stretching east of the present building and containing a large number of rooms, including three libraries, a conservatory, a vast saloon or drawing-room and a dining-room of equal proportions. Much of the building work was, in fact, executed, but it is by no means certain that 'Prinny's' Royal Lodge was actually completed.

With his accession to the throne in June 1830, King William IV demolished his brother's house, save for the Great Saloon, which was afterwards partitioned off into five separate and ill-proportioned rooms and used by Sir Arthur Ellis, Comptroller to Edward VII's Lord Chamberlain. When King George V gave

Royal Lodge to the Duke and Duchess of York, some twenty years later, much work needed to be done, including the restoration of the Great Saloon – 48 feet long, 29 feet wide and 20 feet high – to its former glory. A bedroom wing was added towards the end of the 1930s, together with nursery accommodation, guest rooms and servants' quarters.

Other alterations and additions have been made through the years. A few years ago, a basement kitchen, which had been sealed up a long time before, was rediscovered. Said an Old Windsorian carrying out repair work at the house, 'It was as if somebody had finished work, closed the door and left everything as it was; lovely copper pans and all. Just sealed it all up.'

One of the joys of the Duke of York's existence was gardening, and in exactly the same way that the Prince of Wales had conquered a wilderness at Fort Belvedere with his own hands, so the Duke eagerly took on the task of turning the jungle at Royal Lodge into a supremely beautiful, almost magical garden. It was a formidable and exacting task, but one which the Duke took up with relentless zeal; hacking away at solid banks of rhododendron bushes, wrestling with tangled thickets, shrubs and creepers and trundling the never-ending debris to the huge bonfires. Callers at Royal Lodge were always roped in to lend a hand and everybody worked together weekend after weekend until, eventually, the desired glades and avenues began to take shape and were planted with new trees and flowering shrubs. In connection with this strenuous, even therapeutic but hugely rewarding work, the Duke enjoyed discussing his plans and schemes with the man who was soon to be responsible for planning and founding the famous garden which, as King, the Duke of York insisted should bear his name. He was Sir Eric Savill whose influence, first as Agent of the Commissioners of Crown Lands and later as Deputy Ranger, was to be felt throughout Windsor Great Park for more than thirty years.

A love of gardens was also shared by the Duchess of York, who enthusiastically played her part in helping to clear the way for the tranquil garden – in spring and summer vividly coloured by massed daffodils, azaleas, syringa and pink, white, red and mauve rhododendrons – that she continues to enjoy. Indeed it is a mark of her all-consuming interest in gardening that, as Queen Mother, she began to make tours of designated London boroughs each summer to inspect civic as well as private gardens. It is an engagement in her calendar to which she has always looked forward with as much pleasure as her annual private visits to France, to view the magnificent gardens of personal friends staying, until his recent death, with the Vicomte de Noailles at his home near Grasse.

At Clarence House in London, at the Royal Lodge, and at the Castle of Mey in Caithness, where she planned and laid out a garden hardy enough to endure the fierce winds of the Scottish coast, any number of gardening books may be found in Queen Elizabeth's library. Some she has collected herself, others have over the years been sent to her by friends. Writing to one such friend, the late Ava, Lady Waverley, in December 1959, for example, the Queen Mother thanked her for 'those enchanting flower books – they really are most delightful, and the flowering trees and shrubs one is the sort of thing I have been longing to find . . .'

National and international events during the 1930s marked the decline of the Yorks' 'halcyon' days. The bubble of blissful contentment that had enfolded them since their marriage was shortly to burst, and by the end of the decade the Duke and Duchess had both been catapulted over the heads of the royal 'chorus' to the lonely heights of solo performers.

In the words of Queen Mary, 1931 itself had been, 'a tiresome year, full of anxieties'. Hard on the heels of the collapse of the New York stock market in October 1929, renewed financial disaster caused by the crash of the Kreditanstalt Bank in Vienna sent violent shock waves reverberating throughout Europe. In London that August, King George V advised his Labour Prime Minister, Ramsay MacDonald, to form a National Government – a coalition – to save the country from bankruptcy.

In the hope of trying to help avert even greater catastrophe at home, the King himself surrendered £50,000 from his annual Civil List allowance, and Edward, Prince of Wales, made a corresponding gesture from his very considerable income, notably that derived from the revenues of his Duchy of Cornwall estates. (Princes of Wales are also Dukes of Cornwall and of Rothesay.)

With the inevitability of hardline economics, Britain's families were forced to tighten their belts. In tightening his, the Duke of

York reluctantly put his six hunting horses up for auction.

'It has come as a great shock to me that my hunting should have been one of the things I must do without,' he wrote to the Master of the Pytchley Hunt. Ironically it was as the result of a week-end's hunting that the Duke of York was ultimately to surrender more than his love of chasing foxes. For during the autumn of that 'tiresome year', the Prince of Wales and his brother Prince George were invited to join a hunting party at Melton Mowbray. Among their fellow guests were Mr and Mrs Ernest Simpson. As Duke of Windsor, the Prince recalled:

> Mrs Simpson did not ride and obviously had no interest in horses, hounds, or hunting in general.
>
> Since a Prince is by custom expected to take the lead in conversing with strangers, and having been informed that she was an American, I was prompted to observe that she must miss central heating, of which there was a lamentable lack in my country and an abundance in hers. The affirmative answer that, in the circumstances, any Briton had reason to expect would then have cleared the way for a casual discussion of the variety of physical comforts available in America, and the conversation would have been safely anchored on firm ground. But instead, a verbal chasm opened under my feet. Mrs Simpson did not miss the great boon that her country had conferred upon the world. On the contrary, she liked our cold houses. A mocking look came into her eyes. 'I am sorry, Sir,' she said, 'but you have disappointed me.'
>
> 'In what way?'
>
> 'Every American woman who comes to your country is always asked that same question. I had hoped for something more original from the Prince of Wales.'

Thoughts of that first meeting and the memory of Mrs Simpson's refreshingly straightforward remarks lingered on in the Prince's mind. In time the man who became King Edward VIII, fulfilled his future wife's hopes for 'something more original', and she, in turn, provided him with something so original that it shook the throne to its very foundations.

Although the Prince of Wales' penchant for married women was known by many in high society, nobody present during that week-end house party at Melton Mowbray could have guessed what fate held in store for the Prince and Mrs Simpson. Indeed, had anybody thought it even remotely possible that the couple were to establish an intimate relationship before very long, most would have regarded it as no more than just another romantic episode in the life of the debonair Heir Apparent.

He had, after all, enjoyed a prolonged affair of many years standing with Winifred ('Freda') Dudley Ward, afterwards the Marquesa de Casa Maury, and was currently enjoying the favours of Thelma, Lady Furness, whose own star, incidentally, was already in the descent. She, like Mrs Dudley Ward, was to be ditched ungallantly by the Prince of Wales when he grew weary of her.

Within two years of the Prince's meeting with Wallis Simpson, marriage was indeed in the air. Not theirs, of course, but that of Prince George and Princess Marina of Greece and Denmark. Tall and dark, as beautiful as she was intelligent, the Princess had been born in Athens on 13 December 1906. Her father, Prince Nicholas, was the third son of the Danish prince who became King George I of the Hellenes. Her mother, officially known as Princess Nicholas, was the Russian Grand Duchess Helen Vladimirovna, a niece of Tsar Alexander III and his Empress Marie, whose sister, as we have already seen, was Britain's Queen Alexandra.

'She is a child of destiny, and there is both sunshine and shadow for her', a gypsy woman foretold, shortly after Princess Marina's birth. 'She will be beautiful and make a great marriage with a king's son. Love will be her guiding star. It will bring her sorrow, for she will lose her husband while she is still young and at the height of her happiness. But she will find consolation in her children.'

Raised by an English governess, Princess Marina was fluent in English, Greek, French, Russian and German. As a child, she informed her grandmother Queen Olga that she preferred to pray in English rather than in Greek, saying, 'I have arranged it with God. I told Him I liked to talk to Him in English best, and He said, "Please yourself, Marina".'

The Princess with her sophisticated culture brought both style and elegance to the House of Windsor. The public adored her and not only copied her fashions, but named colours in her honour. 'Marina blue' for example was *de rigueur* for the fashion-conscious.

When the Greek royal family was exiled in 1922, Prince and Princess Nicholas took their three daughters, of whom Princess

Marina was the youngest, to Paris. There the Prince earned a modest living as a painter, his wife worked in the home she had founded in Saint-Germain for Russian orphans and refugees, while Princess Marina found work as a mannequin at the grandest of salons. Indeed, it was the House of Molyneux that made her exquisitely delicate wedding gown of white and silver brocade.

Created Duke of Kent three weeks before his wedding in November 1934, Prince George had, upon leaving the Royal Navy – at the end of another comparatively short service career – been taken under his eldest brother's wing and in fact lived with him at York House for three or four years. It was, no doubt, a tactful move, for the elder Prince had helped the younger conquer his drug addiction, and he was in a position to watch over some of Prince George's other, rather more colourful exploits and activities, perhaps offering a kindly word of caution every now and then.

In his memoirs the Duke of Windsor provided a thumbnail sketch of his favourite brother: 'Nearly nine years younger than I, George was sharply different in outlook and temperament from the rest of us,' he wrote. 'Possessed of unusual charm of manner and a quick sense of humour and talented in many directions, he had an undoubted flair for the arts. He played the piano, knew a good deal about music, and had a knowledgeable eye for antiques. Being somewhat Bohemian by inclination, he had understandably found life in the Navy a bit confining.'

Eighteen months after the marriage of Prince George and Princess Marina, the nation celebrated another, and this time more significant, event in the life of the royal family; the Silver Jubilee of the King's reign.

George V's popularity gave rise to an immense outpouring of loyalty and sentimentality on the occasion of the twenty-fifth anniversary of his accession. Jubilee celebrations across the Empire took many forms, as did the tributes that were paid to the seventy-year-old Sovereign. One example was the illumination of public buildings and places. In Bombay the façade and tower of the Victoria Terminus of the Great Indian Peninsular Railway was floodlit; in Northern Ireland Belfast City Hall was awash with red, white and blue light; the Gothic tower of Bristol University stood out against the night skies like some kind of massive

Victorian wedding cake; while St James's Park in London was described as looking like a 'Fairyland'.

An even greater extravaganza was staged by the Oxford Street store, Selfridges. At a cost of £10,000 the building's entire façade was transformed into a patriotic mural on a gargantuan scale, designed by the distinguished painter William Walcot. The grey stone walls were submerged beneath voluminous Union Jacks, swathed in banners and colonial emblems, hung with crowns, and studded with huge medallions representing the Silver Jubilee medal and showing the crowned profiles of both George V and Queen Mary. On the roof, surmounting the whole and flanked by a pair of lions, was a monumental gilded statue of Britannia, designed by Sir William Reid Dick.

In writing to Count Albert Mensdorff, whose friendship with the royal family went back to the previous century, the King said, '. . . looking back during these last 25 years, I am indeed thankful for all that has been done for me. . . . I do indeed appreciate all the love and affection which my people are expressing, from all over the world. . . . I remember so well both Queen Victoria's Jubilees and can't yet realise that I am having one now.'

Monday, 6 May 1935, the actual anniversary of the King's accession, witnessed all the pomp and pageantry of a full-scale royal occasion, as George V and Queen Mary with their family attended the Jubilee thanksgiving service at St Paul's Cathedral.

The majestic figures of the King and Queen – he wearing the scarlet uniform of a Field Marshal, she dressed in silver – rode in procession to the cathedral in the 1902 state landau, drawn by six Windsor greys, preceded by other members of the royal family. Recalling the flavour of so great a national event, one contemporary newspaper report tells us,

First came the Duke and Duchess of York, the Duke in the uniform of a Rear-Admiral and the Duchess in a dress of aeroplane blue. Opposite them sat their two little girls, Princess Elizabeth and Princess Margaret, both dressed in salmon pink frocks with pink bonnets.

The Princesses captured the hearts of the multitude instantly. The dignified self-possession of Princess Elizabeth and the laughing happiness of her little sister sent the crowds into raptures. While the children waved their hands with an entire lack of self-consciousness the crowd roared with delight.

In the second carriage was the Duke of Kent . . . and his lovely Duchess, dressed in grey with a large hat.

A pause of a few minutes, then came the Prince of Wales, his face scarcely visible under the bearskin he wore with his uniform of Colonel-in-Chief, Welsh Guards.

The clatter of horses' hooves and an imposing military procession went by – lancers, dragoons, artillery, in brilliant dress . . . there were cheers for the Indian Princes [the Maharajas of Patiala, Kashmir, Bikaner, and Sir Umar Hayat Khan, were ADCs to George V, the second Emperor of India] and cheers for the Escort.

'Here comes the King'. Cheering rolled along the bannered way. Bowing and smiling to right and left, the King and Queen slowly passed by. . . .

Late that evening both George V and Queen Mary picked up their pens to record the day's events. To her diary the Queen – who was nearing her sixty-eighth birthday – confided, 'We had a marvellous reception from the crowds of people all the way to St Pauls Cathedral & back – The thanksgiving service at 11.30 was beautiful – Back before 1 & we all went on to the Balcony where the crowds cheered us – After luncheon we had to go on to the Balcony again . . .'. At length the Queen concluded that it had been 'A wonderful day'. Though profoundly moved by the occasion, the King himself was less descriptive. He wrote, 'The greatest number of people in the streets I have ever seen in my life. The enthusiasm was indeed most touching.' Then he added modestly, 'I'd no idea they felt like that about me. I am beginning to think they must really like me for myself.'

Had he but known it, King George V had seen his last parade, for eight months later, on 20 January 1936, he was dead; his end brought on by the recurrence of bronchial trouble that had started to plague him several years earlier.

With the words *'Am brokenhearted'*, Queen Mary began to record the peaceful death of her 'darling husband' in her journal. When she had finished she turned to a fresh page and wrote, 'The sunset of his death tinged the whole world's sky'. Three days later the widowed Queen, accompanied by the newly-proclaimed King Edward VIII, the Duke and Duchess of York, the Princess Royal and other members of the royal family, followed the coffin of George V from Sandringham to London where it was taken to

Westminster Hall to lie in state for four days, before the funeral at Windsor on 28 January.

It was during that time that, in a unique tribute to their father – to their dead King – 'David', 'Bertie', 'Harry', and 'George', each dressed in ceremonial uniform, took up one of the twenty-minute watches that were observed at the foot of the catafalque on which the coffin rested. Later, at Queen Mary's own wish that scene, which became known as *The Vigil of the Princes*, was painted by F. E. Beresford and in June, the Queen gave the picture to Edward VIII as a forty-first birthday present.

So had begun a period known in British history as the 'Year of the Three Kings'.

Was it just an inspired guess or royal 'second sight' that had prompted George V to say that, as king, his heir would 'ruin himself' within a year; adding that he prayed nothing would 'come between Bertie and Lilibet [as Princess Elizabeth was nicknamed] and the Throne'? Certainly the reign of Edward VIII opened on a note of ill-omen. For on the morning that the dead King's coffin was conveyed to Westminster Hall, the diamond Maltese cross surmounting the Imperial State Crown became dislodged from its setting and fell from the gun-carriage, '. . . suddenly out of the corner of my eye, I caught a flash of light dancing along the pavement,' the Duke of Windsor recalled. ' . . . it seemed a strange thing to happen; and although not superstitious, I wondered whether it was a bad omen.'

Of all his sons the most tense relationship always existed between George V and the Prince of Wales. The old King did not approve of the way in which the Prince had introduced a generous amount of informality into his offical life, any more than he liked the hedonistic pursuits of his son's private life. He did not much care for his circle of friends, for their taste in foreign holiday travel, or for the way in which they danced the nights away at fashionable night-clubs such as the Embassy. He did not like the modern stylish way in which his son dressed, and had him sternly lectured on the necessity of preserving the 'mystique' of the monarchy. 'If you bring it down to the people,' argued the King's Keeper of the Privy Purse, Sir Frederick Ponsonby, 'it will lose its mystery and influence.' The Prince did not agree. Nor did he agree with his father when the King warned him, 'You must always remember your position and who you are.' '. . . who exactly was I?' the Prince of Wales asked. 'The idea that my birth and title should somehow or other set me apart from and above other people struck me as wrong,' he explained many years later. 'If the levelling process of Osborne, Dartmouth and Oxford, and the democracy of the battlefields, had taught me anything, it was firstly, that my desires and interests were much the same as those of other people. . . .'

Such is an indication of the gulf that existed between a sovereign of the old school and a disciple of the new. That gulf would never be narrowed and it resulted in an uneasy truce that was never completely maintained. At the close of one confrontation between father and son, for example, George V is known to have bellowed at the Heir Apparent, 'You dress like a cad. You act like a cad. You *are* a cad. Get out!'

Whatever the King's view of his son, Prince Edward had succeeded – as no other has – in proving himself a spectacularly popular and effective Prince of Wales, a man of the people and, as the Duchess of Windsor described him, a man 'ahead of his time'.

Despite all efforts to discredit him in the years since he relinquished the throne, it is the memory of his career as Prince of Wales that has survived what would nowadays be called the 'smear campaign', orchestrated against him by 'Establishment' forces. In the words of Diana Mosley, 'Virtually the whole working class adored him, and a great many others besides. The goody-goodies (as Churchill used to call them) did *not* and they are powerful in England.'

It would serve no useful purpose in this study to enter into a lengthy dissertation of the *known* facts of the abdication of King Edward VIII.

What does seem highly probable, however, is that the young Sovereign's love for Wallis Simpson was not the only reason for making him take the irrevocable step of renouncing the Crown. It has, of course, been regarded and perpetuated as such since that fateful winter of 1936; but almost inevitably, there is much that will ever be concealed by what the Duchess of Windsor once called the 'Velvet and Ermine Curtain', through which the truths of royal lives are rarely perceived by the vast majority in the world outside.

Curiously King Edward VIII's wish to marry Mrs Simpson – although it became a grave constitutional issue – was never put before Parliament. As Prime Minister, Stanley Baldwin seems to have regarded the entire episode as being exclusively his.

The Duke of Windsor himself later painted a frustrating picture of a wall being built around him, isolating him from a paramount right to what might be called a fair hearing and alienating him from his people. In an attempt to quell rising passions somewhat, Wallis Simpson fled to France, from where she begged the King to think again.

The 'official' view of Mrs Simpson's act was that the American-born divorcée, with not one but two former husbands still living, was nothing more than a ruthlessly calculating 'adventuress' who, when it finally dawned on her that she could never become Queen of England – a point which, in any event, had never been insisted upon – turned swiftly on her heels, wanting to wash her hands of the King as well as all her glittering hopes. In subsequent years, she was further vilified as a cold, domineering woman, dedicated to exploiting her semi-royal status to the full.

Among those who have leapt to the Duchess of Windsor's defence are Diana Mosley, who was a personal friend; Michael Bloch, the learned author of two remarkable studies about the Windsors and a latter-day champion of their cause; and Anne Seagrim, who worked as secretary to the Duke and Duchess. With the benefit of an 'insider's' knowledge, each has averred that when Mrs Simpson pleaded with the King to forget her and remain on the throne, she did so not because her personal dreams were never to be fully realized, but from a selfless desire to see Edward VIII fulfil his rightful role as sovereign, secure in the undoubted affection of his people.

Throughout this time, the King remained immoveable in his determination to make Wallis Simpson his wife. During the critical period which led up to the abdication, the idea that the King and Mrs Simpson might marry morganatically was one of the proposals submitted to Downing Street. It was an arrangement that had been employed among the royal courts of Europe, even if there had been no cause for such an arrangement to have been properly tested in England. Indeed Queen Mary's own paternal grandparents, Alexander, Duke of Württenberg and Claudine, Countess Rhédey, had been so married.

When the idea was put to the Prime Minister, he responded by saying that he would, of necessity, have to consult the Dominion premiers. He did so and the proposal was summarily dismissed. The King then requested that he be allowed to broadcast personally to his subjects, in the style of the American President Roosevelt's cosy 'fireside chats'. On this, too, he was overruled. In short, the King's ideas were thwarted at every turn.

'Clear to the end, Mr Baldwin in his exchanges with me followed with scrupulous exactitude the constitutional rhetoric which preserves the fiction of kingly authority,' the Duke of Windsor wrote. 'It was always *my* Ministers who would not let me do what I wished. It was always with *his humble duty* that he did what *he* wished. The Prime Minister controlled all the levers of power.'

In the eyes of Queen Mary, who had referred to the whole abdication saga as 'a pretty kettle of fish', her son had committed the cardinal sin of putting private considerations before his duty. He had abandoned his birth-right, and had brought heartache and disgrace to the royal house and, more especially, upon the monarchy itself. For that the Queen would never extend her forgiveness.

The word 'duty' was, of course, much bandied about. Yet paradoxically it was precisely *through* his sense of duty that Edward VIII abdicated the responsibilities which, in all conscience, he felt unable to discharge.

That no English king had abdicated since Richard II in 1399, may well have made the unhappy events of 1936 so much more unpalatable. In a country where abdication was not unknown, for example in The Netherlands, such an event would never have caused so great a furore. Nevertheless, the story of Edward VIII and Wallis Simpson, like so many stories of human tragedy, was destined to go on captivating European audiences in many forms – books, magazine articles, plays, television soap-operas and documentary films – for generations. Yet perhaps one of the most bizarre by-products of the abdication was its inspirational effect upon the American film-maker Walt Disney. For out of it he created the story of *Snow White* and modelled his heroine on the Duchess of Windsor.

The Instrument of Abdication was drawn up for the King's

approval on 9 December and taken to him at Fort Belvedere. It read:

> I, Edward the Eighth, of Great Britain, Ireland, and the British Dominions beyond the Seas, King, Emperor of India, do hereby declare My irrevocable determination to renounce the Throne for Myself and for My descendants, and My desire that effect should be given to this Instrument of Abdication immediately.

The following morning, in his ground-floor study at the Fort, Edward VIII signed the document in the presence of his brothers: the Duke of York, who would succeed him, and the Dukes of Gloucester and Kent. The actual Act of Abdication, 'A Bill to give effect to His Majesty's declaration . . .' was signed the following day.

As 'His Royal Highness Prince Edward' (the ex-King was not created HRH The Duke of Windsor until 8 March 1937), the man who had so briefly reigned as the second sovereign of the House of Windsor, broadcast to the nation, before rejoining his family at Royal Lodge. From Windsor Great Park, a passenger in an unmarked car, the Prince quietly slipped away shortly after midnight, bound for Portsmouth and the destroyer HMS *Fury*, which was waiting to transport him across the Channel to France.

'And so it came to pass,' the Duke remembered, 'that at two o'clock on the morning of December 12, 1936, HMS *Fury* slid silently and unescorted out of Portsmouth Harbour. Watching the shore of England recede, I was swept by many emotions. If it had been hard to give up the Throne, it had been even harder to give up my country. . . .

'The drawbridges were going up behind me.'

# ∽ 9 ∽

# *King George VI and Queen Elizabeth*

The Duke of York ascended the throne four days before his forty-first birthday. With the exception of his brother, he was the youngest prince to succeed since George III in 1760.

At his Accession Council, held at St James's Palace – the offical seat of monarchic power – on Saturday, 12 December, nine hours after the *Fury* had sailed from Portsmouth, the new King George VI addressed the assembly as follows:

> Your Royal Highnesses, My Lords and Gentlemen, I meet you today in circumstances which are without parallel in the history of our Country. Now that the duties of Sovereignty have fallen to Me I declare to you My adherence to the strict principles of constitutional government and My resolve to work before all else for the welfare of the British Commonwealth of Nations.
>
> With my wife as helpmeet by My side, I take up the heavy task which lies before Me. In it I look for the support of all my peoples. . . .

George VI's first speech as king was delivered haltingly, in a low, nervous voice, which belied the confident sentiments of the words he had spoken. The emotions he felt at his brother's departure were revealed only in private. To his diary, for instance, he confessed that, when discussing the abdication with his mother Queen Mary, he 'broke down & sobbed like a child'.

The new King's distress, summed up in his cry, 'I'm only a Naval Officer, it's the only thing I know about', amply testified to his personal feelings of inadequacy.

The abdication, even if it wasn't immediately apparent, had split wide the question of the hereditary system, whereby the first-born son of a sovereign (or the eldest daughter, when there are no male heirs) is carefully prepared for his ultimate inheritance. It is accepted without question that the heir apparent, programmed from childhood, has no other – or will have no other – desires or ambitions, save to assume the mantle of sovereignty. It is his *duty* so to do.

Edward VIII's nature was not one that could be happily confined within the framework of an office which disallowed the right of free expression. In his own way a king must assume a subservient role, submitting to the will of those who wield the true authority, accepting that his symbolic 'power' extends no further than his three constitutional rights – to be consulted, to encourage, to warn. Edward VIII, as a 'modern king', would clearly not have been content with so ornamental a function. George VI had no choice.

Quite the last thing that King George needed at this traumatic time, no matter how well meant, was the back-handed character reference, broadcast to the nation by the Archbishop of Canterbury. The meddling, even rather sinister Dr Cosmo Gordon Lang, while condemning King Edward VIII's circle, vastly embarrassed the new King by drawing attention to his speech impediment. 'To those who hear it,' he waffled, 'it need cause no embarrassment, for it causes none to him who speaks.' So tactless an observation, and so absurd an understatement, horrified the King and Queen, and outraged Lionel Logue, who had done so much to boost the former Prince Albert's confidence.

There was, too, much talk about George VI's suitability as king. Was he strong enough to be regarded as much more than a 'rubber stamp', some asked? Even more uncomplimentary was the story that Prince George, Duke of Kent, had been proposed to succeed Edward VIII, over the heads of his elder brothers, the Dukes of York and Gloucester. Such an idea scarcely merits in-depth analysis for several reasons. First and foremost, there has never been any evidence to support the 'Kent *v.* York' theory;

second, Prince George, though married and by now the father of a male child, the present Duke of Kent, was still too much the night-clubbing, glamour boy to be regarded as a serious – or even suitable – contender for the Crown; and third, the abdication had shaken the throne to so great an extent that it may not have survived the further upheaval of a confused line of succession.

What both the Crown and people needed in December 1936 was the expedient re-establishment of a stable monarchy. George VI and Queen Elizabeth provided that stability.

Buckingham Palace is often described as a vast, impersonal museum of a place and therefore not at all like a home for its royal occupants. It is perfectly true that Queen Victoria saw very little of it during the long years of her widowhood, and equally true that neither King Edward VII nor King Edward VIII liked it. Conversely Queen Alexandra and Queen Mary loved it, and when both in their turn vacated their apartments to move down the Mall to Marlborough House, which, until Queen Mary's death in 1953, could have been described as the royal dower house, they did so with genuine regret. Upon her departure, Queen Mary lamented the loss of 'Those lovely comfortable rooms which have been my happy home . . . '.

To begin with, the King and Queen Elizabeth might well have said much the same at their enforced move from 145 Piccadilly. Yet the private royal apartments on the first floor of Buckingham Palace, with their views across the magnificent garden in one direction and Green Park in the other, were soon transformed into the warmest of homes; and the impersonal aura of the state rooms and labyrinthine passages might easily have belonged to a different house entirely.

Princess Elizabeth, the eleven-year-old Heiress Presumptive, and her six-year-old sister Princess Margaret moved to Buckingham Palace only after their parents had installed themselves there. It was, as Princess Margaret once explained to the author, deliberately planned that way so that their visits to the King and Queen would help acclimatize them to their new home – a house that was, after all, unfamiliar to them, except for visits to their grandparents' suites – while still retaining the security of the old. Such an arrangement worked well. Yet while the Princesses adapted themselves painlessly to their change in circumstances and surroundings, those same changes took a severe toll on the reluctant new King.

As quickly as the abdication had thrown the royal family into a state of turmoil, so, during the following weeks, did George VI succumb to the effects of his personal emotions and suffer a nervous breakdown. Sir John Wheeler-Bennett described the King's collapse as follows: 'At first he had been emotionally disturbed; then a merciful numbness had supervened, to be followed . . . by a gradual reawakening to the realities of life, which demanded all his courage.'

As we have already noted, King George VI as Duke of York had always been at his happiest in his official work when no 'damned red carpet' hindered his progress. The next ordeal which loomed large on his horizon was far worse than any local authority's display of formal grandeur. The coronation of Edward VIII had been set to take place at Westminster Abbey on Wednesday, 12 May 1937, observing the unwritten law that a new sovereign was not crowned until at least a year had passed since the demise of his predecessor. In this strange and unparalleled instance, it was decided that the coronation of King George and Queen Elizabeth should still go ahead on that day.

'I can hardly now believe that we have been called to this tremendous task,' the Queen wrote to the Archbishop of Canterbury. '. . . the curious thing is that we are not afraid. I feel that God has enabled us to face the situation calmly.'

As the day of the coronation approached, representatives and emissaries of foreign heads of state began flooding into London. The Emperor Hirohito of Japan was represented by his brother Prince Chichibu and his Princess, the former Miss Setsu-Ko Matsudaira; Princess Juliana of The Netherlands and her husband Prince Bernhard represented Queen Wilhelmina; while the Crown Princes and Princesses of Norway, Sweden, Denmark, Greece and Saudi Arabia represented their respective sovereigns. The Prince Regent of Yugoslavia and Princess Paul (sister of Princess Marina, Duchess of Kent), the Grand Voevod of Alba Julia, and the Prince of Preslav were also formally received, as were the representatives of the kings of Egypt, the Yemen, Italy, Rumania, Siam, the Albanians and Iraq; the emperors of Ethiopia and Iran, the Maharajadhiraja of Nepal, the Regent of Hungary, the Grand Duchess of Luxemburg and the Prince of Monaco.

The German Reich, the Soviet Union, the Swiss Confederation, and – among many others – the republics of China, the United States of America, France, Poland, Spain, Portugal, Latvia, Peru, Lithuania, Nicaragua, Estonia, Cuba and Panama, were likewise represented.

On the great day itself the doors of Westminster Abbey were opened almost before the dawn fog of that damp spring morning had lifted. The *Ceremonial* – a kind of handbook-cum-*Who's Who* detailing the proceedings – instructed:

> The Peers, Dowager Peeresses and Peeresses, in their Robes of Estate, and others invited by His Majesty's Command to be present at the Solemnity of the Coronation, will be conducted to the places assigned to them in Westminster Abbey before 8.30 o'clock, at which time the doors of the Abbey will be closed.
>
> The Lords Spiritual will be seated on the Northside of the Area, or Sacrarium, the Lords Temporal in the South Transept, and the Dowager Peeresses and Peeresses in the North Transept.
>
> The Great Officers of State and the Lords appointed to carry Their Majesties' Regalia, in their Robes of Estate, the Archbishops of Canterbury and York, the Bishops who are to support Their Majesties, and those who are to carry the Bible, the Chalice, and the Paten, vested in Copes, and the other persons appointed to take part in the Procession, will assemble in the Vestibule without the West Door.

The 'vestibule' was a specially designed and elaborate annexe attached to the western end of the Abbey, and covering a very considerable area. Not only was it a waiting-room of the most spendid kind for royal and ecclesiastical personages, but through it the royal processions would pass upon arrival and departure. Within its walls the royal regalia would be laid out immediately before the ceremony, and here, too, were to be found the royal retiring-rooms. Closed to the general public from the first week in January 1937, the Abbey's interior took four months to be prepared for the coronation.

Tiered galleries were erected on both sides of the nave leading to the ornate organ screen, on top of which the trumpeters and drummers were to be positioned, while beyond, the raised coronation 'theatre' was constructed before the high altar in the sacrarium. Here a special dais was built, on which were placed the chairs of estate to be occupied by the King and Queen, and in front of them stood the ancient coronation chair, or King Edward's chair. Fashioned in 1300 at a cost of 100 shillings by Master Walter of Durham, it had been built to the order of Edward I to enclose the Stone of Scone, which had been seized from the Scots in 1296, and upon which Scottish kings had been crowned. According to legend, it was upon this stone that Jacob laid his head and dreamed his dream.

Looking across the sacrarium, on the south side of the sanctuary was the royal gallery. Built on four staggered levels over the tomb of Anne of Cleves, fourth wife of Henry VIII, it was reserved almost exclusively for members of the royal family. Here would sit the Queen Mother, Queen Mary, her granddaughters the Princesses Elizabeth and Margaret, her own daughter the Princess Royal, her daughters-in-law Marina, Duchess of Kent and Alice Duchess of Gloucester (in November 1935 Prince Henry, Duke of Gloucester had married the Lady Alice Montagu Douglas Scott), her sisters-in-law Queen Maud of Norway, and Princess Alice, Countess of Athlone; and a bevy of lesser royalties. In the front row of the royal gallery were also accommodated the new Queen's parents, the Earl and Countess of Strathmore.

With her decision to attend the coronation of her son, Queen Mary in fact broke with tradition. Formerly queens dowager were not present at the coronations of their successors. In June 1911, for instance, when George V and Queen Mary herself were crowned, the Dowager Queen Alexandra remained at Sandringham with her sister 'Minnie', her daughter 'Toria' (Princess Victoria, whom the Queen would never permit to marry) and her memories. It has also been said, incidentally, that Queen Mary's attendance at the coronation of George VI was a public sign of her condemnation of her eldest son's abdication.

Queen Mary took an especially close interest in almost every aspect of the solemn celebrations of 1937. She offered sound constructive advice, based on her own memories of 1911, and only a few weeks after Westminster Abbey had found itself over-run by an army of builders, carpenters and workmen, she paid a private visit to see how things were coming along. 'A marvellous sight,' was her enthusiastic judgement. Later still Queen Mary drove round London in her famous, coach-like Daimler, to look at the street decorations. At Marlborough House and at the Abbey itself, she held several rehearsals to instruct her four pages-of-honour (the Earl of Dalkeith, the Marquess of Lansdowne, Viscount Errington, and her grandson the Honourable Gerald Lascelles, second and youngest son of the Princess Royal), on how to carry her voluminous purple velvet train; and she visited Messrs Garrard's, the Crown jewellers.

There she saw her son's crown (the Imperial State Crown) being re-set, and was intrigued to watch part of the creation of a new crown for her daughter-in-law. Although not quite as delicate as that which had been made for Queen Mary's own crowning as consort twenty-six years earlier, Queen Elizabeth's crown was no less a masterpiece. Set with diamonds from a circlet which had once been owned by Queen Victoria, the crown's most magnificent gem was the legendary Koh-i-noor diamond of 108 carats.

Once said to have belonged to the Mogul Queen Mumtaz Mahal, in whose memory the Taj Mahal was built, the diamond is never worn by a male. Popular legend has it that should it be worn by a man certain disaster will befall him. Indeed, history has proven the 'truth' of the legend, for most of the men who have worn the Koh-i-noor – including the famous Persian invader, Nadir Shah – have met violent deaths. The diamond came to Britain during the reign of Queen Victoria, to whom it was presented following the British annexation of the Punjab.

At 10.30 on the morning of 12 May, the massive gilded hulk of George III's four-ton State Coach, drawn by eight grey horses, and attended by four postilions, eight grooms, six footmen and four Yeoman of the King's Bodyguard, all dressed in scarlet and gold state livery, passed through the central arch of Buckingham Palace. Swaying slightly as it proceeded at walking pace across the gravel forecourt, it swung slowly out into the upper part of the Mall and round the Queen Victoria Memorial, on its way to Westminster Abbey.

From inside, the King – robed in velvet and ermine, the rather incongruous Cap of Maintenance upon his head – and his Queen acknowledged the tumultuous welcome of the crowds, as many as twenty deep, along the entire processional route. Down the Mall and through Admiralty Arch it passed, thence into Whitehall and Parliament Street, before turning into Parliament Square which, on that day, with its vast tented stands and banners emblazoned with the royal cypher, set against the Gothic-style architecture of the Palace of Westminster, looked like a scene plucked straight from the Middle Ages.

As the State Coach drew up outside the canopied entrance to the vestibule, Big Ben struck eleven, the appointed time of the Sovereign's arrival. 'Punctuality,' said that 'Grand Monarque', Louis XIV of France, 'is the politeness of kings.' Be that as it may, the long coronation ceremony and its attendant pageantry had been planned with great precision by the Duke of Norfolk, the hereditary Earl Marshal, and, on this of all days, time was of the essence.

Inside the annexe the royal dukes and peers who had followed the State Coach on horseback were robed in their mantles before entering the church to take up their places in and around the sacrarium. With the scene now set, the Queen's procession of more than one hundred figures was formed. There was a brief unscheduled pause while one elderly clergyman who had fainted was revived, and then, with infinite splendour, the procession moved off along the nave to the sound of Psalm CXXII, the anthem 'I was glad when they said unto me, We will go into the House of the Lord', sung by the choir of Westminster.

Immediately preceeded by Maltravers Herald Extraordinary, York Herald and Windsor Herald, the Queen's regalia was borne in: the Ivory Rod with the Dove, the Sceptre with the Cross, and Her Majesty's crown. Then came the Queen herself, dressed in an ivory satin gown heavily embroidered in pure gold thread and diamanté with emblems of the British Isles and Dominions, her short sleeves trimmed with flowing ivory lace. Her embroidered mantle of purple velvet, eighteen feet long, was borne by the Mistress of the Robes, the Dowager Duchess of Northumberland, assisted by six maids-of-honour, the Ladies Ursula Manners, Diana Legge, Margaret Cavendish-Bentinck, Elizabeth Percy, Elizabeth Paget and Iris Mountbatten, and followed by eight ladies-in-waiting, divided equally into four Ladies of the Bed-chamber and four Women of the Bedchamber.

Presently came into view the King's regalia: St Edward's Staff, the Sceptre with the Cross (containing the 530-carat diamond known as the Star of Africa), the Golden Spurs of St George, emblems of knighthood and chivalry, the three swords, chief among them Curtana (the Sword of Mercy); the Sovereign's sceptre with the Dove, representing equity and mercy, St Edward's Crown, and the Orb (perhaps the most sacred ornament of the regalia, symbolizing the dominion of the Christian religion over the world).

And then came the King himself. Flanked by the Bishop of Bath and Wells and the Bishop of Durham, as the Queen had been supported by the Bishop of Blackburn and the Bishop of St Albans, his train was borne by nine pages-of-honour, including his nephew George, the Viscount Lascelles, eldest son of the Princess Royal. Attended by his Groom of the Robes, the Master of the Horse, Gold Stick-in-Waiting, and thirty-six others, including twelve Yeomen of the Guard, the entire royal procession passed through the body of Westminster Abbey and into the coronation theatre for the start of the ceremony.

'Sirs, I here present unto you King George, your undoubted King: Wherefore all you who are come this day to do your homage and service, Are you willing to do the same?' So proclaimed and charged the Archbishop of Canterbury to the four sides of the Abbey. The immense congregation in their turn responded in a shout, 'God Save King George', and each time the trumpets sounded a flourish.

The Recognition completed, the Oath was administered, in which the King promised to govern his peoples 'according to their respective laws and customs'. He then went on to promise that he would 'cause Law and Justice, in Mercy, to be executed', in all his judgements, and maintain 'the Laws of God and the true profession of the Gospel', to 'maintain in the United Kingdom the Protestant Reformed Religion established by law . . . maintain and preserve inviolably the settlement of the Church of England, and the doctrine, worship, discipline, and government thereof. . . . Preserve unto the Bishops and clergy in England, and to the Churches there committed to their charge, all such rights and privileges, as by law do or shall appertain to them, or any of them. . . .'

Then followed the communion service, the anointing of both the King and Queen, kneeling before the high altar, and the performance of the stirring anthem 'Zadok the Priest . . .', which Handel had composed for the coronation of George II more than two hundred years earlier, in 1727. There then followed the solemn presentation of the King's regalia. As the climax of this part of the ceremony was reached, the Archbishop of Canterbury lifted high St Edward's Crown, reciting the prayer; 'O God, the Crown of the faithful: Bless we beseech thee and sanctify this thy servant George our King: and as thou dost this day set a Crown of pure gold upon his head, so enrich his royal heart with thine abundant grace, and crown him with all princely virtues. . . .'

As the crown was lowered and set on to the King's head (an unintentionally amusing note in the order of service advised, 'Here the King must be put in mind to bow his head') the royal dukes and peers put on their coronets, and the congregation repeatedly shouted the words 'God Save The King!'. At that moment the trumpets blared while, beyond the walls of Westminster Abbey, a signal was given and 'the great guns' were 'shot off ' in royal salute.

Enthroned, King George VI received the homage of his two brothers, the Dukes of Gloucester and Kent, and of the peers of the realm, before the coronation of the Queen began. As Her Majesty's crown was lowered on to her head, all the peeresses, their arms clad in long white gloves, and all the royal ladies in the royal gallery, raised their own coronets, causing the young Princess Elizabeth to note afterwards that 'They looked like swans.'

If to the uninitiated the ceremony appeared to have been completed without a hiccup, the King himself knew better – to his cost. Recording the events of 12 May 1937 in his diary, he wrote:

> After the Introduction I removed my Parliamentary robes . . . and moved to the Coronation chair. Here various vestments were placed upon me, the white Colobium Sindonis, a surplice which the Dean of Westminster insisted I should put on inside out, had not my Groom of the Robes come to the rescue. Before this I knelt at the Altar to take the Coronation Oath. I had two Bishops, Durham and Wells, one on either side to support me & to hold the form of Service for me to follow. When this great moment came neither Bishop could find the words, so the Archbishop held his book down for me to read, but horror of horrors his thumb covered the words of the Oath.

Later, recorded the King, the Lord Great Chamberlain shook so much that His Majesty had to fasten the sword-belt himself; St Edward's Crown was very nearly put on the King's head the wrong way round; and one of the attendant bishops trod on the King's robes, almost pulling him down. 'I had to tell him to get off it pretty sharply,' the amused Sovereign noted.

The incident concerning St Edward's Crown, explained the Archbishop of Canterbury afterwards, had been occasioned by the removal of a small piece of red thread, quite deliberately attached to the front of the crown to avoid any confusion. It is interesting to note here that at the coronation of George VI's daughter, the present Queen, sixteen years later, 'some officious person', as Dr Lang had put it, removed another red 'marker'; this time from the carpeting in the annexe, indicating where Elizabeth II should stand before proceeding into the Abbey. It says much for the Queen's retentive mind that she stood in the right place instinctively.

Like her son, Queen Mary described the coronation of 1937 in her own diary, and it is for a final word on the subject that we read, 'Bertie & E looked so well . . . & did it all too beautifully. The Service was wonderful & impressive – we were all much moved . . . A wonderful day.'

# ❧ 10 ❧

# *A Wedding and a War*

In France less than a month after the coronation, the Duke of Windsor married Mrs Simpson, or to be more precise, Mrs Warfield. She had by this time dispensed with 'Simpson' and, by deed-poll, reverted to her maiden name.

In March 1937 the Château de Candé in Touraine, near Tours, a fine old castle set in the middle of its own private park, had been put at the Windsors' disposal by its owner, Charles Bedaux, a wealthy French-American industrialist.

Superstition forbade Wallis Warfield from choosing a May wedding and early June was therefore settled upon. It was, as may have been anticipated, a quiet occasion, attended by about a dozen personal friends: Major Edward 'Fruity' Metcalfe, the Duke's Equerry and best man, his wife, the former Lady Alexandra Curzon, Randolph Churchill (son of Sir Winston), Walter Monckton (the former King's go-between during the abdication crisis), Hugh Lloyd-Thomas, Lady Selby, the bride's devoted 'Aunt Bessie' (Mrs Merryman), Herman and Katherine Rogers, and Eugene and Kitty de Rothschild.

The celebrated Parisian couturier Mainbocher designed the bride's elegant wedding-dress of palest blue crêpe satin, Cecil Beaton took the formal photographs of the bridal couple in their wedding finery the day before, and Constance Spry personally arranged the flowers – lilies and white peonies – the scent of which Beaton was to remember long afterwards as one of his sharpest memories of the Windsors' wedding.

Continental law requires that a civil marriage ceremony should precede any form of religious celebration. This rule was naturally to be observed at the Château de Candé, but the Duke of Windsor earnestly desired a formal religious wedding, too. His wish was granted when the Reverend Robert Anderson Jardine, vicar of St Paul's Church, Darlington, offered his services. (Mr Jardine was, however, to pay a very high price for the privilege of defying his bishop's specific orders against his royal mission. Despite forty years of service, he lost his ministry in England and, when attempting to earn a living preaching in the United States, he and his wife found church doors slammed before them. 'Bigotry and persecution have followed us across the sea,' Jardine declared, 'my wife and I hardly know where to turn . . .'. Such was his reward for having played the Good Samaritan.)

In her diary for 3 June 1937, Queen Mary noted briefly, 'Alas! the wedding day in France of David & Mrs Warfield. We all telegraphed to him.' The King also wrote. In his letter, given to the Duke of Windsor by Walter Monckton, George VI told his brother that while he was entitled to enjoy the rank and status of 'Royal Highness' (something not even the King could deny him), the same distinction was not to be extended to his bride. The Duke was outraged. 'I know Bertie – I know he couldn't have written this letter on his own,' he cried. 'Why in God's name would they do this to me at this time!'

It was as naïve of the Duke to expect his wife to be accorded the rank of royal highness as it was of him to hope that Queen Mary – or at the very least his brother, the Duke of Kent – would attend his wedding.

There have been those, however, who have claimed that the Duchess of Windsor had a legal right to share her husband's royal title. This is not so. Certainly nothing could have been done to deprive Wallis Warfield Simpson of her rightful status as a duchess – or of the courtesy title 'Her Grace' – but the rank of royal highness has to be bestowed by the sovereign and specifically created by letters patent – which the Duke should have realized. He was, nevertheless, absolutely correct on one point. He *did* know his brother, and not only would the King have been unable to write the offending letter 'on his own', but it may never have occurred to him to take so vindictive a stand against his new sister-in-law, had he not been under very considerable pressure to disregard her existence.

The irony of the Crown's vendetta was that the Duchess of Windsor was placed in exactly the same position as if a morganatic marriage had been permitted.

For herself the Duchess did not covet the royal title; she loved and had married the *man*. But she was not oblivious to the insult her husband considered he had been delivered, and went along with the game when the Duke referred to her in public as 'Her Royal Highness', when the bell-pushes to her rooms were so labelled and when, by order, their servants called her by that title. She grew accustomed to being called 'Ma'am', and never batted an eyelid when some curtsied before her.

In a letter to his wife, Vita, dated 5 August 1938, Sir Harold Nicolson provided a witty description of a dinner party given by Somerset Maugham at Cap Ferrat. The Duke and Duchess of Windsor were among the guests, and on this occasion the Duke used the forbidden title to great effect.

> 'Oim sorry we were a little loite,' said the Duke, 'but Her Royal Highness wouldn't drag herself away from the Amurrican orficers.' He had said it. The three words fell into the circle like three stones into a pool. Her (gasp) Royal (shudder) Highness (and not one eye dared to meet another).
>
> Then we went into dinner. I sat next to the Duchess. He sat opposite. They called each other 'darling' a great deal. I called him 'Your Royal Highness' a great deal, and 'Sir' the whole time. I called her 'Duchess', sharplike. We chattered a great deal. You know that tiresome way royalties have of pretending everything is being very amusing when it isn't. . . . But of course one cannot get away from his glamour and his charm and his sadness. Though I must say he seemed gay enough.

It was precisely the Duke of Windsor's 'glamour' and 'charm', his 'Little boy lost' charisma, that hardened Queen Elizabeth's determination never to permit his permanent return to Britain. It has been said from time to time that the Queen did not hold anything against her brother-in-law personally, but bitterly resented everything about his wife.

At all events, when the Second World War broke out and the question, 'What best to do with the Windsors?' had to be resolved, the Queen was adamant that the popular standing of her husband was not going to be jeopardized by the close proximity of his glamorous, enigmatic elder brother. This was seen, for instance, in September 1939, after the Duke and Duchess had offered their services to Britain. 'I will not receive her,' the Queen had remarked. When a friend asked, 'May I make this known?' the Queen had replied, 'You certainly may'.

The abdication had pulverized the Yorks, far more, in fact, than many would ever realize. The new Queen had seen what it had done to her husband, what it had done to their lives, and, in helping to pick up the pieces, great bitterness had entered her heart. The very fact that Queen Elizabeth was unable to discuss the abdication, even with her closest family, until some thirty years after the event, is a considerable indication of the depth of her feelings.

Yet if today the Queen's stand against the Duke and Duchess of Windsor – particularly during the early years of the King's reign – seems at all cold-hearted, then it must be said in her defence that such an attitude was – and is – wholly justifiable. Indeed, is there anywhere a wife who would not do everything within her power to protect and defend the husband she loves? George VI may have been the 'strong' man some would claim, but as King he was also very vulnerable.

Keeping the Windsors at arm's length was not a difficult matter. The question of the Duchess's title has always been widely regarded as the reason for the Duke's prolonged – if self-imposed – exile: no HRH for Wallis, no return to England. Though undoubtedly a consideration at one time, it wasn't the reason that kept them wandering aimlessly between France and the United States for almost three decades. At length the Duke had realized that he and the Duchess would never be permitted to enjoy parity of rank. All he asked, therefore, was that his family, and in particular the King and Queen, should receive his wife just once, and for that meeting to be recorded in the Court Circular. That act, or so he thought, would disperse the cloud of 'disgrace' under which they lived and grant recognition to the Duchess. It was never to be.

Towards the end of the first year of their reign, while the Windsors were visiting Hitler's Germany (despite his mass appeal and hypnotic jingoism, the Führer, with his 'Kaiser-Bill'-like posturings, struck the Duke as, 'a somewhat ridiculous figure'), the King and Queen had agreed to pay a visit to Paris. It was, ostensibly, to be a state visit but, in reality, with another war in the offing, it was an important diplomatic mission – designed to re-affirm and polish Anglo-French relations, promote the British Premier's peace policy and, as Lady Longford put it, 'to demonstrate the strength of Britain in her new Sovereigns'.

Alas, shortly before their departure the following summer, the Queen's mother died. Her death on 28 June meant that the start of the state visit was posponed for three weeks. On 19 July, however, George VI and Queen Elizabeth entered the French capital to a tumultuous reception. Lady Diana Cooper recalled, 'We saw the King and Queen from a window coming down the Champs Elysées with roofs, windows and pavements roaring exultantly, the Queen a radiant Winterhalter.' Well might Queen Elizabeth have resembled one of that painter's glorious portraits of nineteenth-century royalty; that, indeed, was the intention. Norman Hartnell, who was to dress the Queen for more than forty years, had been asked by the King to re-create the 'picturesque grace' of the gowns worn by the French Empress Eugénie and the Austro-Hungarian Empress Elisabeth who, in their vast gilded frames, looked down from the walls of the Long Gallery at Buckingham Palace. 'We have taken the Queen to our hearts,' worshipped the French Press. 'She rules over two nations.'

Ten months later, with the European situation worsening all the time – the Germans had marched into Prague on 15 March – the King and Queen were, perforce, off on their travels again. This time, sailing aboard the liner *Empress of Australia*, they were bound for North America – first Canada and then the United States.

As with the return voyage of the *Renown* from Australia in May 1927, the outward voyage to Canada in May 1939 was not without incident. Fog hampered the liner's progress with the result that a full two days of the royal tour were irretrievably lost. From aboard the German-built vessel, formerly known as the *Tirpitz* (it was given over to Britain by Germany as part of the reparation payments at the end of the Great War), the Queen wrote to Queen Mary:

For three & a half days we only moved a few miles. The fog was so thick, that it was like a white cloud round the ship, and the fog horn blew incessantly. Its melancholy blasts were echoed by the icebergs like the twang of a piece of wire. Incredibly eery, and really very alarming. . . . We very nearly hit a berg the day before yesterday, and the poor Captain was nearly demented because some kind cheerful people kept on reminding him that it was about here that the Titanic was struck & *just* about the same date!

The tragic event of 15 April 1912 was not repeated, and the King and Queen journeyed on to make history as the first British sovereigns to set foot on Canadian soil. There had, of course, been royal visitors in the past: two years before his father created him Duke of Clarence, the future William IV landed there in 1787, and three more future kings, Edward VII, George V and Edward VIII, had visited the Dominion when each was Prince of Wales. But never had a 'King of Canada' come to visit his subjects.

On the morning of 17 May, thousands of French Canadians crowded the high bluffs above the St Lawrence, as the royal liner steamed into port. Cheers and shouts of *'Vive le Roi'* and *'Vive la Reine'* rang out as Their Majesties stepped ashore in Quebec to be greeted by the Prime Minister, Mr Mackenzie King. In that predominantly Catholic region the King gave pleasure to the masses by receiving Cardinal Villeneuve, Primate of Canada, by delivering his addresses in both French and English, and by taking an eight-mile 'state' drive through the city. The rousing reception the King and Queen received set the tone of the entire North American tour, and the following morning they were seen off in style as they boarded the gleaming, ultra-modern, twelve-car train in which they were to cross the continent.

In Vancouver, Canada's third largest city, half a million people greeted the King and Queen (including some 50,000 Americans who had crossed the border from Seattle and Portland) when His Majesty presented colours to the Royal Canadian Navy at Victoria, the island capital of British Columbia. In Winnipeg on 24 May, the King's Empire-Day message was one of peace. Of Canada's geographical location, the King said: 'Her Atlantic windows look to Europe, her Pacific windows to Asia and the Far East. As science reduces the barriers of space, this country will become a thoroughfare between two hemispheres. Some day the peoples of the world will come to realize that prosperity lies in co-operation and not in conflict.'

A week later George VI and Queen Elizabeth arrived at Jasper

National Park, high up in the Canadian Rockies, where they stayed in what was described as 'a log cabin'. It was, however, rather more splendid than the primitive, one-room dwelling of people's imaginations. Indeed, this royal cabin contained a sitting-room of 19 feet by 28 feet, and no fewer than five bedrooms, each with their own private bathrooms. From that 'Paradise resort for the wealthy' (in 1939 it cost holiday-makers over £200 a day), the King and Queen travelled on to Edmonton, Alberta's 'prairie capital', which was still suffering the effects of years of drought and depression. There the King met a 103-year-old philosopher by the name of Joseph Haire. He told the Sovereign, 'You're a great King, Your Majesty, but I'll soon have to go to meet a greater.'

At home the King's mother was involved in a road accident which could well have propelled the seventy-one-year-old Queen Dowager heavenward. Returning to Marlborough House from an engagement in Surrey, the royal car was travelling along Wimbledon Park Road in the quiet suburb of Southfields, when it was struck by a lorry carrying a load of steel tubing. Queen Mary, her Lady-in-Waiting, Lady Constance Milnes Gaskell, and her Comptroller, Lord Claud Hamilton, were flung to the floor in a shower of broken glass, as the vehicle was turned over on to its side. 'It was a wonder we . . . occupants were not killed,' the Queen Mother remarked afterwards. Workmen painting a house nearby rushed across to the scene of the accident and, by pushing one ladder through the car's broken window and steadying another on the outside, helped Queen Mary and her attendants to escape. 'She climbed up and down those ladders as if she might have been walking down the steps at the coronation,' one witness later wrote. 'She had not her hat or one curl out of place. . . . The only outward sign of disorder was a broken hat pin and her umbrella broken in half.' Muttering, 'Oh dear, Oh dear,' Queen Mary was taken by a local vicar to his house, for a cup of tea, while Her Majesty's 'Big Car' was summoned from Marlborough House.

When the redoubtable Queen was attended by her doctor later that day, it was discovered that she had not only suffered from severe bruising and shock, but that a piece of glass had 'brushed off the film' of her left eye. Though her back 'hurt abominably', Queen Mary considered she had had 'a lucky escape', and refused to stay in bed to recover longer than ten days.

On the other side of the Atlantic, King George and Queen Elizabeth were alarmed to hear of Queen Mary's ordeal, but were comforted by subsequent news of her progress.

By the time the King and Queen reached the American border at Niagara Falls, for the start of their four-day state visit to the United States, they had crossed Canada from east to west and very nearly back to the Atlantic again. The only provinces yet to be visited were those of New Brunswick, Nova Scotia and Prince Edward Island. Those regions were not to be forgotten, however, and would wind up the Sovereign's tour in mid-June.

In America the King's simplicity and the Queen's unruffled charm impressed and conquered even the staunchest republican. One magazine reported:

> By many little gestures, the King contrived to show his humanness – as when he took time at a garden party to visit with J.P. Morgan, the banker, and at an embassy reception . . . to chat with John Kareff, a native of Sierra Leone, British African colony; when he earnestly examined the medals of a Boy Scout Fred D. Carl; and later in New York, when he passed the word to the Police Commissioner . . . that he wanted the procession to go more slowly than the 30-mile scheduled clip, so that he and the Queen might see more of the city – and it more of them. The King's crowning gesture was reserved for Mount Vernon. There, at the tomb of George Washington, the descendant of Washington's enemy deposited a wreath and, with bowed head, paid an empire's tribute to the man who wrested from it the greatest colony ever won and lost.

For the duration of the Sovereign's visit, however, the United States might just as well have been the empire's 'greatest colony'. Eulogies flowed in torrents and crowds gathered everywhere the King and Queen appeared. New York police, for example, estimated the turn-out in that city alone to have been somewhere in the region of 3,500,000. Delighted by the success of the visit, the King happily declared, 'This has made us.' In his own mind he and the Queen had *arrived*; their reign was secure.

One of the most outstanding aspects of the royal tour was the bond of friendship cemented between King George VI and President Roosevelt which was soon to bear fruit with American support for Britain during the Second World War. At a White

House banquet, the President said. 'I am persuaded that the greatest single contribution our two countries have been enabled to make to civilization . . . is the example we have jointly set by our manner of conducting relations between our two nations. . . . It is because neither of us fears aggression on the part of the other that we have entered no talk of armaments.' Later on, having bidden farewell to his royal guests, Mr Roosevelt reiterated that point when he told West Point graduates that the significance of the King's visit 'lay in the fact that friendship could exist between two countries without fear'.

On 3 September Britain was once again forced to declare war on Germany.

Little more than a month earlier the King and Queen, with their daughters, that 'small, absolutely united circle', as the late Princess Alice, Countess of Athlone, described them, had started their annual summer holiday at Balmoral Castle. Now, as King George and Queen Elizabeth hastened back to London, the nine-year-old Princess Margaret asked indignantly, 'Who *is* this Hitler, spoiling everything?'

At least to begin with, both the King and the Queen were content that the Princesses should remain safely at Balmoral. It was, of course, a home from home and their parents could keep in touch daily by telephone. The King was also happy for other children to know the safety of Royal Deeside, and by his command, Craigowan House on the royal estate was prepared for the arrival of evacuees from the Glasgow slums. Many of them, however, were unable to adjust to their new surroundings. Balmoral was a totally alien world to them and, as Princess Margaret told the author, 'The sound of the wind groaning through the trees at night terrified them. It was, they said, the sound of witches and devils.'

'After a while,' Princess Margaret went on, 'many of the children were so unhappy that they had to be sent home again.'

Perhaps George VI's chief function from 1939 to 1945 was to help sustain his people's morale, and in this work both he and the Queen were incomparable. Some argue, indeed, that it was during these years that the King really proved what he was made of.

Anxious to do everything he possibly could, the ceaseless visits he and Queen Elizabeth made through the length and breadth of the country, often in extremely dangerous circumstances, led the Prime Minister, Winston Churchill, to say: 'Your Majesties are more beloved by all classes and conditions, than any of the princes of the past.'

Of her countryfolk Lady Donaldson wrote, '. . . it was the spirit of the British that carried them through while they stood alone. This spirit was aroused by Winston Churchill but it was sustained and very much nourished by the King and Queen, and this, as with . . . Churchill, was a result of their courage as well as of their position.'

Position does not exclude royalty from human suffering either directly or indirectly, and at the beginning of the war, the Queen commiserated with a friend who had just lost all her possessions, including Her Majesty's photograph. 'I do feel so deeply for you over the loss of all your personal belongings,' the Queen wrote, 'the small things that one cherishes, each little object means so much in one's memories. I send you my heartfelt sympathy. I shall be very pleased to send you a photograph to replace the one we gave you. . . . I expect it will reach you in a few days from now.'

Worse news was, of course, still to come. The Queen's nephew Patrick, the Master of Glamis, was killed on active service, while another nephew, Andrew Elphinstone, was captured and held as a prisoner-of-war. The King's nephew, George Lascelles, serving as a captain with the Grenadier Guards, was also captured and imprisoned in the notorious Colditz Castle where, because of his royal blood, he was considered perfect hostage material, should the need ever arise.

Over and above these sad and alarming tidings, one of the most tragic events to touch the royal family was the death of the King's brother, the forty-year-old Prince George, Duke of Kent. On Tuesday, 25 August 1942, the Duke, who was serving with the Royal Air Force, set off from the RAF Station at Invergordon in Scotland aboard a Sunderland seaplane to inspect RAF bases in Iceland. At about 1.30 p.m. the aircraft ploughed into the side of a remote mountain. Of the fifteen-man crew only one, a rear gunner, survived.

'The news came as a great shock to me,' the King wrote in his diary, 'and I had to break it to Elizabeth and Harry and Alice [the

Duke and Duchess of Gloucester] who were staying with us.'

The Duke of Kent was buried at Frogmore on 29 August, following the funeral service at St George's Chapel, Windsor Castle. Noel Coward, who was a great personal friend of both Prince George and his young widow Princess Marina, was among the mourners. He wrote later:

> The service was impressive and supremely dignified. I tried hard not to cry, but it was useless. When the Duchess came in with the Queen and Queen Mary I broke a bit, and when the coffin passed with flowers from the garden at Coppins [then the Kents' home in Iver, Buckinghamshire] and Prince George's cap on it I was finished. I then gave up all pretence and just stood with the tears splashing down my face. . . .

To King George VI the funeral of his brother was the most difficult, the most moving, he had ever attended. 'Everybody was there,' he told a friend afterwards, 'but I did not dare look at any of them for fear of breaking down.'

The funeral of her fourth son brought Queen Mary down from the West Country, for she, too, had become a somewhat reluctant evacuee. When war was declared, the King insisted that his mother should leave London for Badminton in Gloucestershire, the estate of her niece's husband, the Duke of Beaufort. To leave, the Queen Mother declared, was not 'at all the thing'. But leave she did when the King pointed out that her continued presence at Marlborough House would only cause needless trouble and anxiety. So it was that, on 4 September, Queen Mary in her limousine swept out of the gates of Sandringham – where she had been spending a few days with her Kent grandchildren – followed by a considerable convoy of vehicles which not only carried the Queen's luggage, but the majority of her Marlborough House staff of sixty-three *and* the majority of their dependants, too!

The stately (and not so stately) caravan completed the journey across country in eight and a half hours, having made a considerable detour en route to take luncheon with Earl and Countess Spencer at Althorp in Northampton. It had been, said Queen Mary at the end of the day, 'A lovely drive'.

It is entertaining to note that during her wartime stay at

Badminton House and despite her years, Queen Mary allowed herself barely an idle moment. She gleefully stripped walls of ivy, in outdoor coat and toque hat had herself photographed sawing wood, wrote endless letters, completed a filing-system for her prodigious collection of paperwork, organized the collection of salvage, served in canteens, attended to her embroidery – for which she was justly famous – carried out official engagements, visited nearby hospitals and factories, inspected bomb-sites, helped out at garden fêtes and, to her immense pleasure, was forever giving lifts to any servicemen she met on the road, enjoying their frequently earthy, breezy conversation.

During a visit to Bath she encountered a happy group of Australian soldiers and airmen who asked if she would be photographed with 'the boys'. Describing the meeting in a letter to her brother 'Alge', Queen Mary said, '. . . they crowded round me and I suddenly felt an arm pushed through mine and an arm placed round my waist in order to make more room, I suppose. It really was very comical and *unexpected* at my age.'

# ∼ 11 ∼

# *War and Peace*

None had wanted to avert the catastrophe of war more than King George VI and, in his anxiety to do so, he had put forward several suggestions which he considered to be workable alternatives.

During the late summer of 1938 the King pressed to be allowed to make a personal appeal to Hitler as 'one ex-Serviceman to another'; he suggested that the services of his cousin, Philip of Hesse, might be engaged to convey to the Führer a conciliatory message, 'that we are really in earnest'. Later still, the Permanent Under-Secretary for Foreign Affairs heard from the King's Private Secretary, Sir Alexander Hardinge, that His Majesty, having kept a vigilant eye on the effects of the German-Soviet Pact on Japan, wondered if, 'at an opportune moment', anything were to be gained by his sending a 'friendly message' direct to the Japanese Emperor, Hirohito. Finally, just one month before war was declared, George VI made it known that he wished to follow the lead set by Pope Pius XII, President Roosevelt and the Belgian King, Leopold III, in making a direct appeal to Hitler.

Perhaps not surprisingly, none of the King's proposed measures was approved, largely because it was deemed unwise to test the 'prestige' of the Sovereign and risk the almost inevitable embarrassment of rejection.

So it was that Britain entered a second world war, and the King scribbled down, 'The schoolboy's definition of courage: That part of you which says "stick it" while the rest of you says "chuck it".' Then quoting the Book of Isaiah, he noted a verse which summed up the British resolve in adversity: 'They helped every one his neighbour and every one said to his brother, Be of good courage.'

Both the King and Queen remained 'of good courage' throughout the years of war, something which they publicly demonstrated time and time again. Nor were they ever oblivious to the sufferings of others, whether among their own people or those whose countries had been invaded. One to whom they offered shelter was the indomitable Queen Wilhelmina of The Netherlands who, clutching a handbag and a tin hat, arrived at Buckingham Palace with nothing but the clothes she stood up in. With her came her daughter Princess Juliana and her two young granddaughters Beatrix and Irene. The latter, still an infant, was christened in the private chapel of Buckingham Palace which the Luftwaffe was so soon to demolish.

Presently the Dutch Princesses were on the move again, this time to Canada, which was also to be the destination of the British royal family in the event of invasion. When such plans were first put forward, neither George VI nor Queen Elizabeth were in favour of anything that would necessitate leaving their people at a time of even greater peril. Indeed, the Queen – who had been taught how to use a gun, and who bravely declared, 'I shan't go down like the others' – was never more determined to stay put. One of her most famous wartime statements, retold innumerable times since, was, 'The children could not leave without me, I could not leave without the King, and the King will never leave.'

With his slight build and unprepossessing air, George VI could scarcely be described as an imposing figure, any more than he could justifiably be said to have fitted the role of a 'warrior king', an image which could not have been further removed from the twentieth century. There can be no doubt, however, that he was nothing if not a brave man, and as a sovereign, none was more dedicated. It has been asserted, indeed, that in the event of an invasion, the King himself was fully prepared to lead a resistance movement.

In May 1940 'the children', Princess Elizabeth and Princess Margaret, now returned from Balmoral, were installed in the comparative safety of Windsor Castle. To some, wartime exigencies made that vast ancient pile a gloomy mausoleum of a place; its windows were protected, as far as possible, by 'stuck-on' mesh, overlaid with wire-netting, and at night were lost behind thick black-out curtaining, the lifelessness of which was relieved only by the dim light provided by reduced voltage electric bulbs. Outside the grounds were scored with trenches, laced with barbed-wire fences. Of these 'defences' Princess Margaret was later to say, 'They wouldn't have kept anybody out, but they kept us in!' Although only fifteen in 1945, one of the Princess's keenest memories of Windsor at that time was the 'tremendous spirit' that existed among all those who lived in the castle: 'Everybody was always cheerful.' Not 'everybody' concurred with Princess Margaret's remembrances, however. The late Lord Adeane (then Assistant Private Secretary to the King) who served with distinction in Northwestern Europe with the Fifth Battalion, Coldstream Guards, said of the atmosphere upon his return, 'It was rather like that of a convent.'

Despite such minor differences of opinion, there were certain occasions that dissipated the oppressiveness of the war for brief periods, and none more so than the now-famous royal pantomimes staged each Christmas in the Waterloo Chamber. Watching his daughters take part in *Cinderella*, *Sleeping Beauty*, *Aladdin*, or some such traditional show filled the King with inordinate pride, and when, during the Nativity, the first of these productions, Princess Margaret sang 'Gentle Jesus, meek and mild', her father was so moved that he confessed afterwards, 'I wept through most of it.'

Of these lighter moments of royal family life, many retain their own vivid memories. Herbert White served at Windsor Castle for eighteen months as a member of the King's Bodyguard, furnished by the Grenadiers. In 'civvy street' a violinist and antique restorer, Mr White was one of five guardsmen who volunteered to join the choir in the royal family's private chapel. After one service he and his colleagues were invited to the royal apartments to meet the King and Queen.

'I mentioned to the Queen that I came from Norwich,' he recalled. 'The Blitz had started by then, and after that she was always genuinely interested in any news I had from home. She would make a point of chatting to me to find out how the [local] people were standing up to the bombings.'

On another occasion, Guardsman White was asked to join the small band of musicians when the King and Queen gave a concert in aid of the Red Cross. During the performance he played a violin solo while Princess Elizabeth danced a French minuet and then a

Scottish reel. That evening was made the more memorable for Herbert White by the presence of his wife, and the thoughtfulness of the Queen herself. Mrs White's first reaction at finding herself invited from Norwich to Windsor was one of undisguised delight. But concern at making the long journey alone, particularly since she was expecting her first child, made her think of declining. However, when the Queen heard of the problem, she immediately despatched a second invitation in order that Mrs White's sister could accompany her. 'That was typical of the Queen's kindness,' Mr White said. 'If she could do anything to make life easier for you, she would.'

Buckingham Palace represented a daytime base to King George and Queen Elizabeth, while Windsor Castle was the home to which they returned of an evening. This system of commuting by armoured car between London and Berkshire was, of course, constantly interrupted by the morale-boosting trips the King and Queen undertook. Then the royal train became 'home', often for days on end, and details of its routes and timetables remained top secret until the last possible moment. In total the sovereigns made 300 such journeys within Great Britain and covered 40,000 miles.

Almost without exception the King was accompanied by his wife as they picked their way through devastated streets, consoling, encouraging, sympathizing. They toured hospitals, ARP centres, Home Guard stations, barracks, munition factories, feeding centres, stood in stunned silence on the edge of vast craters, and shared shelters with ordinary men and women when the sirens wailed. There was one visit, however, which the King insisted upon undertaking alone. That was to Coventry, where he toured the still smouldering ruins of that decimated city only five hours after the German bombers had released their loads. On that occasion it was the King's own wish that Queen Elizabeth should be spared such harrowing sights.

The gallantry which the King witnessed among the civilian population on his travels touched him profoundly. It was not simply the courage and fortitude of all those who suffered so terribly as a result of air assaults that impressed him, but that of the men and women whose manifold activities would almost certainly have gone unrewarded, if not unnoticed. It was this that moved George VI to institute two new honours bearing his name;

thus the George Cross and the George Medal – designed by the King himself – came into existence.

Meeting as many ordinary people as possible during visits was always the royal couple's prime consideration. One example of this stratagem was given to Harold Nicolson by Lord Harlech, the Midlands Commissioner, who was with the King and Queen in Sheffield one winter. As their car stopped, he said, 'The Queen nips out into the snow and goes straight into the middle of the crowd and starts talking to them. First they would just gape; then they all started talking at once – "Hi! Your Majesty! Look here." '

On one occasion, however, the Queen received a far from ecstatic welcome from a little girl in a hospital bed, the start of whose birthday 'celebrations' the royal visitor had unwittingly delayed. Noticing a small cake on the bedside locker, the Queen stopped to talk to the young patient who regarded her with a solemn and unsmiling expression. After a few moments Queen Elizabeth asked when she would be having her birthday cake and was very firmly told, 'When *you've* gone!'

The protection of public figures has always been a major consideration to all those responsible for security arrangements. That task has never been more onerous or complex than in the times through which we now live. In March 1974, shortly after her marriage, Princess Anne was ambushed as she drove towards Buckingham Palace along that most public of thoroughfares, the Mall. Rarely had the life of a member of the royal family been so dangerously threatened than on that near fatal occasion.

Some years later, two further incidents, which involved the present Queen herself, brought the whole question of royal protection into sharp focus. The first of these occurrences emphasized the extreme vulnerability of the Sovereign at the annual ceremony of Trooping the Colour. In June 1981 as Her Majesty reached the junction of the Mall and Horse Guards Approach Road, a youth – out to become a footnote in royal history books – fired several blank shots at the Queen. A year later, in July 1982, Michael Fagan achieved notoriety by slipping through a loop-hole in the Buckingham Palace security system, and finding his way into the Queen's bedroom.

Though such things cause a furore today, neither incident was very far removed from two unpublicized, but no less dramatic, events in the wartime lives of King George VI and Queen Elizabeth. It happened that on one occasion in the Queen's bedroom at Windsor Castle a half-crazed deserter sprang out from behind the curtains, threw himself to the floor and seized the Queen's ankles. 'For a moment my heart stood still,' she told a friend. But then, with the same quick presence of mind that was to be displayed by her elder daughter forty years later, Queen Elizabeth quietly said, 'Tell me about it', and as she listened, backed slowly and calmly towards the servants' bell. 'Poor man,' the Queen said later, 'I was so sorry for him.'

On 12 September 1940 the King and Queen together experienced the kind of attack which, had it been successful, would have severely damaged the morale of the nation. It was an audaciously conceived scheme to kill the royal couple as they worked at Buckingham Palace. On that day a German bomber, taking full advantage of low cloud cover, flew straight up the Mall and deposited two sticks of six bombs each on the palace building. '. . . all of a sudden,' recorded the King, 'we heard an aircraft making a zooming noise above us.' Then he saw '2 bombs falling past the opposite side of the Palace, & then heard 2 resounding crashes as the bombs fell in the quadrangle about 30 yards away. We looked at each other & then we were out in the passage as fast as we could get there. . . . We all wondered why we weren't dead . . . ' A little later the King began a tour of inspection of the palace to see for himself what damage had been caused. When he arrived at the kitchens, he discovered the chef, M. René Roussin, covered in grime and surrounded by the debris of a collapsed ceiling. As an amusing aside, the King was relieved to see that the cooker had been spared and, peering in, he expressed his gratitude that nothing had happened to his lunch, adding, 'I'm very hungry.'

That day, the King sent a message to his Prime Minister, Winston Churchill, in which he said, 'We have now had a personal experience of German barbarity, which only strengthens the resolution of all of us to fight through to final victory'; to the Queen the bombing of Buckingham Palace meant that she could now 'look the East End in the face'.

The destruction and disruption of life in Britain and in Europe were ever on the minds of both King George and Queen Elizabeth throughout the war, as Her Majesty revealed in March 1943,

when she again received a gift of two books from her friend Ava,
Lady Waverley. In a handwritten letter of thanks, the Queen said:

> The 'words' book is delightful, and I am enjoying it enormously.
> How dull we all are in our choice of words, when the English
> language is so rich in lovely and vivid ones!
> 'Les lilas et les roses' is very touching & poignant – I think it is
> odd that *our* poets were dumb at that glorious moment when the
> British Isles stood alone against the oppressor, it is disappointing
> that they do not seem to see the significance of our crusade against
> slavery and lies – do you not agree? I know that the cruelty & the
> ugliness & bestiality of the bombing in 1940 must have been
> difficult to write about, but through all the horror shone such
> courage & hope & trust – perhaps our poets will rise to the occasion
> soon. . . .

Between June 1943 and October 1944 King George VI was finally
able to widen his travels to encompass a number of battle fronts,
including those in North Africa, France, Italy, Malta and the
Low Countries. And nine days after D-Day he crossed to the
Normandy beaches.

'He feels so much at not being more in the firing line,' the
Queen had written to Queen Mary. Yet when the King set off by
air at the start of his first official visit to North Africa, in the wake
of the 8th Army's defeat of Rommel's forces, the Queen herself
was to endure hours of agonizing tension. The King's first visit
was, in fact, the longest he undertook during the war – stretching
across eleven days and 6,000 miles.

Following his departure Queen Elizabeth wrote to her mother-
in-law:

> I have had an anxious few hours, because at 8.15 I heard that the
> plane had been heard near Gibraltar, and that it would soon be
> landing. Then after an hour & a half I heard that there was a thick
> fog at Gib. & that they were going on to Africa. Then complete
> silence till a few minutes ago, when a message came that they have
> landed in Africa & taken off again. Of course I imagined every sort
> of horror, & walked up and down my room staring at the
> telephone.

Not all those commanding the British Forces on the various
fronts, however, were overjoyed at the prospect of the King's

presence. Yet while those who wanted the monarch to be kept at home in nominal leadership concealed their displeasure, there was no disguising the unbridled delight felt by the men at having their King among them. One report of his meeting with 3,000 soldiers ran:

> As he walked out on the verandah of his villa, first one man, then another, recognized him.
>
> And as if called by one voice, the thousands of men, most of them semi-nude, many of them still dripping with water, raced up the beach like a human wave.
>
> Then, as if the wave had suddenly frozen, they stood silently below the verandah, a solid mass of tanned and dripping men.
>
> There was one of those strange silences one sometimes gets among a huge crowd. A voice started 'God Save The King'. In a moment the National Anthem was taken up everywhere. It swelled deep-throatedly from a mass of soldiers.
>
> As the last notes of the Anthem died out, the King suddenly turned, stepped down from the verandah. He stood there, surrounded by hundreds of men, talking to them, asking them about their experiences. Then the men broke into song again, this time with 'For He's a Jolly Good Fellow'.

Peace – at least victory in Europe – was proclaimed on 8 May 1945, and the King told his peoples:

> Today we give thanks to Almighty God for a great deliverance.
>
> Speaking from our Empire's oldest capital city, war-battered but never for one moment daunted or dismayed – speaking from London, I ask you to join with me in that act of thanksgiving.
>
> Germany, the enemy who drove all Europe into war, has been finally overcome. In the Far East we have yet to deal with the Japanese, a determined and cruel foe. . . .

Three months later the dreadful matter of that 'cruel foe' was resolved. On 6 August an atomic bomb, the very first, was dropped on Hiroshima; on the 9th another was dropped on Nagasaki; and in between, Russia had declared war on Japan and that nation capitulated. It was the end of a long and ghastly saga.

On 15 August 1945 – VJ Day – George VI again broadcast to the Empire. In part he said:

Japan has surrendered, so let us join in thanking God that war has ended throughout the world. . . .

Our sense of deliverance is overpowering, and with it all, we have a right to feel that we have done our duty . . . from the bottom of my heart I thank my Peoples for all they have done, not only for themselves but for mankind.

# 12

## The King's Decline

The world at peace in 1945 was a very different world to that George VI had known at the end of the Great War. Then, in the reign of his father King George V, Britain was to have become a land fit for heroes to live in. It was a splendid dream, a vision of Utopia. But a dream, a vision, was all that it was.

On VJ Day, the King had called for men to 'turn their industry, skill and science' to repairing the war's 'frightful devastation', and in so doing, to build 'prosperity and happiness'. All this and more the average man wanted, but not under a Conservative administration. Men and women now called for greater social justice, for far better conditions than ever they had known between the wars. Thus, when the votes were counted and the results of the General Election of 5 July 1945 were finally announced, Winston Churchill – for all his inspired leadership – was not returned to 10 Downing Street.

The Tories had lost 160 seats, while Labour, under the leadership of 'Clem' (Clement) Attlee, had gained 230 seats and a majority of 180. The King, not surprisingly, was stunned by news of Churchill's defeat, not least because it deprived him of the comfortable and harmonious unity of like minds, which he cherished. The King wrote to Churchill, 'For myself personally, I regret what has happened more than perhaps anyone else. I shall miss your counsel to me more than I can say. But please remember that as a friend I hope we shall be able to meet at intervals.'

To George VI – despite his humanity and his concern for the

underprivileged – a Labour government, and with it the prospect of social revolution, was a chilling consideration, one which was totally alien to all he knew, believed in and represented. For while the sovereign is ostensibly apolitical, he or she stands at the apex of a system built on and around the ideals of the old ruling class.

Grave though the King's misgivings were at the installation of Mr Attlee's government, and though his relations with his new Prime Minister were, at first, predictably cooler than would otherwise have been the case, George VI fulfilled the 'conditions' of his apolitical role to perfection.

To Clement Attlee, 'The old pattern was worn out and it was for us to weave a new. . . . We had not been elected to try to patch up an old system but to make something new. Our policy was not a reformed capitalism, but progress towards a democratic socialism.' To the King – distrustful and suspicious of unnecessary haste and political extremism in any form – the Labour party 'were going too fast in their [reforming] legislation . . . and were offending every class of people who were ready to help them if they were asked to, but were swept aside by regulations. . . '. Two years later, at the beginning of 1947, the King was no happier about the strain dealing with his new ministers imposed.

Writing to Queen Mary, he said, 'I have asked Mr Attlee 3 times if he is not worried over the domestic situation in this country, but he won't tell me when he is when I feel he is. I know I am worried.' Still later he told his mother, 'I do wish I could see a glimmer of a bright spot anywhere in world affairs. Never in the whole history of mankind have things looked gloomier than they do now, and one feels so powerless to do anything to help.'

In time relations between the King and members of his government, especially those with Attlee himself, grew more cordial. The long awkward silences that were a feature of their regular meetings grew less frequent and by and by the King reached a better understanding and appreciation of his ministers. All the same, nothing would persuade him that what he regarded as Labour's 'radical policies' were not being introduced too fast. Even the survival of the monarchy – and how many kings had lost their thrones since the end of the First World War – sometimes troubled him. 'Everything is going nowadays,' he once said, 'Before long, I shall also have to go.' In that King George was mistaken.

It is true, of course, that the monarchy had passed, and would pass again, through phases of near-indifference on the part of the people; there were times when it seemed as if kings and queens, princes and princesses, were ill-cast in a modern and progressive society. All that was really nothing new. A sovereign, however, cannot remain blind to the needs of change and, through the years, Queen Elizabeth II was to continue the programme of reforms within the monarchy that were begun by her father. Barriers were slowly and imperceptibly lowered, the starchy formality of life at 'Court' (a word the King always disliked) was gradually diluted, and the Crown moved far closer than ever before towards its people. King George V may have been aghast at such 'revolutionary' moves, but all were implemented without impairing either the prestige of the Crown or the standing of its royal representatives.

For certain George VI would have delighted in the strength and affection of the monarchy today, had he but guessed the extent of its appeal.

As Duke of York, King George VI had once said, 'I am only a very ordinary person when people let me be one.' This was, in fact, the view he was always to have of himself. Yet while some shared that same view, others went still further.

During the 1920s 'Chips' Channon, an ambitious American who had come to England from Chicago in 1918, married into the aristocracy, entered Parliament, scaled the heights of London society, and was eventually knighted, described the future Sovereign (who, incidentally, never cared for Channon) as, 'good, dull, dutiful and good-mannered'. Many years later, Frances Donaldson was to respond, 'no one who did not know [George VI] well could say that this was not an adequate description of him.' The King's character, however, as Lady Donaldson implied, went far deeper than many would ever have suspected.

Writing to his wife Vita, Harold Nicolson disclosed, 'Alec Hardinge [the King's former private secretary] told me that George VI had the most tortuous mind of any man he ever knew. He never began to understand what was at the back of it. Extreme diffidence twisting itself into fantastic shapes. . . .' Later still, the King's official biographer, Sir John Wheeler-Bennett, bemoaned the fact that certain aspects of King George, notably that he 'never kept records of dictated talks with his Ministers . . .' made 'biographizing difficult'.

From time to time, as had always been the case, the King's irritability flared in fits of temper, but these were invariably quelled by Queen Elizabeth's gentle reproof, 'Now, Bertie', or, if she were present, by some amusing antic or aside on the part of his younger daughter Princess Margaret, in whom the King saw so much of himself.

King George VI was certainly a complex man but, nevertheless, a man of simple tastes who enjoyed a simple life; a man whom few, beyond his own intimate circle, ever properly knew. As we have already noted, the King was at his most relaxed and contented when at home with his wife and daughters, or when out in the field, participating in his best-loved sports with those whom he looked upon as his closest friends. Such a lifestyle may have seemed 'dull' to so gregarious, if egocentric, a personality as 'Chips' Channon, but by and large it suited the British temperament.

Of all the King's sporting activities, shooting has most often been referred to as the 'great passion in his life'. As Prince Albert he first joined his father and elder brother at Sandringham, on 23 December 1907, nine days after his twelfth birthday. That evening he recorded in a fresh Game Book, 'My first day's shooting. I used a single barrel muzzle loader with which Grandpapa, Uncle Eddy and Papa [Edward VII, Albert Victor, Duke of Clarence, and George V, respectively] all started shooting. I shot 3 rabbits.'

During the next forty-four years King George never lost an opportunity to indulge in his favourite pastime and, indeed, as with his love of hunting, tennis and golf, he established a formidable reputation among his contemporaries. Aubrey Buxton, who was to publish a book of rosy prose entitled *The King in His Country*, shortly after George VI's death, was of the opinion that, 'No more accomplished expert, no man with a more sensitive understanding of his quarry, has trodden the hill and bog of Scotland, or the broad acres and marshes of East Anglia.'

Whether shooting rabbits, hare, pheasant, grouse, partridge or woodcock, the King was in his element, and his Game Book observations provide a permanent record of his successes: 'I shot my first pheasant' (1909); 'I shot my first grouse', 'I shot my first partridge', 'My first woodcock' (all during 1911); 'My thousandth woodcock' (New Year's Day 1951), are all examples. Then finally, on 25 January 1952, it was noted that George VI had shot his last woodcock, 'No. 1055'.

In later life the King also took up and became an enthusiastic wild fowler which, since it depends on the movement of migratory duck, is an even more unpredictable sport. His prowess with a gun on such occasions was not the only memory to survive the King, however. Indeed, his kindness and sensitivity towards the feelings of others is constantly spoken about. To one young man who clearly knew little about shooting, but who didn't like to say so, the King – embarrassed and irritated by the taunts and jibes of other members of the party – explained the art with infinite sympathy and patience. Equally, in the presence of an inexperienced shot he would always minimize his own claims.

That the King hated those within his orbit to feel embarrassed or uncomfortable doubtless stemmed from painful memories of his own experiences and, whenever possible, he did all he could to put people at their ease.

In retrospect the last full decade of the King's life brought to the royal family an unpleasantly full measure of anxiety. The trauma of war was followed by the ugly nature of the King's declining health. There were political anxieties, too, where the Empire was concerned. By the mid-1940s the old idea of colonial rule had soured considerably in the minds of Western democracies. The British government, therefore, embarked on a gradual programme of granting independence to her colonial territories.

In 1947 Clement Attlee took the decision to send Lord Mountbatten, a cousin of the King, to India – the greatest of Britain's 'possessions' – as Viceroy to stage-manage the last days of British rule and thus negotiate the transfer of power. For some time the King had been deeply perturbed by the question of Indian independence and its possible effect on her peoples, but eventually became reconciled to the necessity of withdrawal.

So it was that from 15 August 1947, George VI ceased to reign as Emperor of India. It was just over seventy-one years since his great-grandmother, having been proclaimed Empress, first signed herself 'Victoria R.I.' (Regina et Imperatrix). Henceforth the King would simply sign himself 'George R' instead of the familiar

'George R.I.'. His mother, Queen Mary, who for twenty-five years had been the consort the second of India's four emperors, lamented the loss of so great a 'jewel'.

On 18 August the Queen Dowager received a letter from her son and, no doubt for posterity, she wrote on the back of the envelope, 'The first time Bertie wrote me a letter with the I for Emperor of India left out, very sad'. It was indeed the end of an epoch. Yet through it the structure and identity of the Commonwealth itself was redefined and strengthened. For shortly after attaining independence, India declared her intention of becoming a republic, but added that she did not wish to leave the Commonwealth.

So was posed the problem none had anticipated. Since 1926 the Commonwealth – save for the various colonies and dependencies – had been composed of white (or white-ruled) nations who, although independent, owed a common allegiance to the Crown. How then could a republic owe such allegiance? The solution was found in 1949 when it was decided that the British Sovereign should be designated *Head* of the Commonwealth, and in that capacity India would owe allegiance to the King.

George VI's last overseas journey was to South Africa early in 1947. The idea of a royal tour had been planted in the King's mind by Field Marshal Jan Smuts, the South African Prime Minister, during his wartime visits to England. Not fifty years earlier Smuts, then a staunch republican, had acted as supreme commander of Queen Victoria's enemy forces during the Boer War. Now, by a curious about-turn, Smuts had become a vigorous royalist. Not only did he proclaim an absolute belief in the power of monarchy, but stoutly maintained that kings and queens were capable of influencing public opinion. With a general election due in South Africa in 1948, the Field-Marshal's point was duly noted.

At Westminster there were the inevitable back-bench grumblings about the royal visit, but otherwise both the King and the government were of one mind: His Majesty's presence would reaffirm the bond between the Crown and South Africa, and though strenuous – the royal party covered 23,000 miles in a packed twelve-week schedule – it was hoped that the tour would revitalize the King, whose energy had been so severely taxed during the years of war.

Queen Elizabeth naturally accompanied her husband to South Africa, but perhaps more significantly, this tour marked the début of their daughters as royal ambassadors, providing the Princesses Elizabeth and Margaret with an important foretaste of something that was to become a prominent feature of their official lives. When the royal family returned to England at the end of April, the King, though looking fit and well, had lost a stone in weight. Nonetheless he was of the opinion that the tour had done him 'a great deal of good'.

Although grounds for concern at the King's health were not long in coming to the fore, the royal family's private life during 1947 was relatively untroubled. Amid all the matters of state with which George VI had to contend that year, he and the Queen experienced great personal joy at the marriage of their elder daughter to the tall, handsomely-Nordic (former) Prince Philip of Greece and Denmark. Born in Corfu on 10 June 1921, the only son of Prince Andrew of Greece and Denmark and the former Princess Alice of Battenberg, he was five years older than Princess Elizabeth.

The announcement, on 10 July, of the Princess's engagement to her distant cousin brought to an end months of rumour in which the media had linked the Heiress Presumptive's name with those of some highly unlikely 'suitors', including one or two European princes – such as Charles of the Belgians – who were almost old enough to be her father.

Dr Geoffrey Fisher, the Archbishop of Canterbury, married Princess Elizabeth and the newly created Philip, Duke of Edinburgh, at Westminster Abbey on the morning of 20 November. So 'new' a royal creation was the young Duke, in fact, that the formal *Ceremonial*, describing him less grandly as 'Lieutenant Philip Mountbatten, Royal Navy', had to stand unaltered.

The royal wedding – the first occasion of its kind for ten years – aroused great passions. The overall emotion, though not surprisingly, was one of delight, and Winston Churchill declared it to be, 'A flash of colour on the hard road we have to travel'. Yet there was also an underlying current of public disappointment, on which the Left-wing Press seized, that the future Queen had chosen a husband of foreign origin. Indeed, in an opinion poll conducted at the time, forty per cent of those questioned were found to be opposed to the Princess marrying a 'foreigner', albeit one already serving Britain in the Royal Navy, and whose naturalization, finally granted in March 1947, had been raised with George VI as early as the autumn of 1944.

During the week which led up to the day of the wedding, the King and Queen found themselves travelling hither and thither to greet their European royal guests. The kings of Norway, Romania, Denmark, Yugoslavia and Iraq, the Queen of the Hellenes, the former Queen Victoria-Eugenie of Spain, the Prince Regent of the Belgians, the Princess Regent and Prince Bernhard of The Netherlands, the Crown Prince and Crown Princess of Sweden, princes and princesses of Denmark, Greece, and Bourbon-Parma, together with the Duchess of Aosta, poured into London to join the celebrations.

Yet at the heart of all the pomp and pageantry there lay something that was, essentially, a family occasion. This could not have been illustrated more clearly than by two small – but in their own way memorable – incidents. First, the remonstrations of the eleven-year-old Princess Alexandra of Kent, a first cousin of Princess Elizabeth (and after Princes Margaret the next senior-ranking bridesmaid), *not* to be made to sit through the showing of a film of the royal wedding with her term-mates from Heathfield School, on the grounds that it would embarrass her; and second, part of a letter King George VI wrote to his daughter on the very evening of her marriage:

'I was so proud and thrilled at having you so close to me on our long walk in Westminster Abbey but when I handed your hand to the Archbishop, I felt I had lost something very precious. You were so calm and composed during the Service and said your words with such conviction, that I knew everything was all right.'

Within the year, however, it became apparent that everything was far from 'all right' with the King. Masked by such public celebrations as the Sovereigns' silver wedding anniversary in April 1948 and the birth of their first grandchild, Prince Charles, that November, anxiety over the King's health had nevertheless been gradually rising.

From the beginning of the year – though he kept it to himself – King George had been suffering from cramp in both legs. By early autumn his left foot was continuously numb and at night intense pain prevented him from sleeping. By the end of November his right foot had been similarly affected.

When, at last, the King's doctors were brought in, the diagnosis was plain: arteriosclerosis; hardening of the arteries. That he had not said anything much earlier meant that there was the threat of gangrene and the distinct possibility that the King's right leg would have to be amputated. In the event such drastic measures were averted, but surgery was not. In March 1949 the King underwent a right lumbar sympathectomy. The results of the operation were considered satisfactory, but postponement of the Antipodean tour, which King George, Queen Elizabeth and Princess Margaret were to have undertaken the following spring, was deemed advisable. The King, though upset by the decision, had no choice but to concur with his doctors when they announced shortly afterwards that 'It would be hazardous for His Majesty to embark upon a long journey'.

By June of that year – 1949 – the King's condition had improved to the extent that he was able to take the salute as usual at the Sovereign's annual Birthday Parade, Trooping the Colour. There was, however, a significant departure to the established ceremonial in that the King was seated in a State Landau, rather than on horseback.

The suggestion that her father should spare himself the added strain of riding was put forward by Princess Margaret. At first the King would not hear of such an idea. The sovereign, he argued, had always *ridden*. Undeterred Princess Margaret remonstrated that, since a carriage was drawn *by* horses, it would surely not matter too much if, for once, the King were to review his troops on Horse Guards Parade from such an equipage. At length the King gave in and with Princess Elizabeth riding side-saddle alongside, George VI attended what was to be his penultimate Trooping ceremony.

Taking life at a somewhat slower pace, the King was able to continue with much of his official programme of events. But in plain terms doctors had told him that his future lay in his own hands. The threat of another thrombosis, he was warned, would be ever present. The King heeded his physicians' advice and assured them that he would take care not to over-tax himself.

After the Birthday Parade on 9 June, the King and Queen took up residence at Windsor Castle for Ascot week and King George had the great satisfaction of watching his horse Avila race to victory in the Coronation Stakes. Later in the year the royal family attended 'a show that was never a duty' – the Royal Variety Performance, staged at the London Coliseum. The following day, 8 November, King George put on his Admiral-of-the-Fleet's uniform and travelled down to Portsmouth on a visit to the United States Ship *Columbus*, the flagship of Admiral R.L. Conolly, commanding the US Naval Forces in the Eastern Atlantic and Mediterranean.

As the King was piped aboard, yet another footnote of royal history was written as the royal standard was raised on an American warship for the first time. During the following year George VI, true to his promise, was careful not to over-exert himself, even though his schedule was no less full. Yet if 1950 passed at a steady pace in the King's life, 1951 brought with it renewed alarm.

In May – a month during which the King had opened the Festival of Britain and had entertained King Frederick of Denmark upon his state visit to England – George VI wrote to his mother of 'a condition on the left lung known as pneumonitis'. He told Queen Mary, 'I was X-rayed and the photographs showed a shadow.' Though the King remained in an optimistic mood, he was irritated at 'not being able to chuck out the bug'. Five months later his left lung was removed. Though he is said not to have realized it, the operation had been for malignant cancer.

Still King George remained hopeful. 'An operation is not an illness,' he said stoically as he approached his fifty-sixth birthday on 14 December, and prepared for the royal family's Christmas visit to Sandringham.

The last time the King appeared in public was when he, the Queen and Princess Margaret travelled from Norfolk to bid farewell to Princess Elizabeth and the Duke of Edinburgh at Heathrow Airport. The date was 31 January 1952 and the Heiress Presumptive was flying out to East Africa, thence to Australia and New Zealand, deputizing for the King on the long-postponed tour he had hoped to undertake himself.

At Sandringham six days later, the life of King George VI came full circle when, sometime during the early hours of Wednesday 6 February – the precise time is unknown – His Majesty died peacefully in his sleep.

'For fifteen years,' Winston Churchill told the stunned nation,

131

'King George the Sixth was King; never at any moment in all the perplexities at home and abroad, in public or in private, did he fail in his duties; well does he deserve the farewell salute of all his governments and peoples.'

# 13

# *Queen Elizabeth the Queen Mother*

'I must go to him', was Queen Elizabeth's immediate reaction when the news of her husband's death was brought to her by Sir Harold Campbell, the Equerry-in-Waiting. After she had sat beside the body for a time, the royal widow who would soon choose to be known officially as Queen Elizabeth the Queen Mother, rather than by the outmoded, but perfectly correct style, 'Queen Dowager', instructed that a constant vigil should be kept by the open door to the King's room.

At that time Queen Elizabeth's thoughts were not of herself, but of those around her – of her daughter Princess Margaret, who worshipped her father (and who would always ask, 'Why did he have to die so young?'), and the youngest members of the family at Sandringham, the three-year-old Prince Charles and his sister Princess Anne, born eighteen months earlier, in August 1950.

There were also any number of arrangements to be considered – from the small, personal jobs which face any family at a time of bereavement, to the major ceremonial aspects of the King's state funeral. There was, too, the homecoming of the new Sovereign, the second Elizabeth who, like the first, had ascended the throne at the age of twenty-five.

In Africa on 6 February, it was already early afternoon before the news was confirmed and the Duke of Edinburgh quietly took his wife aside to tell her of her father's death. At 4.30 p.m. the following day, Queen Elizabeth II, a slight figure in black, stepped on to the tarmac at London Airport after the long flight from Entebbe. The first to greet her was Winston Churchill, back in office as prime minister, then – among others – Clement Attlee, Anthony Eden and Lord and Lady Mountbatten. A few minutes later, the new Queen and the Duke of Edinburgh (he was not to be re-created *Prince* Philip until 1957), climbed into a Daimler limousine for the journey to Clarence House, their official London residence, a few hundred yards down the Mall from Buckingham Palace.

Waiting there to greet and console her granddaughter, and to pay homage to her new Sovereign, was Queen Mary. 'Her old Grannie and subject must be the first to kiss her hand,', George V's Queen, who was nearing her eighty-fifth birthday, had said.

On 8 February as her accession was ceremoniously proclaimed in London from St James's Palace, Whitehall, Temple Bar and the Royal Exchange, from Queen Victoria's statue on Castle Hill in Windsor, from Cardiff City Hall, and from the Mercat Cross in Edinburgh, the young Elizabeth II was travelling to Norfolk to join her mother at Sandringham. There, as darkness fell, she followed her father's coffin by torchlight to the church of St Mary Magdalene and, there, knelt in prayer by its side. For the next two days, draped with the royal standard and bearing the Queen Mother's wreath of white orchids, lilies and carnations, the King's coffin rested in front of the altar. Throughout that time estate workers, gamekeepers, foresters, carpenters and others kept watch in groups of four, and those who had known George VI more as 'the Squire of Sandringham' than as King of England passed through the church to pay their last respects.

On Sunday 9 February, the new Queen, the Queen Mother, Princess Margaret and other members of the royal family attended a short, private service conducted by the rector. Two days later, by means of the traditional gun-carriage, the King's remains were borne away from the church by the King's Troop of the Royal Horse Artillery and taken to the nearby Wolferton Station at the start of the journey to Westminster Hall in London. There, high on a purple catafalque, King George VI was to lie in state for three days and four nights.

Now on the oak coffin, in addition to the royal standard and his widow's flowers, were placed the Imperial State Crown, the Orb and the Sceptre, together with the King's Insignia of the Order of the Garter. At the four corners of the dais, and at the head and at the foot, amber candles burned in tall golden sticks. Four officers of the Household Troops, two from the Life Guards, two from the Blues and Royals, together with four Yeomen of the Guard, and two of the King's Gentlemen-at-Arms, stood watches of twenty minutes each, each party being succeeded by the next in silence, save for the sound of marching feet and the clink of sword scabbards.

Through that ancient hall, where early kings had lived and held great councils of state, where King Charles I was tried and sentenced to death, where Oliver Cromwell's disinterred head had been hung from the south gable, where George VI's father and grandfather had lain in state before him, 305,806 ordinary men and women filed past. In freezing temperatures most had waited five and six abreast for up to five hours, in a queue – at one point four miles long – that crossed and re-crossed the River Thames in a vast human rectangle, surrounding the Palace of Westminster.

Unobtrusively, members of the royal family came to West-minster Hall and stood in the shadows of the east door, gazing at a scene which, despite its mournful nature, was both colourful and supremely majestic. Among the last of the royal visitors were Queen Mary, her daughter the Princess Royal, and the Duke of Windsor, who had recently arrived from New York. For several minutes the old Queen and her daughter stood with bowed heads, and upon their arrival and departure the former King Edward VIII knelt on one knee in homage to his late brother.

Last of all, on the eve of the state funeral, came Queen Elizabeth the Queen Mother, who arrived at 11.25 p.m. and stayed until a little before midnight.

At 9.30 the following morning – 15 February – a bearer party of the King's Company of the Brigade of Guards carried the King's coffin at shoulder height from Westminster Hall and placed it on a gun-carriage, drawn by over one hundred naval ratings. Big Ben chimed fifty-six times (one stroke for each year of the King's life) and, to the beat of muffled drums and the sound of familiar funeral marches, the procession finally moved off on its two-hour prog-ress through London (witnessed it was estimated by crowds totalling one million) to Paddington, where the royal train waited to convey the dead King to Windsor.

As the cortège passed along the Mall, Queen Mary, unable to attend the committal service, appeared at a window of her sitting-room at Marlborough House. 'Here *he* is,' she murmured to her old friend Mabell, Countess of Airlie, as the coffin came into view. As it went by, the Queen, tall and erect in a long black dress, raised her arm in a gesture of farewell to her son. The Queen, the Queen Mother, Princess Margaret and the Princess Royal, veiled and shadowy figures following the gun-carriage in the Irish State Coach, turned their heads in Queen Mary's direction and bowed. The royal Dukes – of Edinburgh, Gloucester and Windsor – walking behind the coach and dressed in service uniform saluted, while the young 'civilian' Duke of Kent doffed his black top hat.

Then followed the rest of what must have seemed an interminable procession of mourners. Four kings, twelve princes, three presidents, nine peripheral members of the royal family, Commonwealth high commissioners and heads of foreign delegations, preceded six royal carriages containing yet another king, three more queens, four duchesses, three princesses, and a host of courtiers, known collectively as 'the Suites in Attendance'. Escorting the entire funeral procession – and numbering hundreds – were guards' bands, massed pipers, the Household Cavalry, detachments of all the British and Commonwealth armed forces, and officers representing the armies, navies and air forces of more than thirty countries around the world, quite literally from East to West.

At Paddington Station, swathed in purple and white drapes, the funeral party entrained for Windsor Central where, an hour later, the procession formed up once again and made its slow, dignified way to St George's Chapel.

There at exactly twenty-two minutes past two o'clock, at the conclusion of the funeral service, and almost five hours after leaving Westminster Hall, the mortal remains of King George VI were lowered into the royal vault. The Lord Chamberlain, Lord Clarendon, as tradition decrees, had broken his wand of office in two, and the new Queen – watched by her mother, her sister and all those congregated in the choir – sprinkled earth on to the coffin as the Archbishop of Canterbury, Dr Fisher, intoned the words of committal.

For the last time Garter King-of-Arms proclaimed all the King's titles and a prayer was said for 'Our Sovereign Lady, Elizabeth the Second . . . '. The Queen curtsied to the place where her father had lain throughout the service and the Queen Mother bowed. Then while the organist played the Dead March from *Saul*, the royal mourners departed, to seek solace with one another at the end of what surely had been a particularly gruelling test of endurance.

King George's coffin, having been lowered from a place before the high altar in St George's Chapel by means of a hand-operated lift mechanism, was borne into the royal tomb-house which lies beneath the Albert Memorial Chapel. Comparatively few, save members of the royal family, have ever seen it.

The tomb-house, originally created for George III and eventually altered by his granddaughter Queen Victoria, contains the remains of a large number of kings and princes for whom memorial chapels or alternative resting places were not to be found. These royal figures include King George III himself and four of his sons, George IV, William IV, Frederick, Duke of York and Edward, Duke of Kent (the father of Queen Victoria). Their coffins, protected by carved screens, lie to this day on shelves which occupy the length of the north and south walls of the tomb-house.

On a stone platform in the centre of this subterranean chamber, George VI was to rest for the next seventeen years, until 1969. In that year the King George VI Chapel was constructed to the north of the north choir aisle – or in plain terms, to the left of the organ screen if viewed from the west door. The King George VI Chapel, designed by the architects George Pace and Paul Paget, was to be the first addition to St George's Chapel since completion of the vaulting in 1528. Set into the floor, the black ledger stone covering the King's final resting place and bearing the simple legend 'George VI', recalls that which covers the tomb of King Henry VI. On the wall beyond, a portrait medallion bears a profile relief of the King, while behind the altar, on which stands a modern cross commissioned by Princess Margaret, light filters through stained-glass windows, the work of the celebrated painter John Piper.

The gates to the chapel are a modern interpretation of Edward IV's grille, and affixed to them – on either side of the entrance steps – are a pair of engraved brass plates, their lettering picked out in red. One plate provides details about the late King, while on the other is inscribed the poem which became his epitaph. In 1939 His Majesty received a copy of a poem entitled 'The Gate of the Year'. Written by Miss 'Minnie' (Marie Louise) Haskins, a lecturer at the London School of Economics, and privately published in 1908 as part of a collection called *The Desert*, it so impressed the King that he included its message of faith in his first Christmas Day broadcast of the war. It reads:

> *I said to the man who stood at the Gate of the Year,*
> *'Give me a light so that I may tread safely into the unknown,'*
> *And he replied, 'Go out into the darkness,*
> *And put your hand into the Hand of God.*
> *That shall be to you better than light,*
> *And safer than a known way.'*

One of the Queen Mother's first acts following the King's death was to compose a message of thanks,

> To a multitude of people, to you whom from all parts of the world have given me sympathy and affection throughout these dark days. I want you to know how your concern for me has upheld me in my sorrow, and how proud you have made me by your wonderful tributes to my dear husband, a great and noble King. No man had a deeper sense than he of duty and of service, and no man was more full of compassion for his fellow-men. He loved you all, every one of you, most truly. That, you know, was what he always tried to tell you in his yearly message at Christmas; that was the pledge he took at the sacred moment of his Coronation fifteen years ago. Now I am left alone, to do what I can to honour that pledge without him.
>
> Throughout our married life we have tried, the King and I, to fulfil with all our hearts and all our strength the great task of service that was laid upon us. My only wish now is that I may be allowed to continue the work that we sought to do together.
>
> I commend to you our dear daughter: give her your loyalty and devotion: in the great and lonely station to which she has been called she will need your protection and your love.
>
> God Bless you all: and may He in His wisdom guide us safely to our true destiny of peace and goodwill.

It was a mark of Queen Elizabeth's resilience, her enormous

strength of purpose, that she did not break down at the time of her husband's death. Though her instincts were, of course, much the same as those of any other widow, her fortitude prevailed to such an extent that her doctor is on record as having said, 'If only Queen Elizabeth could break down. This incredible self-control will take its toll.'

Queen Elizabeth the Queen Mother, as many who know her well confirm, has always been regarded as a 'tough' individual. One who has known her for more than thirty years said, 'She *is* a remarkable woman. But you know, underneath all that smiling and waving that she puts on for the crowds, lies a ridge of steel.' Another confided, 'Queen Elizabeth really does personify the idea of an "Iron Fist in a Velvet Glove".' Equally euphemistically, the journalist Ann Morrow wrote, 'There is polished marble under the cream.'

In marked contrast to the rather superficial image, therefore, observations such as these shed a very different light on Queen Elizabeth; one that reveals her to be every bit as formidable as her predecessor, Queen Mary. In fact, it is possible to draw remarkably similar parallels between Queen Elizabeth and her mother-in-law; the most obvious being that both had married second sons – both Dukes of York – whose ultimate and unexpected inheritance was the Crown.

Admittedly Queen Mary had realized, first with her engagement to her husband's elder brother, Albert Victor, then after his death to Prince George, that hers would one day be the role of consort. Queen Elizabeth, of course, had no such knowledge. Nevertheless, when called upon, both Queens Consort set themselves rigid personal standards of behaviour, born of a belief that exalted rank demands unfaltering loyalty and supreme dignity. At the same time both re-dedicated themselves anew to the insuperable call of duty, according it unswerving devotion.

Comparisons begin to diverge, however, when considering the nature of the relationships Queen Mary and Queen Elizabeth had with their husbands. There were inevitably certain inescapable similarities since, in outlook, father and son were very much of the same mould. Neither knew or much cared for intellectual or cultural pursuits, much preferring the hearth to the salon.

Yet of the two marriages it is clear that Queen Elizabeth's was the more demanding. For while Queen Mary certainly had to release her husband from his mother's possessive grasp, nurturing and encouraging his inner strength, Queen Elizabeth had to extricate her husband from the formidable inhibitions of his youth, and to help establish a confidence and a belief in himself. In short, her task was very much to rehabilitate the man. The enormous level of support that George VI required of his consort, his 'helpmeet', as he referred to her in his accession speech, therefore, was by far the more exacting. Nor should we forget that the circumstances in which George VI ascended the throne led the monarchy into a distinctly new and, for the most part, uncharted phase of its history. From that time on – as witness the royal family today – more was to be required not only of the sovereign, but of royalty in general.

During the reigns of George V and George VI fundamental differences in character and attitude ensured marked differences in the respective Queens' portrayal of the consort's role. Afflicted by a withering shyness that threw up difficulties in communication, Queen Mary – revered though she became – appeared detached and regally aloof. Yet in private, in her relationship with George V, we find a kind of dutiful subservience rising to the surface; seen, for example, in her husband's relations with their children. When they fell from grace – as seemed to happen all the time – Queen Mary would never intervene, much less remonstrate on their behalf, saying that she had always to remember that their father was also their King.

George VI and Queen Elizabeth's partnership was founded on a very different footing. Throughout their married life the Queen's positive presence, her potently decisive mind, acted as the perfect counterbalance to the King's more diffident nature. Indeed if it ever crossed her mind, Queen Mary may well have secretly envied the strength and confidence she saw in her daughter-in-law. Thus to the role in which she seemed to be so perfectly cast, Queen Elizabeth brought an air that was at once warm and approachable. It not only commanded people's respect and affection, but engendered a new and spontaneous kind of adoration never before experienced by a member of the royal family, save for the possible exception of the Duke of Windsor when Prince of Wales.

By nature Queen Mary and Queen Elizabeth were poles apart. Even within the spectrum of private family life, it is impossible to imagine that Queen Mary was ever a great deal warmer than the bastion-like image presented to the world. In female company, for instance, she was always decidedly ill at ease, and this alone built a wall between herself and the young Princesses Elizabeth and Margaret in whom she unwittingly instilled fear.

'Whenever we had to visit Granny . . .', Princess Margaret has said, 'we always felt that we were going to be hauled over the coals for something we had done. But we never were.' All the same neither Princess was ever to conquer feelings of dread at receiving a summons from Queen Mary or to forget 'the hollow, empty feeling' their grandmother inspired.

In her grandchildren Queen Elizabeth was to inspire devotion. It is inconceivable to picture Queen Mary with any one of her grandchildren riding in an open carriage smiling and waving to the crowds, whilst all the time exchanging jokes with her companion to see who would be the first to dissolve in a fit of giggles. This, however, is exactly what happened in May 1981 when, accompanied by Lady Sarah Armstrong-Jones and escorted by a travelling party of the Household Cavalry, Queen Elizabeth drove the short distance from Windsor Castle to the Home Park nearby where, in a public ceremony, she received the Freedom of the Royal Borough.

If, as consort, Queen Elizabeth exerted a powerful influence in establishing the authority of her husband's reign, that influence remains just as strong to this day. In fact, the very force of her personality meant that, even in widowhood, Queen Elizabeth would never have been content dozing on the royal back-benches.

At family councils – let's say, the debate over the young Prince Charles's education, or even on everyday issues relating to her family, the Bowes Lyons included – the Queen Mother's is ever an authoritative voice, as much alive to the support she receives as to the opposition. Yet whatever the stakes, it has been said, sometimes with surprise, that while capable of making acidic remarks, she has never been known to lose her temper. This may well be so. Certainly she has no need of anger or vehement expression in order to make a point, deliver a rebuke or achieve an objective. For Queen Elizabeth's strength, her power, has always been found in the gentle, consummate, art of persuasive manipulation.

★

Heartbroken though Queen Mary was at the death of George V, nobody saw it. Sixteen years later that same royal dignity forbade the release of Queen Elizabeth's grief, except in the privacy of her room.

It was only when the full impact of the King's death began to dawn on her that, for a moment, she faltered and allowed thoughts of withdrawing from public life to cross her mind.

The King and Queen's 'togetherness', as it were, had become paramount to each other's existence, and one small act that illustrates their complete devotion to one another was inadvertently witnessed at Buckingham Palace, moments after their Majesties had retired at the end of a long and tiresome function. In Lady Donaldson's words, 'someone opened a door on to a corridor and caught sight of the King and Queen, hand in hand, skipping gaily down it together'.

That same 'loving' which the King displayed for his Queen was naturally apparent in his role as a parent. At Easter time 1952, in a letter to her mother's friend Ava Waverley, Princess Margaret provided a daughter's view of the King. 'He was such a wonderful person, the very heart and centre of our happy family,' she wrote. 'Everything seemed to come from him and no-one could have had a more devoted and thoughtful father.

'He was always so very much *alive*; so that at this lovely Easter time he doesn't feel so very far away and one is comforted by all thoughts of happiness for him and his love for us all.'

Such ideas as Queen Elizabeth had entertained for retirement were soon to vanish. Among those who spoke to her of the future, compassionately, but no doubt plainly, perhaps even reminding her of her publicly stated 'wish' to 'continue the work' she and George VI had 'sought to do together', was Winston Churchill. Whatever passed between them the Queen Mother's sense of duty was very clearly revived and, resolved to carry on, she stepped back into the public arena in May 1952.

Her first official engagement that month, as Colonel-in-Chief, took her to Crail in Fife, to inspect the First Battalion of the Black Watch (Royal Highland Regiment) before its departure for Korea, whither it had been ordered. On that occasion, with the pitch black of her mourning outfit relieved only by a pearl necklace and her diamond regimental brooch, Queen Elizabeth reviewed the five hundred men on parade and told them, 'The Black Watch, so dear to my heart and to many of my family [the Bowes Lyons] . . . has for more than two hundred years played a distinguished part in the battles of our country . . . and I know well that whatever may face you, you will win new honour for the Black Watch and for Scotland.'

Getting back into the swing of her official duties and thus rebuilding a new life for herself as a queen dowager was not the only way in which Queen Elizabeth helped herself counterbalance the King's loss. Indeed the sense of renewed stability in her life was to be afforded to a large extent by the acquisition of two new houses: Clarence House, St James's Palace, which was now to become her official residence, and the Castle of Mey in Caithness, which she was to buy and maintain from her considerable private funds as a much-loved holiday retreat.

The question of alternative accommodation for Queen Elizabeth was, of course, one that had to be raised upon the accession of the new sovereign. Marlborough House, had it been vacant, may well have received its third queen mother. As it was, Clarence House – so recently refurbished for Princess Elizabeth and the Duke of Edinburgh – seemed ideal.

The Queen Mother's transfer from Buckingham Palace was not imminent, however; and in fact she and Princess Margaret did not move in until 18 May 1953, the day that Queen Elizabeth's distinctive personal standard was flown from the crown-topped masthead for the very first time.

The Castle of Mey, on the other hand, seems almost to have been put in the Queen Mother's path by Providence, not only to help distract her from her grief, but as a focus for her energies, a kind of threshold to the future.

It was during the very early days of her widowhood, while staying with her friends Commander and Lady Doris Vyner at their house on the coast of Caithness, known as the House of the Northern Gate, that Queen Elizabeth chanced upon the small, decaying Barrogill Castle. In the absence of a purchaser, she was told, it would almost certainly be demolished. The Queen Mother paid seven visits to the near-ruins, then declared, 'Pull it down? Never! I shall buy it.'

Some years later she explained why:

I found the Castle of Mey, with its long history, its serene beauty and its proud setting, faced with the prospect of having no one able to occupy it. I felt a great wish to preserve, if I could, this ancient dwelling. It is too common an experience to find that once a house becomes deserted its decay begins and it is a happiness to me to feel that I have been able to save from such a fate part of Scotland's heritage.

For some four hundred years the Castle of Mey, for such was its original name, was the seat of the earls of Caithness. It did not become known as Barrogill Castle until the nineteenth century, when John Sinclair, 14th Earl of Caithness, a lord-in-waiting to Queen Victoria, was created a peer of the United Kingdom. He then adopted the title Lord Barrogill.

As with so much of Britain's history, romance and tragedy are the main ingredients of the story of the Castle of Mey. One such tale, marked by a memorial in the castle grounds, tells of Lady Fanny Sinclair's thwarted love for one of her father's servants. Locked away in her room – the uppermost chamber of the tower – by her outraged parent, the unfortunate Lady Fanny leapt to her death from the window. Though the window frame was retained, the casement itself was bricked up and it is now indistinguishable from the rest of the wall in what, today, is used as a servant's bedroom.

Located in the most northerly parish of mainland Great Britain, known as Canisbay (John O'Groats lies only six miles to the east), the Castle of Mey commands fine views across the Pentland Firth – with its two whirlpools, the 'Men o' Mey' and the 'Well of Swona' – to the Orkney island of Hoy.

Described as 'an enchanting house' (to the royal family even castles and palaces are 'houses'), the Castle of Mey was finally ready to receive its new royal owner in October 1955, when Queen Elizabeth gave a house-warming party. Among the guests were the Queen and the Duke of Edinburgh, who had sailed up in the Royal Yacht *Britannia*, and the Vyners.

Here at Mey, luxuriating whenever she can in splendid isolation, the Queen Mother takes long walks with her corgi dogs along the shore. It is said that she never tires of watching the seals who, or so the story goes, come closer inshore when she sings Scottish ballads to them.

During her visits Queen Elizabeth worships in either the small, white-washed Canisbay Parish Church, or further afield at Dunnet. The castle itself was not, however, the Queen Mother's only purchase in the early 1950s; she also bought a nearby croft, complete with sheep, and the 120-acre Longgoe Farm where she keeps a herd of pedigree Angus cattle.

Of her personal Scottish retreat, one visitor has said, 'It remains for Queen Elizabeth a haven from the world.'

## 14

# A New Direction

No sooner had Court mourning ended for King George VI than it began again with the death, on Tuesday 24 March 1953, of Queen Mary. Two months later, almost to the very day (26 May) the Queen would have attained her eighty-sixth birthday.

All through the last day of her life friends and relations called at Marlborough House. Queen Mary's eldest son, the Duke of Windsor, visited three times; the Queen and the Duke of Edinburgh, accompanied by Princess Margaret, arrived during the late afternoon, following Queen Elizabeth the Queen Mother, who had just spent an hour with her mother-in-law. Fifteen minutes after the departure of the Duchess of Kent with her children Edward and Alexandra, at the end of a three-hour visit, the old Queen's third son, Henry, Duke of Gloucester, with his Duchess, drove through the tall black gates of the house that Sir Christopher Wren originally built for the first Duke of Marlborough, and which is today, alas, no more than a Commonwealth conference centre.

Of Queen Mary's closest friends, her devoted Lady-in-Waiting, Mabell, Countess of Airlie, postponed a trip to her home in Scotland to sit by the bedside and chatter about idle things. Much later on she was to recall her royal mistress as she lay dying from a combination of old age and hardening of the arteries:

> . . . the exquisitely embroidered soft lawn night gown – the same as those she had worn in her youth – the nails delicately shaped and polished a pale pink; the immaculately arranged grey hair. Her face

had still a gentle beauty of expression; no trace of hardness as so many faces have in old age, only resignation. As I kissed her hand before leaving her I noticed the extreme softness of her skin.

Outside in Pall Mall the crowds mustered, anxious to read the briefly worded bulletins. At 7 p.m. it was stated that, 'Queen Mary's strength is ebbing, but Her Majesty is sleeping peacefully.' At 11.15 p.m. the final bulletin was posted: 'While sleeping peacefully Queen Mary died at twenty minutes past ten o'clock.' Both notices were signed by Sir Horace Evans (the arterial specialist) and Lord Webb-Johnson (Queen Mary's surgeon) who had attended her.

No doubt to the royal family's intense relief – and especially that of the Queen Mother – the ceremonial ritual surrounding the passing of Queen Mary was very much briefer than that observed only thirteen months earlier. For although the dead Queen, whom 'Chips' Channon had referred to as 'a kind of Olympian Goddess', was borne to Westminster Hall on the by-now familiar gun-carriage, amid all the attendant pageantry befitting the occasion, the royal obsequies – at Queen Mary's own wish – were dealt with decorously but, above all, expediently.

Wise to the end, she had instructed that nothing, not even her death, should be allowed to mar or interrupt the progress of arrangements, already well in hand, for her granddaughter's coronation, now only five weeks hence.

At Westminster Hall, therefore, while Queen Mary was the first queen consort to be so honoured, the public lying-in-state lasted no more than thirty-two hours. Then the coffin was transferred privately, by motor hearse, to Windsor where, on the morning of 31 March, Queen Mary was interred at St George's Chapel. She lies entombed beside her husband, King George V, in the simple, yet magnificent sarcophagus of white Clipsham stone designed by Sir Edwin Lutyens. Sir William Reid Dick's recumbent effigies of the King and herself – so reminiscent of Marochetti's effigies of Queen Victoria and the Prince Consort at Frogmore – lie above.

The coronation of Elizabeth II took place at Westminster Abbey on Tuesday, 2 June. Though somewhat shorter – there was no consort to be crowned this time – the ceremony followed the same lines as that of her father and any number of her ancestors.

Following the precedent established by the late Queen Mary, Queen Elizabeth the Queen Mother attended the coronation of her daughter. Travelling with Princess Margaret in the Irish State Coach, she was greeted by exultant crowds. At the Abbey Queen Elizabeth, dressed in diamanté-embroidered white satin fringed with gold, her long purple train – which had belonged to Queen Mary – supported by her pages-of-honour, and the diamond base of her own crown upon her head, processed along the nave to the sound of Sir William Walton's *Orb and Sceptre*.

'On she came,' wrote Anne Edwards of the *Daily Express*, 'with a bow here to Prince Bernhard, a bow there to the row of ambassadors, and up those tricky steps [of the coronation theatre] with no looking down like the Duke of Gloucester, no half turn to check her train like the Duchess of Kent, no hesitation at the top like Princess Margaret, no nervous nods of her head like Princess Mary.' At the steps of the royal gallery her voluminous mantle was folded into a parcel and placed over her arm, and then, with consummate grace, the Queen Mother took her place in the first row, seated between her younger daughter and her sister-in-law, the Princess Royal.

During the ceremony the young Prince Charles, known at that time as the Duke of Cornwall, joined his grandmother for an hour in the royal box. Between them Queen Elizabeth and Princess Margaret explained aspects of the coronation to him and, at the moment of his mother's crowning, before she, too, put on her own velvet-capped coronet, Princess Margaret bent down and whispered to her nephew, 'Always remember that you saw this.'

Almost thirty years later, Princess Margaret explained to the author, 'Nobody bothered to tell me what was going on at my parents' coronation. My grandmother and my Aunt Mary were too preoccupied with their tears, so I just had to sit and watch, waiting for the end. That's why at my sister's coronation, I tried to explain certain things to Charles.'

Four weeks later on 30 June, Queen Elizabeth set out on her first overseas tour as Queen Mother, accompanied by Princess Margaret. Their destination was Southern Rhodesia and before them lay a sixteen-day schedule covering 1,500 miles of territory not visited by the royal family six years earlier in 1947.

From Salisbury on 2 July, the royal party travelled southwest to

Bulawayo, thence to Gwelo, Que Que, and Hartley; east to Umtali, Nyanyadzi, and Birchenough Bridge; south to Rhodesia and Fort Victoria; finally winding up the tour in Salisbury where it had begun. Fifty-four formal engagements had been planned, each lasting between two and four hours. There were nine ceremonies of welcome, twenty-eight presentation lines of unspecified numbers of dignitaries to be greeted, and twelve guards-of-honour to be inspected in as many different locations.

Save for a severe attack of 'Bulawayo 'flu', to which Princess Margaret succumbed at Umtali seven days into the tour, the visit was highly successful and did much to sharpen Queen Elizabeth's confidence in herself, so soon after the King's death, as one of Britain's leading royal ambassadors.

The following year, during the months of October and November, an even longer official journey awaited her – this time to the United States and Canada.

The purpose of Queen Elizabeth's second American visit was in connection with a fund commemorating the life of King George VI, which had been set up by Lewis Douglas, the former American ambassador to the Court of St James's, and warmly supported by the President, Dwight D. Eisenhower.

Those responsible for the tribute to the late King had amassed sufficient capital to finance technical training programmes in the United States for young people from the Commonwealth. Thus the Queen Mother was invited to 'receive' the cheque for the King George VI Fund, at a banquet held at the Waldorf-Astoria Hotel in New York. At first Queen Elizabeth had certain reservations about making the trip, not least that, even given the extent of her personal success in Southern Rhodesia, she was in many ways still finding her feet as a 'solo artiste'. With a little gentle persuasion, however, she sailed forth aboard the *Queen Elizabeth*, the liner she had launched in 1936, and found herself at the centre of a reception few had envisaged.

Those who had said, 'No American is going to be very interested in the middle-aged widow of a King', found their predictions thoroughly humiliated. To use one contemporary newspaper slogan, Queen Elizabeth, 'Wowed New York', and if the Queen Mother had harboured any hopes of seeing Manhattan as lesser mortals see it, then those hopes were unquestionably dashed.

When, for instance, she attempted to visit Sak's of Fifth Avenue, shoppers and sales assistants alike stampeded to catch a glimpse of her. So impossible did the situation become that Queen Elizabeth sought sanctuary in a 'boutique', where samples of Sak's merchandise were brought to her.

In Washington the entire Pentagon saluted her, while the Annapolis Naval Academy mounted a full parade in her honour. What the nameless officials of New York had presumably overlooked when they foresaw a low-key reception for Britain's 'Queen Mother Elizabeth', as she is frequently, if quaintly, referred to by the American Press, was the enormous – sometimes almost fanatical – interest untold numbers of Americans have in the British royal family.

During the remaining years of the 1950s Queen Elizabeth undertook several more official overseas visits. But again, because of their unremarkable and repetitive nature (recounting details of royal tours is often as tiresome as looking at other people's holiday snaps), we need only briefly note that in 1956 the Queen Mother visited Paris to open the Franco-Scottish Exhibition, and the following June she returned to France to unveil the Dunkirk War Memorial.

During 1957 she also undertook a three-week tour of the Federation of Rhodesia and Nyasaland (now Zimbabwe, Zambia and Malawi), in the course of which she was installed as the first President of the University College of Rhodesia and Nyasaland, an office which she relinquished in 1970. The following year, leaving London at the end of January, Queen Elizabeth toured New Zealand and Australia, and in the course of her journeys, flew round the world. On the outward flight she paid visits to Montreal and Vancouver, Honolulu and Fiji, and en route back to Britain that March, she travelled via Cocos, Mauritius, Uganda and Malta. At the start of 1959 Uganda was again visited, this time as part of an extensive tour which also encompassed Kenya.

The Queen Mother's travels that year were wound up by a purely private visit to Rome which she undertook – once again accompanied by Princess Margaret – at the invitation of the British Ambassador.

Over and above her official commitments and obligatory public performances, Queen Elizabeth's thoughts, at least to some

Prince Albert of York ('Bertie') in 1899

Lady Elizabeth Bowes Lyon,
aged about two

Prince Albert (left) and his elder brother Prince Edward (right), riding
with Stratton, the groom, at Sandringham, 1902

Lady Elizabeth in 1909

Prince Albert at Dartmouth in 1912

An engagement study of 'Bertie'
and Elizabeth, January 1923

26 April 1923: the newly created Duke of York with his bride. King
George V and Queen Mary and the Earl and Countess of Strathmore join
the bridal couple in this formal wedding photograph

The Duke of York and Sir Louis
Greig playing at Wimbledon
1926 in a championship doubles
match

The Duchess of York
with Princess Elizabeth,
1926

Coronation Day 1937. King George VI and Queen Elizabeth with the Princesses Elizabeth and Margaret

The King and Queen leave Ottawa's Parliament building during their North American tour in May 1939

The King with his daughters at Buckingham Palace

Their Majesties inspecting bomb damage at Buckingham Palace, 1940

Wedding day for Princess Elizabeth and Philip, Duke of Edinburgh, 20 November 1947

A Silver Wedding
portrait, 1948

One of the last photographs of
the King

George VI lies in state at Westminster Hall, February 1952

Queen Elizabeth The Queen Mother with Prince Charles
after the Coronation of Queen Elizabeth II, 1953

May 1960. Princess Margaret and Antony
Armstrong-Jones after their wedding

The Duke and Duchess of Windsor join the royal family in London, June 1967 for the unveiling of the memorial plaque to Queen Mary

Queen Elizabeth and Lord Mountbatten with the King of Sweden during his state visit to Britain, 1975

Victory in the Oaks 1977, with the Queen's horse, Dunfermline, at Epsom

An eightieth birthday photograph by Norman Parkinson. Queen Elizabeth The Queen Mother with the Queen and Princess Margaret

The Queen Mother with her grandchildren after the Service of Thanksgiving to mark her eightieth birthday

The Prince and Princess of Wales at the time of their engagement, 1981, in a photograph by Lord Snowdon

Queen Elizabeth The Queen Mother cradling her fourth great-
grandchild Prince Henry of Wales after his christening, 1984

extent, were concentrated on family issues and the comfortable feeling of anticipation of things to come.

By the end of 1959 two events to which she looked forward were the birth of her third grandchild and the marrige of her younger daughter. Both, in their own way, were significant events in the history of the monarchy. On the one hand, not since Queen Victoria had given birth to her tribe of nine had a child been born to a reigning sovereign; on the other hand, the marriage of a senior-ranking princess – the daughter of a King and the sister of a Queen – to a commoner indicated a further progressive change in royal attitudes.

Princess Margaret's engagement to Lord Snowdon, then Antony Armstrong-Jones, a talented society photographer, five months her senior, was sanctioned by the Queen at Sandringham in December 1959. 'I'm *so* pleased you are going to marry Margaret,' the Queen Mother, in ebullient mood, told her future son-in-law. Others were less pleased. Prince Philip was never enamoured of Armstrong-Jones nor, for that matter, was Princess Marina, Duchess of Kent. It should be stated however, that this Princess – with her awe-inspiring Russian and Scandinavian ancestry – had very clear-cut ideas about the calibre of person royalty should marry. Indeed, of the Queen Mother and Princess Alice, Duchess of Gloucester, Princess Marina had once remarked, 'Och! Those common little Scottish girls.' In return, it has been said that Queen Elizabeth's 'fondness' for her sister-in-law did not become manifest until after the Princess's unexpected death in August 1968.

Such things aside, Princess Margaret and her fiancé decided to keep their engagement a family secret until 'after the birth of that beautiful child', as the Princess fondly described Prince Andrew, who was born at Buckingham Palace on 19 February 1960.

Like her parents and sister before her, Princess Margaret chose to be married at Westminster Abbey. The wedding, solemnized on Friday 6 May, the warmest day yet in 1960, with a midday temperature of 72°F, attracted the biggest crowds in London – estimated at 150,000 – since the coronation.

The simple splendour of her daughter's wedding undoubtedly evoked memories of Queen Elizabeth's own wedding almost forty years earlier. Remembrances of her father were indisputably brought to the bride's mind, too, when she decided to have her eight young attendants dressed in copies of her first ball gown, which happened to be a particular favourite of the late King.

When Queen Elizabeth met the television and radio broadcaster Audrey Russell shortly after the royal wedding, she was full of feminine questions: 'Didn't my daughter look beautiful?', 'Did the bridesmaids keep in line?', and so on. In fact the Queen Mother had found herself so caught up in the day's events that, in her excitement, she declared that she wanted to accompany the bride and bridegroom to the Pool of London to watch them set sail aboard the royal yacht *Britannia*, at the start of their Caribbean honeymoon. It was only when the police advised her that the density of the crowds thronging the narrow city streets made such an exercise impracticable that Queen Elizabeth settled for watching the departure on television.

Princess Margaret and her husband had scarcely begun their six-week cruise in the West Indies before talk of another royal romance was buzzing through Fleet Street. Rumour and gossip about members of the royal family have always been staple ingredients of many a newsman's diet, and indeed, given the proliferation of such stories, it is interesting to reflect on how few ever give rise to official response.

In May 1960, however, the rumour that Queen Elizabeth the Queen Mother was about to marry her Treasurer, the bachelor Sir Arthur Penn, gathered such momentum that it became front-page news and caused indignation at Clarence House. Queen Elizabeth herself was not only furious at the escalation of idle speculation, but offended by the very idea that, as the widow of a man whose memory she revered, she would ever contemplate re-marrying. The result was an official statement issued on the Queen Mother's behalf which denied that there was so much as a grain of truth in the Press reports. The communiqué was widely published on 21 May and the entire issue was soon forgotten.

The relationship between the Queen Mother and her daughters, as we shall see shortly, was never quite as intimate as outward appearances would seem to suggest. Nevertheless, it is no doubt true that she missed the presence of Princess Margaret at Clarence House after she married and moved to No. 10 Kensington Palace (which is today the London residence of Prince and Princess Michael of Kent).

It was, however, to Clarence House that Princess Margaret

returned at the end of 1961 to give birth to her first child. David, Viscount Linley, was born beneath his grandmother's roof on 3 November that year.

As we have already noted, Clarence House has been the Queen Mother's home since the spring of 1953 and perhaps at this point, we should pause to take a closer look at it. The only house Queen Elizabeth owns in her own right is the Castle of Mey. Her London residence, like the Royal Lodge in Windsor Great Park (which the Queen Mother has left virtually unaltered since her husband's death) belongs to the Crown, while Birkhall – on the Balmoral estate – belongs to the Queen.

Clarence House, though it appears to be distinctly separate, forms part of St James's Palace, originally built by Henry VIII for Anne Boleyn on the site of the fourteenth-century Convent of St James the Less, founded for 'fourteen leprous maiden sisters. . . '. In the seventeenth century Clarence House was no more than an outbuilding of St James's Palace, and so it remained until George III's third son, William, Duke of Clarence, took it for himself a century later. Content to live in it more or less as it was until he married, the Duke then decided that it was inconvenient and unfit, and complained to his brother, the King (George IV), about its 'wretched state and dirt'. In 1825, despite his work on both Buckingham Palace and the King's seaside folly in Brighton, the Royal Pavilion, John Nash was instructed to rebuild Clarence House.

After William IV's death, Queen Victoria's mother, the Duchess of Kent, lived there and, five years after her demise in 1861, the house was given over to 'Affie', the Queen's second son, Prince Alfred, Duke of Edinburgh. The present appearance of the building in fact dates from that time.

At the turn of the century Clarence House became the residence of Queen Victoria's youngest son, Prince Arthur, Duke of Connaught, whose Duchess (formerly Princess Louise Margaret of Prussia) died there in March 1917. It remained the Duke's principal residence until his own death in January 1942, at the age of ninety-two. The house did not become a royal residence again until, following her marriage, it was allocated to the present Queen, then still Princess Elizabeth.

Clarence House is entered today, as it was a hundred years ago, from beneath the pillared portico on the south front, next to the sovereign's entrance to St James's Palace proper. Glass-panelled doors lead directly into a long, wide hall – the Lower Corridor – carpeted in red and overlaid with Persian rugs. Settees, one brocaded, another simply upholstered in red, *jardinières*, tables and pedestals, one surmounted by a 'head' of King George VI, are ranged along both sides. A vast tapestry, a number of paintings, including portraits of sovereign forebears, and heavy, gilded mirrors, hang against palest cream walls, the door recesses picked out in gold. Beyond, where the corridor bends, red flock walls are hung with paintings of horses and sporting scenes, which (if the visitor could not guess) represent Queen Elizabeth's passionate interest in racing. Near the foot of the staircase, a pair of early eighteenth-century Nubian figures, originally intended as torchères, stand sentinel.

On the ground floor, the Morning Room, with its pale grey/blue walls inset with display alcoves, its brocaded sofas and armchairs, and gilded wooden lamp pedestals, is connected to the Library by double doors, from where the long, apricot-coloured Dining-room, with its original Nash ceiling, may be entered. In this room a white and grey marble fireplace, which dates from 1770, perfectly complements the Spanish walnut dining-table.

Queen Elizabeth enjoys entertaining lavishly in a style better suited, in fact, to earlier, more prosperous days, and this room – particularly when decked out for dinner-parties with gold and silver plate from the Queen Mother's impressive collection – vividly evokes the splendour of times gone by.

Yet, perhaps the most graceful of all the rooms is the Drawing-room on the first floor. Originally designed by Nash as two distinctly separate rooms, it has, for more years than most can remember, run uninterrupted along the length of the west front. The original ceiling and cornice-work, architraves, panelling and pillars have been retained, the former picked out in gold. The creamy-buttermilk walls provide a comfortably mellow background for the eighteenth-century, English gilt-wood furnishings, the large number of paintings – including one by Sir William Richmond of three girls (Queen Elizabeth's mother and her two sisters) and another of the child Princess Elizabeth by Edwin Brock – and the Regency looking-glasses. Here, too,

Waterford crystal chandeliers pick up the delicate colours of two well-worn Aubusson carpets.

On the same floor is the Queen Mother's private sitting-room. As elsewhere throughout Clarence House, personal objects and furnishings that have moved when she has moved bear testimony to the rich and varied quality of Queen Elizabeth's long life. In this room, a kind of sanctuary, where the walls are covered in blue silk, embossed with a classic design of flower arrangements and birds, the Queen Mother attends to her paperwork.

Her desktop is awash with family photographs, predominantly of the King and herself. A silver dish, always at hand, contains pens and pencils, while a black metal angle-poise lamp, an incongruous object in such a setting, looks down on in-coming and out-going papers – typewritten scripts (with or without the firm signature 'Elizabeth R') as well as handwritten letters to family and friends. For her personal correspondence, Queen Elizabeth - unlike the Queen, who uses standard Buckingham Palace letter-heading – uses stationery printed with her own cypher, and entwined letters 'ER' surmounted by a crown, and completed by the words 'Clarence House' in block-lettering alongside.

The focal point of the Queen Mother's desk is a crystal triptych. Designed by Laurence Whistler and given to Her Majesty by Major Tom Harvey, her Private Secretary during the early 1950s, this object is a holder for Queen Elizabeth's daily programme of engagements.

At Clarence House, as in her other homes in England and Scotland, visitors cannot conceal their astonishment at the sheer volume of Queen Elizabeth's personal possessions, many of which, stored in various Crown properties for safekeeping during the last war, continue to be discovered to the present day.

Pictures form a large part of the Queen Mother's private collections. But while there are, as might be expected, a few Old Masters, the strength of the picture collection originally encouraged, as we saw earlier by Kenneth Clark's enthusiastic tutelage, is to be found in the work of twentieth-century painters, represented by Augustus John (whose unfinished portrait of the Queen Mother as Queen was presented to her after his death), Sir William Nicholson, L.S. Lowry, Graham Sutherland, Edward Seago (of whose works the royal family are especially fond), and John Piper, who received a royal commission to paint scenes of Windsor Castle during the war.

Yet for all the splendour of Clarence House, the Queen Mother's guests invariably speak of its warm and informal atmosphere, of the way in which – in all her homes – she helps her visitors relax, and of her excellence as one of the last great hostesses.

'Queen Elizabeth's care for her guests is something that deserves attention,' said one who has enjoyed her friendship for some years:

> As a young man, in the 1960s, I found myself sitting on Her Majesty's left at luncheon and she was, as you would expect, paying attention to the guest on her right. Some delicious meat was being served and I noticed that Queen Elizabeth had taken one slice and that her principal guest had, in conversation with her, done the same thing. When my turn came, I took a single slice at which Queen Elizabeth turned and looked at my plate and asked. 'What's the matter? Don't you like it?' I replied, 'I didn't want to be greedy, Ma'am. I noticed that you yourself had taken only one slice.' She quietly called the footman back to her with the tray of meat which she asked him to show her; whereupon, she took the spoon and fork and put another two slices on my plate and said, 'Eat it up. It will do you good.'

This same guest went on to tell of another luncheon gathering at Clarence House at which he was present:

> Her guests were told that lunch would begin at a certain hour. The party was very talkative; rather noisy, in fact, and we were all going at it madly when I heard a little voice at my side saying, 'Do you think we might go in for lunch now? The cook's going mad.' I don't wonder. We were twenty-five minutes late and Queen Elizabeth was trying to get her ducks in a row.

Others also glow with appreciation when recalling the Queen Mother's hospitality: 'In her presence everybody melts and relaxes. She has such a sense of fun' (Lord Astor of Hever); 'I shall always cherish the memory of the Queen Mother and me singing as a duet "My Old Man Said Follow the Van" ' (Noël Coward); 'I like the fact that the carpets are threadbare in places; the food is very, very good and the martinis are wonderful. She knows I love port and always plonks the decanter in front of me' (Sir Frederick Ashton).

Queen Elizabeth's enjoyment in her friends is paramount and in return their devotion to her is total. As one said:

> I have always found her to be one of the easiest people in the world to talk to . . . the almost magical effect of her personality has never failed to move me to be both protective and gallant. She has this extraordinary capacity for bringing out of a man the most remarkable desire to be noble. I could, I know, make her laugh with a slightly risqué remark, but I could not contemplate causing her any sort of pain. I find myself in my soul devoted to her.

As an afterthought, this same friend went on to say:

> The royal family are smart to be as reserved as they are with people they don't know very well. The glass wall is rightfully there. I have a suspicion that if they like and trust you they can be extraordinarily frank.
>
> I have sat with some of them, hoping to God I wouldn't be hit by a bus and repeat, in my delirium, some of the comments I had overheard when they talked across me, as though I wasn't there.

# 15

# The People's
# 'Queen Mum'

On 4 August 1960 Queen Elizabeth celebrated her sixtieth birthday and moved still closer to the kind of veneration that surrounds popular personalities as they grow old. This was also the dawning of the age in which Queen Elizabeth was to assume the guise of invincible royal matriarch, a process which seemed to begin when, with Prince Charles and Princess Anne looking on, she posed for her sixtieth-birthday photographs in the garden of Clarence House, dandling Prince Andrew on her knee.

This image was soon encouraged by the births of three more grandchildren, Viscount Linley (who, as we have already seen, was born at Clarence House in 1961), Prince Edward and Lady Sarah Armstrong-Jones, who were both born during the spring of 1964. An ever-growing number of great-nephews and great-nieces and, in the fullness of time, great-grandchildren, were to re-affirm the Queen Mother's matriarchal role.

For Queen Elizabeth the 1960s were years which brought a fair share of mixed blessings to her door. At the start of the decade there was a spate of family weddings: Princess Margaret's was followed by that of the Duke of Kent who married the enchanting Miss Katharine Worsley in June 1961, and in April 1963 Princess Alexandra married Mabell Airlie's grandson, the Honourable Angus Ogilvy. There were partings, too. An old and valued friend, Sir Winston Churchill, died in January 1965, and at the end of March that year, the Princess Royal suffered a fatal heart-attack while walking with her son George in the grounds of Harewood House, her home in Yorkshire.

Three years later in August 1968, at the age of sixty-one, Princess Marina, Duchess of Kent, died suddenly of an inoperable brain tumour. But indisputably the most grievous losses Queen Elizabeth sustained during these years were those of her brother David, the soul-mate of her youth, who died in September 1961 at the early age of fifty-nine, and her sister Rose, the Countess Granville, who was seventy-seven when she died in November 1967.

Through all these sorrows the Queen Mother was of comfort to those most directly concerned. Ava, Lady Waverley, who we encounter for the last time through her exchange of correspondence with Her Majesty, was herself widowed in 1958 with the death of Sir John Anderson, 1st Viscount Waverley. The following winter Queen Elizabeth had written to her, 'I do hope Christmas time did not make you feel too sad. It is such a thing of memories I find, and one is thankful when it is over. . . .' Widowhood was not the only bond the two friends had in common. Another was that both had had the lives of their husbands commemorated by the same distinguished biographer, Sir John Wheeler-Bennett.

In the autumn of 1962 Ava Waverley sent a copy of Lord Waverley's life to Clarence House. Queen Elizabeth's response, though one of sympathy, undoubtedly tells us much about herself:

I am so greatly touched by your dear thought in sending me a copy of Sir John Wheeler-Bennett's book, [she wrote] . . . I am reading it with much interest & also with much emotion, for so many memories of past days come flooding back. What a wonderful life of service it was, & how *much* you must have helped him. Your heart must feel *torn* when you read & remember events & moments which remain so vivid in one's mind. To be lonely in spirit is as hard as missing the dear presence – but I know that you are full of courage, & face life most bravely. . . .

Facing the rest of her own life 'most bravely' meant that by the time of the tenth anniversary of the King's passing (an anniversary which she likes to observe privately at the Royal Lodge), Queen Elizabeth had steadfastly consolidated her position as a front-liner in royal affairs, both public and private. That she did so with an outward appearance of such ease, came as no surprise to those about her. But as she grew more advanced in years, the fact that there was no trace of letting up in her annual programme did give rise to a kind of mild astonishment, and it was, perhaps, her determination and stamina which led *The Times* to comment that it was impossible to over-estimate the value of Queen Elizabeth's continuing services to her country and to the Commonwealth. Certainly friends far younger than she marvel at her ability to keep going.

'I simply do not know where she finds the energy to do all the things she does,' said one. 'It is not only unusual, it is extraordinary. After a terrific lunch, for instance, when all we ordinary humans want to do is to have a nap, Queen Elizabeth will go and change and emerge radiant for an engagement to which she brings her own particular brand of enthusiasm and gift of friendliness.'

Through the years, first as Duchess of York, then as Queen and subsequently as Queen Mother, Queen Elizabeth became actively associated – as president or patron – with more than three hundred organizations. To list them all – or to cite instances of her 'enthusiasm' in her work for them – would be an almost impossible task. Indeed a separate book could be written on that aspect of Queen Elizabeth's life alone. It is right, however, to give some indication of the scope of Her Majesty's official obligations, and among those who benefit from her interest are: the British Red Cross Society, the Women's Section of the Royal British Legion, the Royal Academy of Music, the British Drama League, the Friends of St Paul's, the Hostel of God (in Clapham), the Royal School of Needlework, the Victorian Order of Nurses for Canada, the National Trust, the Royal Society for the Prevention of Cruelty to Animals and the Young Women's Christian Association.

To the list of such organizations as these must be added Queen Elizabeth's honorary appointments within the armed services. As colonel-in-chief, as colonel or as commandant-in-chief, she holds some twenty 'commissions'. They include, as we saw earlier, the Black Watch (Royal Highland Regiment) and its Canadian counterpart, the Queen's Own Hussars, and the Royal Australian Army Medical Corps, the Women's Royal Naval Service and the Women's Royal Air Force.

To the crowds who gather to catch sight of her, however, the reasons behind Queen Elizabeth's visit to this place or to that are of little importance – tell them, and they will have forgotten in a trice. All the public sees and, naturally, wants to see is 'the Queen Mum', not the president of this, the patron of that, or the colonel-in-chief of the other. One of the Queen Mother's most outwardly colourful and impressive appointments – though she has since retired from it – was as Chancellor of London University – colourful because, despite her myriad other appointments, Her Majesty possessed no other 'uniform' save the robes of this office: the black brocade redingote heavily sewn with intricately worked panels and borders of real gold thread (her train invariably carried by a scarlet-clad page-of-honour), her black mortar-board similarly trimmed and tasselled in gold.

Queen Elizabeth was fifty-five when she accepted the chancellorship. She relinquished it twenty-five years later, at the age of eighty. In 1955, as her Private Secretary, Sir Martin Gilliat, has said, becoming associated with London University was, 'the spark which set off this tumultuously varied way of life'.

As Chancellor Queen Elizabeth proved herself indefatigable in all the ramifications of her office and of university life – from delivering her 'Charge' (or 'address') while presiding over the long yearly degree ceremonies, to attending the foundation day dinner and the student ball; from visiting the colleges which make up the university, to providing constructive help with fund-raising activities, as when, in 1972, she launched the 'Grand Appeal' for a new building in which to house the British Library of Political and Economic Science. Within six years, spearheaded by the royal Chancellor, the Appeals Committee had raised more than £1,800,000 towards the new library which was opened in July 1979 by Queen Elizabeth herself.

Perhaps one of the Queen Mother's most outstanding contributions to the university in its long history, however, was her personal intervention in the fate of the 'Marjon' site, which occupies a considerable area in London on the Fulham/Chelsea border. The site, so named because of its former occupation by the colleges of St Mark and St John, was to be disposed of during the 1970s and Chelsea College, a part of London University, had put in a bid to acquire the land it had always owned in years gone by. But, as Elizabeth Longford tells us in her own biography of the

Queen Mother, 'it seemed that rival claimants to the site might "gazump" Chelsea's offer, and, if successful, demolish the ancient buildings and park.'

In an attempt to avert disaster, therefore, Queen Elizabeth bade her Private Secretary to write to the then Secretary of State for the Environment, Michael Heseltine. Sir Martin Gilliat's letter read in part:

> . . . In the twenty-four years that she has held the appointment Queen Elizabeth has identified herself in a very personal way with the affairs of every College, Faculty and School, and it is in regard to the hopes of Chelsea College to acquire the 'Marjon' site that The Queen Mother feels a very special concern.
>
> The long and intricate history of the negotiations is well known to Her Majesty, and Queen Elizabeth readily appreciates the complexities of the problem. Many representations have been made to The Queen Mother to help the College to acquire the facilities it so urgently needs and at the same time to ensure the preservation of an historic site.

As a result of the royal 'SOS', rival bids – and potential 'gazumpers' – were all rejected and Chelsea College re-established itself on the site it might easily have lost for ever.

'Your work is the rent you pay for the room you occupy on earth.' With this philosophical statement Queen Elizabeth the Queen Mother is said to rebuff her daughters' remonstrations that she undertakes far too much work for a woman of her years. It may well be true, who can tell? What is certainly true is that the Queen Mother has always maintained an official schedule which, even today, continues to compare favourably with those of the hardest-working members of the royal family. In 1983, for example, she fulfilled 119 engagements, compared to the Princess of Wales' 113, Princess Margaret's 117, the Duchess of Gloucester's 64, and the 40 knotched up by her contemporary, Princess Alice, Duchess of Gloucester.

Queen Elizabeth's friends smile wryly at the very idea that Her Majesty may not enjoy *all* the duties she performs. She is, after all, the star of any show. The organizers of functions that do not go down too well will never know, be they hosts of relatively major events or simply local charity performances. Other members of the royal family may grow weary and a little restless, but in such an instance, the Queen Mother will feign pleasure to the bitter end.

One example of an evening which failed to live up to its 'gala' billing took place in a typically busy month for Queen Elizabeth. The engagement in question – her fourteenth and last of that particular month – was a performance, by a largely amateur operatic society, of Mascagni's *Cavalleria Rusticana*, incongruously teamed that night with a Gilbert and Sullivan operetta. That the handful of musicians provided a rather distorted version of the national anthem as the Queen Mother entered the auditorium unfortunately set the tone for what was to come.

During the interval, which mercifully separated the two performances (and which was enlivened by one character rushing through the distinctly chilly foyer, repeatedly crying in a sonorous voice, 'Has anybody seen Her Majesty's wrap?'), part of the audience seized the opportunity to beat a hasty retreat homeward. The same luxury was not, of course, afforded the royal guest-of-honour who sat through part two of the evening before offering her congratulations to the cast who, incidentally, had already busied themselves congratulating one another!

It is conceivable that Queen Elizabeth *may* have enjoyed herself, but if she called for a fortifying glass of gin and Dubonnet on her return home few could have blamed her. We shall never know what her true reaction was nor, for that matter, will the organizers or, happily, the cast. What is indisputable, however, is that the Queen Mother dispensed a vast amount of pleasure to a great many people that night, and perhaps, essentially, that is what it was all about.

Earlier that same month Queen Elizabeth, as usual, attended the races at Cheltenham and, on her way, fulfilled a private 'engagement' which has now become as much of a tradition as her appearance at the gates of Clarence House on her birthday. For fourteen years the Queen Mother had paused at Philip Delaney's grocery store in Leckhampton, where she received from him gifts of flowers and mint chocolates. In 1982, however, Delaney moved to the village of Prestbury, a few miles away, to run the local store and, as a result, he wrote to Clarence House to advise the Queen Mother.

'I assumed she wouldn't be able to see me,' he said. Then, to his delight, he received a letter which said that his move would not deter Her Majesty and, en route to Cheltenham on Gold Cup day, she would make a detour to see him, his new shop and the new neighbourhood. Queen Elizabeth's meetings with Mr Delaney began during the late 1960s. He explained:

> Her car used to go past my shop in Leckhampton on its way to Badminton, where the Queen Mother stayed the night with the Beauforts. I thought it would be nice for the local children to see her and so I wrote to Clarence House. I was told that if there was a crowd the car would slow down for us. On that day I was handing out daffodils to the children to wave, when around the corner she came . . . and continued on up the road.

Shopkeeper and children alike were reeling from disappointment, when Queen Elizabeth asked her chauffeur to turn back – leaving her police outriders to journey on until they, too, turned back in search of the lost royal car.

Philip Delaney was still clutching his dripping bunch of daffodils when the door of Her Majesty's maroon limousine opened. 'Oh, Mr Delaney,' she said, 'are those flowers for me?' 'Yes, Ma'am,' he replied, 'but I'm sorry they are not properly arranged.' 'That's exactly how I love flowers,' she smiled. Later, a further letter arrived from the Queen Mother's office at Clarence House, assuring him that Her Majesty would look forward to their next meeting the following spring.

'Ever since that first stop at Leckhampton, I have always presented her with a box of mints because I had been told that she was very fond of them. Once she asked me how I found out. I told her a little bird told me.' 'Well,' she whispered, 'I do.'

Queen Elizabeth the Queen Mother has, for most of her life, enjoyed excellent health. In recent years she has been troubled less by colds or chills – or any other ailments – than by an ulcerated leg, a condition particularly noticeable when she attended the Falklands thanksgiving service at St Paul's Cathedral in 1982 – and one not much helped by a series of heavy falls, like the one she took at the Horse Guards building in June 1981, when having watched the Queen's Birthday Parade, she lost her balance and fell down a flight of stairs.

A great advocate of what Prince Charles calls 'complementary medicine' (like the late King and the present Queen, she prefers homoeopathic remedies, even to the extent of having them administered to an ailing race-horse), Queen Elizabeth yields to surgery only when essential. It will be recalled that such an instance occurred in 1982 when, at dinner, a salmon–bone became lodged in her throat, necessitating an emergency dash from Royal Lodge to the King Edward VII Hospital for Officers in London.

Sixteen years earlier, however, major surgery was unavoidable when in 1966, a fortnight before Christmas, she entered the same hospital to undergo an operation to 'relieve a partial obstruction of the abdomen' – in short, a colostomy. Naturally, on the day of the operation – 10 December – the public statements, economically worded and somehow as evasive as ever, maintained that Her Majesty was 'comfortable'. The Queen Mother herself is said to have quipped that the word inevitably has a different meaning to the surgeon than to the patient.

The following month when Queen Elizabeth left London for a holiday at Sandringham, news cameramen waited at the gates of Clarence House to record her departure, while at Liverpool Street Station, where the royal train awaited her, the Queen Mother – by now much slimmer and still looking a little tired and pale after her ordeal – was enthusiastically cheered by a large crowd of on-lookers.

Despite her extreme discomfort at this time, hospital personnel had been amused by Queen Elizabeth's determination to keep abreast of her greatest passion – horse racing. Unlike the Queen, who is deeply interested in absolutely everything to do with horses – her own and other people's – the Queen Mother's interest in 'my darling boys', as she calls them, is one of competitive ownership: technique and performance, first and foremost.

Her absorption in 'the sport of kings' started, as with so many things in all our lives, by chance. In 1949 Lord (Lordy) Mildmay of Fleet, a gentleman rider and breeder of steeplechasers, enthusiastically recounted to Queen Elizabeth how he had ridden a horse called Cromwell in the Grand National. The Queen's own excitement spurred him on to ask why she did not become an owner herself. 'Shall we?' she asked Princess Elizabeth.

Steeplechasing has always gripped the Queen Mother more than flat racing, and the late Peter Cazalet, who became her first trainer, was asked to find a suitable horse which mother and daughter could race in partnership. Cazalet came up with the Irish-bred Monaveen, half-brother of Anthony Mildmay's Cromwell. 'He was a very sound horse, tremendously bold and freegoing and he jumped like the wind,' his trainer enthused. Monaveen won several races for his royal owners at Sandown and Hurst Park, where he emerged victorious, aptly enough, in the Queen Elizabeth Steeplechase.

In the same race a year later, Monaveen broke a leg and, to Princess Elizabeth's great distress, had to be destroyed. In 1950 Queen Elizabeth, whose interest many believe has brought 'a new respectability to the sport', bought another horse – one of the best from the estate of the late Anthony Mildmay, who had drowned that May. This time the horse was Manicou who brought his royal owner yet more success, winning at Kempton Park and achieving the first ever National Hunt win for a queen. Manicou also sired The Rip and he, Laffy and Double Star were responsible for winning Queen Elizabeth's first racing hat-trick. Her second, won by Arch Point, Gay Record and Super Fox followed a few years later.

By 1964 the Queen Mother had celebrated her 100th win; by 1970 that score had been doubled and at Ascot, in February 1976, Sunnyboy brought in her 300th victory. The sweet taste of success is almost inevitably tempered by the bitterness of defeat or plain bad luck. Perhaps the most disastrous event to befall the Queen Mother occurred in 1956 when Devon Loch 'threw away the Grand National by fly jumping a shadow' and unseating his jockey (the thriller-writer Dick Francis) just two hundred yards from the winning post. 'That's racing,' said Queen Elizabeth stoically.

Since 1973 when Peter Cazalet died, Queen Elizabeth's horses have been trained by Fulke Walwyn at Saxon House, in Lambourn, Berkshire. 'During the season I telephone Her Majesty two or three times a week to discuss the horses,' he says. 'We decide between us where they'll run and where she might be able to attend.' Yet while Fulke Walwyn is in frequent touch with the Queen Mother, she herself always follows races by listening to the 'blower' commentaries which are 'fed' to Clarence House.

The only sporting activity in which Queen Elizabeth is still an active participant is fishing, something in which she has taken great pleasure since the days of her youth. Salmon fishing in the Dee, and preferably during spring when the river is at its best, occupies a fair amount of the Queen Mother's time when, in waders and floppy hat, she spends many contented hours casting her line.

Some years ago now a story was told by Dorothy Laird of how Her Majesty waited all day for river conditions to improve. They did at about six in the evening, whereupon the Queen Mother sallied forth. By dinner time when it was, of course, already dark and there was still no sign of her, the household became anxious and set out with hurricane lamps to look for her. No sooner had they started than Queen Elizabeth appeared triumphant, dragging along a twenty-pound salmon. 'This,' she exclaimed, 'is what kept me late.'

## ❧ 16 ❧

# A Time to Reflect

On 7 June 1967, Londoners, jostled by curious tourists, witnessed an historic scene as members of the royal family led by the Queen and Queen Elizabeth the Queen Mother assembled on a blue-carpeted dais at the garden wall of Marlborough House on the Mall. The occasion was the unveiling by the Queen of a handsome memorial plaque to Queen Mary, commemorating the centenary of her birth.

In itself the unveiling was of little or no real significance; what made it a day for royal historians to remember was the presence not only of the Duke of Windsor, but of the Duchess. On that warm summer's morning crowds gathered steadily in Marlborough Road as well as on the Mall. Assuming the best kerb-side places, some had waited for up to three hours, determined not to miss the unique opportunity of glimpsing the Duke and Duchess of Windsor.

As on all such occasions the time-table was scheduled almost to the last second; the royal ceremonial governed as rigidly as ever by the order of precedence. Thus the junior members of the royal family and their assorted semi-royal relations arrived first to take up their places on the dais. Princess Alice, Countess of Athlone, with her daughter and son-in-law, Lady May and Colonel Sir Henry Abel Smith, sat alongside the Duke of Beaufort and his Duchess who was a niece of Queen Mary. They were joined by the Duke of Fife and Captain Alexander Ramsay, the Earl of Harewood and the Honourable Gerald and Mrs Lascelles. Princess Marina, accompanied by the Duke and Duchess of Kent and

Prince Michael preceded the Duke and Duchess of Gloucester and their younger son Prince Richard. Then came the Windsors. As Queen Mary's eldest son, the Duke was accorded the right to arrive after his only surviving brother, his sisters-in-law and his nephews.

As the Duke and Duchess alighted from a maroon Rolls-Royce built for King George VI in 1948 as part of the royal fleet of 'state' cars, the crowd's roar of approbation so surely swelled the heart of the Duchess of Windsor as much as it filled the Duke himself with obvious pride. Minutes later the arrival of Queen Elizabeth the Queen Mother, dressed in a lilac silk coat and a veiled hat of massed blue and lilac flowers, was watched intently. With a smile she walked past her late husband's predecessor and his wife and took up her own position opposite the curtained memorial.

With the arrival of the Queen, dressed in a coat and hat of tangerine, the scene was set for the brief ceremony to begin. The Bishop of London, Robert Stopford (the incumbent of that office is also, by tradition, Dean of the Chapels Royal), assisted by the Sub-Dean James Mansell and attended by the choir of the Chapels Royal, officiated at a religious service before the Queen stepped forward and pulled a cord to release the velvet curtains, veiling the splendid bronze profile of her grandmother.

Presently, as she left the platform, the Queen paused to kiss the Duke of Windsor and to exchange a few words with the Duchess who, in her slim navy-blue coat and long white mink scarf, a matching navy straw pillbox perched on the crown of her head, looked particularly, if incongruously, elegant among the cluster of pastel-shaded coats and garden-party hats that surrounded her.

In turn the Queen Mother also kissed her brother-in-law, acknowledged his wife and, with a wave to the crowds, climbed into her car to be driven the few hundred yards back to Clarence House.

Thirty years earlier members of the royal family would have recoiled in horror at the very suggestion that the reviled Mrs Simpson would one day stand among them in public as one of their number, especially at a ceremony to honour the mother-in-law who barely acknowledged her existence.

At about this time the Queen Mother is reputed to have said, 'The only regret one has as one grows older is that things do not matter so strongly.' Was it that thought that had resulted in the

Duchess of Windsor's name being added to the Duke's formal invitation? There can, of course, be no doubt that Queen Elizabeth had been consulted on the matter.

Was this overture, then, intended to act as a panacea to the Duke's long-harboured desire to see the Duchess received by the royal family? If so it was a compromise; royal hardliners still had not mellowed to the point of acceptance and the Court Circular the following day made no mention of the Windsors' presence. Nevertheless, history had recorded the occasion, observing, too, that this was the very first time that all four of Queen Mary's daughters-in-law – Queen Elizabeth, the Duchess of Gloucester, Princess Marina *and* the Duchess of Windsor – had met together.

The late sixties – when attitudes were becoming freer and people in general were becoming more unfettered – was perhaps a period of reflection for older generations. Anachronistic though the idea of monarchy sometimes appeared during those 'revolutionary' years, when England seemed to be the mecca of everything exciting and innovatory, the younger members of the royal family proved that they, too, fitted into the modern idiom. Following the moods of fashion, for example, Princess Anne at eighteen had her hemlines raised well above the knee, drove fast cars, and was shortly to be responsible for the 'fab' revival of dramatically styled, wide-brimmed hats. The young Duchess of Kent and Princess Alexandra also raised their hemlines, as did Princess Margaret, who often danced the night away at fashionable parties to the sound which epitomized the era, the music of the Beatles.

Only the royal menfolk failed to make much of an impression; although in the summer of 1969, with the approach of his ceremonial investiture as the twenty-first Prince of Wales, media attention was focused very largely on the young Prince Charles.

More than a decade earlier, at the time of the British Empire and Commonwealth Games in Cardiff in 1958, the Queen had bestowed on her son the title traditionally held by the Heir Apparent. Then she had promised the people of Wales that, when he was old enough, she would present him at Caernarvon. That formal presentation, in the form of his investiture, took place on 1 July 1969. Of its kind it was only the second royal event to be celebrated in the Principality this century. The first had been the investiture of the Duke of Windsor as the twentieth Prince of Wales, more than fifty years before.

During the intervening years, however, attitudes had changed and it wasn't every Welshman who now wanted the 'gift' of a Prince who was anything but Welsh. It was therefore against a tense scenario of threatened disruption, bomb hoaxes and real explosions, orchestrated by Plaid Cymru, the National Party of Wales, which claimed 40,000 members, that the royal family assembled within the walls of Caernarvon's medieval castle to hear Prince Charles's oath of allegiance, made on behalf of his Principality, and to watch the Queen crown him with a golden coronet.

From start to finish the investiture was a masterpiece of the highest theatricality. In 1963 the Queen had appointed her brother-in-law Lord Snowdon, who is by descent three-quarters Welsh, to the office of Constable of Caernarvon Castle. The responsibilities of that appointment would, as a matter of course, have involved him in Prince Charles's investiture, come what may. But it was entirely fortuitous that Snowdon was steeped in the world of the arts, and in particular that of the theatre, whence came a large number of his personal friends and contacts.

In retrospect it might seem that asking him to control the venture as designer-in-chief was as natural as daylight. In fact the idea of harnessing Lord Snowdon's talents was nothing short of inspirational. His participation and that of the designers and technicians he engaged, ensured that flair and ingenuity contributed a fresh dimension to an act of ancient feudal ritual. Nevertheless Lord Snowdon and his team had to accept that overall control lay in rather more conventional hands; those of the Duke of Norfolk who, as Earl Marshal, was traditionally responsible for stage-managing state occasions such as this. Left to him, however, the ceremonial would have followed much the same lines as that of 14 July 1911, when the inner walls of Caernarvon Castle were hidden by stands accommodating 11,000 spectators, lawns suffocated beneath miles of red carpet and the actual investiture of Prince Edward by King George V was conducted on a heavily-tented dais, which meant that only those closest to it caught so much as a glimpse of the ceremony.

In 1969 Lord Snowdon would have none of it. 'This is going to be completely different', he had said – and it was. Nothing obscured the castle walls, red carpets and tented pavilions were disqualified from the very start and the number of spectators was restricted to 4000. Aesthetically brilliant, Snowdon's 'set' was in complete accord with the thirteenth-century surroundings of King Edward I's castle. On a slate throne in the centre of the circular dais sat the Queen, whose 'Command' brought Prince Charles to 'Her Presence', preceded by two Heralds, Wales and Chester, and followed by five Peers bearing the regalia. During the ceremony the Letters Patent, by which the Queen created her son Prince of Wales and Earl of Chester, were read aloud; in English by the Secretary of State for the Home Department, and in Welsh by the Secretary of State for Wales.

The Prince then paid homage to his sovereign and she, in return, invested him with the symbols of princely authority; the Coronet, the Sword, the Ring, the Golden Rod and the Mantle, borne in by the Lords Ogmore, Lloyd George, Heycock, Maelor and Harlech.

If Prince Charles felt at all uncomfortable in his royal robe, he might have spared a thought for his great-uncle. At his home on the Route du Champ D'Entrainement in Paris, the Duke of Windsor, now seventy-five, watched the event from North Wales on his television with rapt attention. Fifty-eight years earlier he, too, had accepted all the ritual pageantry and, like Prince Charles, had mastered a brief speech in Welsh. But he felt that things 'had gone too far' when measured for what he called a 'preposterous rig' of white satin breeches and a mantle and surcoat of purple velvet edged with ermine.

Prince Charles fared rather better in that respect. His 'rig' was the plain dark uniform he wore as Colonel-in-Chief of the Welsh Regiment, adorned with the Star and sash of the Garter, which he had received at Windsor the previous year. All the same, by the end of the ceremony the scene was not without its comic-opera touch. For, draped in a ground-length velvet and ermine mantle, the Coronet set firmly on his head, the Rod clutched in one palm, his mother's hand in the other, he was traipsed through the castle to the sound of trumpets, in order that the Queen could show him to the people from three designated points.

Royal costume in general has always caused great interest and, of course, this occasion proved no exception. Even Lord Snowdon had designed himself something new; a bottle-green, zip-fronted, high-neck 'jump suit', tied with a double-tasselled belt of black cord. While some nicknamed him 'Buttons', the Earl Marshal wondered why he didn't have a matching cap, complete with feather, 'and be Robin Hood'. Only the Queen Mother, who had rarely taken her eyes off her beloved grandson, looked her inimitable self; her soft green dress with floating shoulder panels, overlaid with lace, was worn with a hat of toning osprey feathers.

Like Queen Mary, Queen Elizabeth the Queen Mother has firmly established her own particular style of dressing, and in the past forty years or so, it cannot be said that she has ever made any real concessions to popular fashion. Indeed the 'Look' that is so universally associated with Queen Elizabeth today is a natural evolution of a definite, personal style which began to emerge in the late 1930s.

The Queen Mother is invariably dressed by the House of Hartnell; first by the late Sir Norman himself, now by his successors. The majority of her outfits have always been created from soft fabrics such as chiffon, georgette, organdie, silk and lace, following a generous but basic pattern, allowing plenty of material for freedom of movement, as well as for comfort. If the style rarely varies – it was once said that the Queen Mother will be remembered as 'The Queen of the cross-over bodice' – then neither does the range of preferred colours. Pastel shades predominate; blues, pinks, yellows, greens, lilacs and mauves are constantly repeated.

It has been said the closets at Clarence House contain every dress ever made for Queen Elizabeth. Can this be so, or is it simply that favourite designs – as with her hats, those famous veiled confections of feathers or flowers, her shoes with their slight platforms and very high heels, and her long, buttoned gloves – have known very many incarnations? Of all her outfits, the Queen Mother's evening dresses appear to serve her especially well. One reason why this should be so speaks plainly for itself; the lavish embroidery. Every pearl, crystal, sequin and bead, every last detail of a motif in gold or silver, is sewn by hand and that isn't something that can be recreated every day of the week.

It was the arrival of sixties fashion – mini-skirted dresses and so on from such popular designers as Mary Quant, modelled by gamine cover-girls like Twiggy – that first emphasized

Queen Elizabeth's total devotion to something that she has made uniquely her own. The same was true of Queen Mary, though in her case it took the daringly modern 'flapper' of the 1920s to highlight the bizarre, even absurd, styles to which she remained so faithful. Yet as with Queen Elizabeth, Queen Mary dressed more to please her husband – and George V did not want his consort to change the way she looked. One experiment failed abysmally when Queen Mary decided to test the water and asked a lady-in-waiting to raise her skirt a little – as most women were doing – and to wear it in the King's presence. She did and the King, as he made emphatically clear to Queen Mary afterwards, didn't like it. That, then, was the end of any aspirations she may have had to a more modern look.

From that time on the Queen stuck rigidly to her ankle-length skirts and coats often with massive fur collars, buckram bodices, moulded to a regally ample bosom, high Edwardian hats or the familiar, plainer toques, parasols and long pointed shoes. During the day, though more particularly of an evening, when dressing for dinner or for an official engagement, Queen Mary would put on her jewels, but not just a few discreet pieces. Indeed, from her vast collection, some of which had belonged to women of the Russian imperial family, the Queen would deck herself out in a tiara, a deep choker together with one or more necklaces, a brooch or two, a stomacher, diamond bracelets and ear-rings which hung like pendulums from her long earlobes. Frequently added to all that would be the blue sash of the Garter – with another brooch to secure it at the shoulder – and her diamond and ruby Garter Star.

In her use of jewellery, and she owns a large number of magnificent pieces, many of them given originally to Queen Victoria, the Queen Mother is rather more circumspect. It is very doubtful, for instance, that Her Majesty has ever attended a morning function, as did Queen Mary, dressed in a gown of white lace with diamond accessories, 'Glittering in the sun like the Jungfrau', as one who saw her put it.

Yet no matter how many diamonds she chose to wear by day or by night – in fact the more she put on, the more magnificent she looked – and no matter how bizarre her outfits, Queen Mary was solidly Queen Mary and that was all there was to it. Never could she have been mistaken for anything less than a Queen; well, perhaps not quite never. . . . On 29 September 1949, although she did not entirely approve of the match, she joined the rest of the royal family at the wedding of her eldest grandchild, George, the Earl of Harewood, to his first wife Miss Marion Stein, now Mrs Jeremy Thorpe. The reception afterwards was held in the state apartments at St James's Palace, where E.M. Forster, the elderly and very short-sighted novelist, was seen bowing to the wedding-cake in the belief that it was Queen Mary.

In not too dissimilar vein, Queen Elizabeth's own fashions, or more precisely their fondant hue, sparked off good-natured banter among London's Café Society and earned for their royal wearer the light-hearted, nickname, 'the Cake'.

The years 1970-80 yielded a number of memorable events in the life of the Queen Mother and, indeed, in the life of the royal family as a whole. But by no means all of them were occasions for celebration; inevitably there were those which brought sorrow.

On 28 May 1972 the Duke of Windsor died of cancer of the throat. Only ten days earlier during her state visit to Paris, the Queen, together with Prince Philip and Prince Charles, called on the Duke and Duchess at their mansion, a twenty-minute drive from the centre of the city. The Duke was too ill to come downstairs and, as she sat with him in his room, the Queen must have guessed that her uncle was dying. In her telegram of condolence to the Duchess, Her Majesty said, 'I am so glad that I was able to see him . . . ten days ago.'

Earlier that year, the Duchess of Windsor had written to her old friend 'Foxie', Lady Sefton, 'We are not well. I have a flood of nerves and the Duke is having X-ray for his throat.' A little later she reported that while the treatment had done the Duke some good, she was having, 'a painful time with my old friend the ulcer'. The Duchess added, 'There is nothing to be said for growing old.'

The responsibility for bringing the Duke of Windsor's body home to England that summer lay with the Royal Air Force. The mission had been tactfully rehearsed over a period of time, as these things often are, so that when the need arose formal procedure was put into operation in a smooth, well-ordered manner. At RAF Benson in Oxfordshire, the Duke and Duchess of Kent, representing the Queen, headed the offical delegation neatly assembled on the tarmac to receive the coffin upon its arrival. It was a simple dignified scene of which the Duke himself would doubtless have approved.

Next day the remains were taken by road to Windsor. There in the nave of St George's Chapel, within sight of the tomb of King George V and Queen Mary, the Duke's coffin was placed on a deep blue catafalque and draped with his personal standard. The Duchess of Windsor's wreath was placed on top and the tall amber candles at each corner were lit. From then until the night before the funeral, arranged for Monday 5 June, the Duke of Windsor lay in state. In that time 60,000 people filed past the bier to pay their respects. That quite so many had made the pilgrimage to Windsor testified not to idle curiosity, but to admiration. The floral tributes sent from strangers and the volume of letters addressed to the Duchess of Windsor bore witness to the same.

Not unexpectedly the Duke's death had re-kindled many old loyalties and had aroused many an old argument. That the ceremony of Trooping the Colour had taken place in the middle of official Court mourning and only two days before the Duke's funeral was thought shameful by some, despite such marks of respect as the issue of black arm-bands to officers and the observance of a minute's silence at the start of the parade. Others felt that the Queen's invitation to the Duchess to stay at Buckingham Palace as her guest was far too little and much too late. Speaking at a formal dinner in Burton-on-Trent, Ian Mikardo MP declared that the royal family 'with sickening hypocrisy' were 'falling over themselves to show the corpse the charity which they denied the man.'

On the evening of 4 June Prince Charles and Lord Mountbatten accompanied the Duchess of Windsor to St George's Chapel. The public lying-in-state had ended, the fleeting, but intensely private, ceremonial had just begun. 'He was my entire life', the Duchess said sadly. 'I can't begin to think what I am going to do without him; he gave up so much for me. . . . I always hoped that I would die before him.' After she had left, the Duke's coffin was removed to the Albert Memorial Chapel. The following morning, wearing the elegant black coat Hubert de Givenchy had had made for her in a single night, her face covered by a full black veil, the Duchess left Buckingham Palace for Windsor shortly after 10 a.m.

As the Duchess arrived at the deanery at Windsor Castle to await the Queen and the rest of the royal family, the State

Trumpeters of the Household Cavalry moved to the west end of the nave in St George's Chapel, while officers of the bearer party, The Prince of Wales Company, 1st Battalion Welsh Guards, halted at the door to the Albert Memorial Chapel until joined by King Olav of Norway, the Duke of Edinburgh and the Prince of Wales, the Duke of Kent, the Princes William and Richard of Gloucester and Michael of Kent, Lord Mountbatten and the Duke of Beaufort.

With the congregation in place in the nave and the royal family settled in the Choir, the Duchess of Windsor was seated next to the Queen to the right of the altar, a signal was given and the coffin, followed by the royal princes, was borne in on the shoulders of the bearer party. Less than an hour later it was driven slowly through the park to Frogmore. There in the family cemetery dominated by the Royal Mausoleum, where simple ledger stones in an immaculate garden setting are looked down upon by a bronze figure of Christ, His arms open in blessing, the Duke of Windsor was privately interred.

The royal family then returned to the Castle for luncheon and as the Duke's widow, her thoughts confused at times, rambled a little, Queen Elizabeth the Queen Mother patted her hand. 'I know how you feel' she said, 'I've been through it myself.' Later that afternoon the Duchess of Windsor returned to Paris aboard an Andover of the Queen's Flight. While the Queen herself had privately expressed her farewells at Windsor Castle, the Lord Chamberlain, Lord Maclean, in accordance with protocol, formally took leave of the Duchess on Her Majesty's behalf at the foot of the aircraft steps.

Two months later, one of the royal princes who had walked in the Duke of Windsor's funeral procession at St George's Chapel was also dead. Prince William of Gloucester, the elder son of Prince Henry, Duke of Gloucester, whose own death occurred in June 1974, was killed in a flying accident on 28 August. He was thirty.

An occasion to lift royal spirits after the gloom of family mourning was the silver wedding anniversary of the Queen and the Duke of Edinburgh, which was celebrated on 20 November 1972. That morning a service of thanksgiving was held at Westminster Abbey, followed by a formal celebratory luncheon, hosted by the Lord Mayor of London at Guildhall.

As with all such royal occasions, it was a day of pleasure for the nation as much as the royal family, and this was neatly summed up in the Queen's Guildhall speech. For years she had spoken in her broadcasts of 'My husband and I' until the expression had become a jokey catch-phrase and one to be gradually phased out in favour of something less impersonal.

At the Guildhall, however, the Queen said, 'I think everyone will concede that today, of all occasions, I should begin my speech with "My husband and I".' It was a clever and extremely well-constructed speech in which the Queen also made witty reference to the royal 'We' – particularly associated in people's minds with Queen Victoria. 'We,' said Her Majesty, 'and by that I mean both of us. . . .'

A year later, almost to the very day, the royal family re-assembled at Westminster Abbey – together with some 2,000 guests – for the wedding on 14 November of Princess Anne and Captain Mark Phillips, 1st the Queen's Dragoon Guards. Of Queen Elizabeth's six grandchildren Princess Anne was the first to marry. This time the spectacle of royal pageant helped to dispel the gloom of industrial unrest which led to the declaration of a state of emergency and the subsequent collapse of Prime Minister Edward Heath's Tory government.

So precarious was the political climate during that winter of 1973 that certain Labour back-benchers called for the cancellation of the royal wedding. Such an idea was dismissed as lunacy and, on the morning of the fourteenth, as she rode beside the Queen in the Scottish State Coach cheered by all those lining the procession-al route, the Queen Mother, who was so obviously enjoying herself, remarked, 'Everybody looks so happy.'

Yet as one royal marriage began, another, which had got off to a dazzling start thirteen years before, was coming to the end of its woefully unhappy course.

Princess Margaret had first met Antony Armstrong-Jones at a private dinner party given by Lady Elizabeth Cavendish in Chelsea in 1958, three years after Group Captain Peter Townsend had rescinded his proposal of marriage to the Princess. It is perhaps worthwhile taking a brief look at this point at the story of Princess Margaret's love for Peter Townsend. First, it highlights with tragic irony the outcome of the marriage the Princess did enter into. Secondly, it shows clearly how the Queen Mother's response to personal problems of those close to her had changed fundamentally since the death of the King.

Group Captain Peter Townsend had been brought to King George VI's attention as a distinguished fighter pilot, and in March 1944 he was appointed equerry to His Majesty. At that time Townsend was still married to his first wife, Rosemary Pawle, by whom he had two sons. Eight years later they were divorced on the grounds of her adultery with the export merchant John de Laszlo – son of the celebrated painter – whom she married.

Princess Margaret had been attracted to the slim, dark-haired Group Captain from their first meeting, but the hero-worship some insisted had struck her didn't fade away as she grew older, it matured. Well did she know the meaning of her feelings long before Townsend could put a name to his own. At length his proposal, made at Windsor in the spring of 1953, led Princess Margaret to tell the Queen that she and Townsend, by now Comptroller of the Queen Mother's Household, would like to marry. The Queen's personal delight was gradually dissipated by the invidious position in which she was placed as temporal Governor of the Church of England. As Defender of the Faith, she could scarcely ignore canon No. 107 established as long ago as 1603, which quite specifically forbade divorce. Moreover, any member of the royal family wishing to marry had first to obtain the sovereign's consent under the edicts of the Royal Marriages Act, passed into statute by George III in 1772.

By the autumn of 1955, when Princess Margaret issued her now-famous statement in which she declared that she had decided not to marry Peter Townsend, the entire issue had reached fantastic proportions. Initially the Queen had asked her sister to wait a year and the Princess had waited. She was then asked to wait another year, which she did. In all that time it had been hoped that an equitable solution to an almost impossible situation would somehow be found. Indeed, to that end the couple had received enough promises, not the least of them from the man assigned to explore every possibility. He was Sir Alan Lascelles, or 'Tommy' as he was more familiarly called. By now an elderly bachelor, Lascelles had begun his royal career as Assistant Private Secretary to the Prince of Wales in 1920, became Private Secretary to King

George VI and served the Queen in that capacity during the first year of her reign. Something of a misogynist, he did not approve of Townsend's wish to marry the Queen's sister and once told him, 'You must be either mad or bad.'

At the end of the day, with the opposing forces of the Court, the Prime Minister Winston Churchill, his Cabinet, every one of the Commonwealth Premiers and, of course, the Church ranged against them, both Princess Margaret and Group Captain Townsend saw the futility of trying to find a loop-hole through which they might climb. As the Princess herself put it, after two years they were 'thoroughly drained, thoroughly demoralized.' The only alternative, if they still intended to marry, was for Princess Margaret to renounce her birthright, as her uncle had done in 1936, and doubtless to follow the Windsors into exile.

Townsend gallantly forbade any such action and, withdrawing his proposal of marriage, told the Princess that he was not prepared to remove her from the only kind of life she knew. The future was far too uncertain for so great a sacrifice. So ended an episode which the popular press, moved to poetic wistfulness, hailed as 'One of the greatest romances of history'.

Four years later, when Princess Margaret became privately engaged to Tony Armstrong-Jones, or the 'Taj Mahal' as he was code-named until the wedding (the name had been derived from his three initials and a flight of fancy), most of the couple's friends reeled in disbelief, some in horror. All were unanimous in believing that such a marriage could never work, no matter how passionately in love the Princess and Tony might be. It was one thing to drive down to Rotherhithe in the heart of Dockland, where Armstrong-Jones rented a room overlooking the Thames, for cosy romantic evenings; it might even be fun to walk down Waterloo Road with the Queen Mother and not be recognized, but marriage was quite another matter. They were too much alike, quite apart from which Tony would never settle comfortably in a world of rigid protocol and royal ifs and buts.

Within four years of the couple's wedding, forecasts of disaster were beginning to ring horribly true. By early 1964 the marriage, to Princess Margaret's utter bewilderment and profound distress, had very definitely run aground. Indeed, during the period in which she was expecting the birth of her daughter Sarah (which took place on 1 May 1964) Lord Snowdon 'had begun to reveal characteristics which not only took [the Princess] by surprise but literally by storm'. So great was Princess Margaret's misery that her doctors expressed their concern over the effects it might have on her pregnancy.

There can, of course, be no doubt that Lord Snowdon did experience enormous difficulty in his attempt to reconcile his two identities; while resisting the constraints placed on him as the husband of the Queen's sister, he was also very much an artist who needed freedom to pursue his career. In short, Snowdon wanted the best of both worlds. 'One gets the impression,' wrote David Sinclair his most recent biographer, 'that he believed he should have been able to wear his royal aura like an overcoat, taking it off when it became inconvenient or restricted his freedom of movement.'

'It could not be said that Princess Margaret was to blame for the problems,' Sinclair went on. '. . . Indeed, the idea of blame in such circumstances is probably invalid – we are all prisoners of our personalities.' Nevertheless, by the Princess's own admission, Tony was no longer the man she had married and the changes she saw in him alarmed her.

The Queen's concern for Princess Margaret in her unhappiness was naturally acute. But while ready to do everything she could to help diffuse a tense and increasingly difficult situation, her love for her sister and her warm affection for Lord Snowdon – feelings the Queen Mother also shared – meant that she took a carefully considered middle line, favouring one party no more than the other.

By the early 1970s it had become obvious that the Snowdon marriage, if as such it could be called by then, would not survive the decade. At Kensington Palace Princess Margaret and her husband lived beneath the same roof as virtual, even hostile strangers, each leading separate lives and appearing together in public only when obliged to do so. At the start of 1976 matters were finally brought to a head and, amid a blaze of publicity, the couple parted. Two years later, on 24 May 1978, they were divorced.

For the past thirty years, the Queen Mother's stance towards crises in the lives of her daughters has invariably been one of practiced evasion. From about the time of King George VI's death, it became increasingly apparent to her family that Queen

Elizabeth resolutely refused to recognize, much less acknowledge, the existence of disturbing factors in any of their lives. Thus when Princess Margaret was torn between her love for Peter Townsend and her duty to the Crown, the Queen Mother affected oblivion and stolidly sailed on, as if nothing untoward were happening. So it was, too, with the desperately unhappy decline of the Princess's marriage.

'You've been told that Queen Elizabeth plays "ostrich", haven't you?', the author was asked. '. . . The family realizes that it's hopeless trying to approach her with problems, because she really doesn't want to know.' Such a trait seems out of place in one who has always taken, indeed still does take, so prominent a part in the life of her family. Yet it is not unreasonable to suppose that Queen Elizabeth's method of tackling emotionally disturbing or profound issues by pretending they do not exist, originated as a reaction to the King's death. That it survives today assuredly preserves inviolate the measured reality of the Queen Mother's private world.

For most of their lives the Queen and Princess Margaret have always had one another in whom to confide. Moreover, for the Queen there was also another to whom she could turn; her mother-in-law. Now a largely forgotten figure, she was Princess Andrew of Greece, elder sister of Earl Mountbatten.

The daughter of Prince Louis of Battenberg, 1st Marquess of Milford Haven and Princess Victoria of Hesse, granddaughter of Queen Victoria, she was born Princess Alice of Battenberg at Windsor Castle on 23 February 1885. Generally regarded as deaf from birth, though some maintain deafness occurred during infancy, Princess Alice nevertheless learned to lip-read in several languages, including English, French and German. In 1903 she married Prince Andrew of Greece and Denmark, younger brother of Prince Nicholas, father of Princess Marina, and gave birth to five children, of whom the youngest, her only son, is Prince Philip, Duke of Edinburgh. Formally known as Princess Andrew, she led a remarkable and often dramatic life which, alas, would be beyond the scope of this book to study here.

It is worth noting briefly, however, that Princess Andrew was not only a niece but a close friend of the last Russian Empress, Alexandra Feodorovna, and her elder sister the Grand Duchess Elisabeth. Though in recent years investigations into the fate of the Romanovs have cast doubt on history's official version of savage butchery at Ekaterinburg in 1918, the discovery of the Grand Duchess Elisabeth's body at the bottom of an abandoned mineshaft in the Urals township of Alapayevsk, bore tragic and unarguable witness to her barbaric execution. Not surprisingly these events had a devastating effect on Princess Andrew and, indeed, in years to come she was to emulate the example set by her Aunt Elisabeth and establish a part religious, part nursing order, dedicated to the welfare of the poor and underprivileged.

Following the assassination of her husband, the Grand Duke Serge Alexandrovitch, on 4 February 1905, the Grand Duchess relinquished all material possessions and founded the Order of Martha and Mary of which she became Abbess. Her work took her into the squalor of the Moscow slums where she spared herself nothing in the cause of relieving human suffering. Princess Andrew witnessed her aunt's work during her own visits to Moscow and in 1949, five years after the death of her husband, founded the Christian Sisterhood of Martha and Mary of which she became Life President. Like the Grand Duchess Elisabeth Feodorovna, Princess Andrew renounced all but her basic requirements and dressed to the end of her life in the grey habit of her Order. Her last years were spent living as a guest of her son and daughter-in-law at Buckingham Palace, where she died on 5 December 1969 at the age of eighty-four.

Of his sister's relationship with Elizabeth II, Lord Mountbatten once said, 'The Queen adored her, and she adored the Queen. She [Her Majesty] is fond of her mother, but she got on infinitely better with my sister.'

# 17

# *To the Present*

One of the most invaluable services the Queen Mother renders her 'dear daughter', as she often refers to the Queen, is when she is called upon to act as a Counsellor of State, deputizing for the sovereign during her overseas tours or for reasons of incapacitation. On such occasions it falls to the two most senior ranking members of the royal family available to perform certain functions on the Queen's behalf. These include granting audiences to ambassadors and emissaries newly accredited 'to the Court of St James's', and attending to all but the most confidential of issues that would, in the normal course of events, be put before the Queen.

From time to time Queen Elizabeth has also deputized at Buckingham Palace investitures, ceremonies in which men and women who have performed distinguished service receive honours – from knighthoods through the ranks and divisions of various Orders – at the recommendation of the Prime Minister. Otherwise as Queen Dowager, Her Majesty is not required to become involved in affairs of state. Apart from formal courtesy calls received from kings, queens, presidents and other potentates on state visits to the Queen, any VIPs who enjoy the Queen Mother's hospitality do so in an entirely private capacity.

One slight exception to this rule, however, took place a few years before the Shah of Iran was deposed by the Ayatollah Khomeini, when his consort, the Shahbanou Farah Pahlavi, was welcomed to London as Queen Elizabeth's semi-official guest. In April 1975 Her Majesty had enjoyed a six-day tour of Iran as the guest of the Shahanshah and this third wife Empress Farah. On the Queen Mother's itinerary was a visit to Persepolis where four years earlier, in October 1971, Prince Philip and Princess Anne had joined a host of royal visitors from East and West, invited to attend the lavish celebrations marking the 2,500th anniversary of the Persian monarchy.

Cordial relations had existed between the British and Iranian royal families for a long time and Queen Elizabeth's invitation to the beautiful, thirty-eight-year-old Shahbanou to visit her at Clarence House was a mark of her personal affection. As she left London at the end of her stay, the Queen Mother told her imperial guest, 'Let us kiss as sovereign sisters'. It seemed an oddly archaic expression, but not nearly as archaic as the wording found on the Order of Service issued to all those invited to St Paul's Cathedral in 1977 to attend 'A Form of Prayer and Thanksgiving to Almighty God commemorating the blessings granted to THE QUEEN'S MOST EXCELLENT MAJESTY during the Twenty-Five years of Her Majesty's Reign'. The last time Britain celebrated a royal Silver Jubilee had been in 1935, the last year, as it happened, of George V's life. In 1976 it was announced from Buckingham Palace that the twenty-fifth anniversary of Elizabeth II's accession would be formally acknowledged on 7 June 1977. Of course that was not the date on which she had succeeded her father, but a national celebration such as this was better suited to a summer's day, rather than early February. The irony was that Jubilee Day itself was as cold – and often as wet – as any late winter's day. Though the sun broke through in occasional bursts, the skies were hostile, the showers heavy and the blue and silver banners in the Mall hung limp and unimpressive. Nevertheless the one million people who lined the royal route from Buckingham Palace to St Paul's Cathedral, and the crowds who waited for the Queen's subsequent walkabout to the Guildhall, passed the long and uncomfortable hours in good humour, tempered by excitement, patriotism and pure grit.

The Jubilee had got off to a slow, almost indifferent start. To the bulk of the nation, or so it seemed, it was something 'officialdom' would observe whether the public was there to watch or not. Then suddenly there was 'lift-off': bonfire beacons, Thames pageant, magnificent firework displays, street parties, floodlit buildings, flags and jubilee posters in the windows of ordinary people's homes – the works! Indisputably the highlight of the proceedings was the spectacle of the Queen and Prince Philip seated in the massive golden State Coach, riding to St Paul's on 7 June. The Silver Jubilee had brought people together and, moreover, it re-affirmed the nation's loyalty to the Crown and more specifically to the Queen as an individual.

The year drew to a close on a suitably fitting high note, too, with the birth of a son to Princess Anne on 15 November, the day after her fourth wedding anniversary. The advent of Master Peter Phillips (some royal historians threw up their hands in horror that he should have no title) of course meant that the Queen and the Duke of Edinburgh became grandparents for the very first time.

The occasion was no less unique for Queen Elizabeth the Queen Mother who, at the age of seventy-seven, became a great-grandmother for the first time. 'This is one of the happiest days of my life,' she said. 'It's wonderful news, isn't it? I am absolutely delighted.' Two days later Princess Anne and her son left the Lindo Wing of St Mary's Hospital, Paddington, (where Peter had weighed in at 7 pounds 9 ounces) for Buckingham Palace, accompanied by a large Paddington Bear, the gift of the hospital staff.

On 22 December five generations of the royal family attended the infant's christening in the Music Room of Buckingham Palace. The oldest guest present was the remarkable Princess Alice, Countess of Athlone, the last surviving grandchild of Queen Victoria. At ninety-four she had earned the singular distinction of being the longest-ever living member of the royal family. Princess Alice lived on for another three years; she died at her home, Clock House, Kensington Palace, on 3 January 1981, a few weeks short of her ninety-eighth birthday.

If 1977, with its exhausting round of Jubilee tours and celebratory functions, had been the 'year' of the Queen, 1980 was most decidedly the year of the Queen Mother. So many events were, in fact, organized to mark her eightieth birthday on 4 August that Queen Elizabeth herself had said, 'If they arrange much more for me, I shall be dead before then.' The honours so richly bestowed were not, of course, lost on the nation's favourite octogenarian and, indeed, no queen dowager had ever been so favoured.

Stressing the esteem in which Queen Elizabeth is held, Tuesday

15 July was set aside as a day of national celebration, formally observed by a service of thanksgiving at St Paul's Cathedral that morning. Such a service, however, could not fail to assume the tone of a memorial service, as Queen Elizabeth herself was to remark afterwards. Certainly the laudatory nature of the prayers, the lessons, the Bible readings and the obsequious address, delivered by the Archbishop of Canterbury, Dr Robert Runcie, did little to dissipate the mood of *in memoriam*. Only the fact that Queen Elizabeth was present in body as well as spirit prevented the descent of too great a degree of solemnity.

Together with the Queen, Prince Philip and the Prince of Wales, Queen Elizabeth entered the cathedral to the sound of a trumpet fanfare, and while the choir and the congregation sang the hymn, 'Praise, My Soul, the King of Heaven', made her way along the nave to her chair beneath the dome.

Welcoming all those present, the Dean of St Paul's said:

We give thanks today for Her Gracious Majesty Queen Elizabeth The Queen Mother, for her long life of service to the peoples of this Country and Commonwealth, for her warmth, resilience, courage and love shown in time of peace and war.
We rejoice in qualities of sparkling greeting and loyal service. We acknowledge concern for young and old, shared with her husband, His Majesty King George VI, and we remember with gratitude their achievements and their new vision. . . .

The Metrical Psalm, 'I to the hills will lift mine eyes', preceded the lessons – from Joshua I; 7,8,9 and Revelations XXI; 10,11,23,24 – which were read by the Moderator of the Church of Scotland. The anthem, 'Jubilate Deo', the words of which had been set to music by the late Benjamin Britten, was performed and, following Archbishop Runcie's address, Dom Basil Hume, Cardinal Archbishop of Westminster, continued:

We pray especially on this day for Her Majesty Queen Elizabeth The Queen Mother, giving thanks for her life and the life of her family. We give thanks for that great partnership with her devoted husband George, King and leader of Nation and Empire in peace and war. We pray for her today, as she enjoys the affection and loyalty of our people, and for her happiness in the years to come.

187

Presently the formal aspect of the service was concluded by Gordon Jacob's arrangement of the national anthem, whereupon the royal family, led by Queen Elizabeth, returned to Buckingham Palace for luncheon and for the almost obligatory balcony appearances; first Queen Elizabeth by herself, then joined by her daughters, a scene which led one elderly woman in the crowd to remark, 'Ah, 'ere she is with 'er two gels', and finally a last glimpse of the Queen Mother acknowledging the cheers alone, before the tall glass-panelled doors of the balcony-room were closed behind her.

As always on such an occasion, the pageantry was at its most memorable and dramatic that day; and the three carriage processions – those of the royal family, the Queen, and Queen Elizabeth herself – demanded the participation, quite literally, of *all* the Queen's horses and *all* the Queen's men. Retired horses, fit enough for one last parade, were brought to London from Windsor, in order that both the Queen and her mother might each be accompanied by a sovereign's escort of the Household Cavalry. In fact it called for some very clever reorganization of ranks to ensure that both escorts looked 'all present and correct'. In reality both were a few men short, but the visual impact was achieved and that was probably all that mattered. Horses, too, were at such a premium that, at the last minute, the Queen had to ask her family to squeeze themselves into state carriages that were not built to accommodate more than four persons in comfort. This was particularly evident in the case of Princess Anne and Princess Margaret who shared their semi-state landau with Captain Mark Phillips, Viscount Linley and Lady Sarah Armstrong-Jones. So tightly packed were they that both Princesses found it awkward to raise their arms to wave.

In yet another unique tribute to Queen Elizabeth, the Queen withheld her right to arrive last and leave first, which meant that minutes after the rest of the royal family had left the palace for St Paul's Cathedral, Her Majesty and the Duke of Edinburgh were on their way. Finally, riding with the Prince of Wales in the maroon and gold 1902 State Landau, drawn by four of the famous Windsor Greys in State Harness, came Queen Elizabeth the Queen Mother, dressed in lilac and mouthing the words 'Thank you very much' in acknowledgement of the crowds' cheers.

One colourful personality tragically missing from St Paul's was

Earl Mountbatten of Burma, who had been assassinated by the IRA on 27 August 1979, while holidaying at his home in the Irish Republic.

From the days of his youth to the celebration of the Queen's Silver Jubilee, 'Dickie' Mountbatten had rarely missed a royal show. Indeed, on occasion he was the star of the show in his own right, as when, for example, a television series made about his life was 'premiered' at the Imperial War Museum in December 1968, before the entire royal family.

Mountbatten was justifiably proud of his life's achievements; Supreme Allied Commander, South-East Asia; Viceroy of India; Commander-in-Chief, Mediterranean Fleet; First Sea Lord; Chief of the Defence Staff; Colonel of the Life Guards and Gold Stick-in-Waiting, were just a handful of the offices to which he was appointed. Born a Prince of Battenberg at Frogmore House, Windsor, in 1900, a great-grandson of Queen Victoria, he was equally proud of his royal heritage. Yet if modesty seemed never to be one of Mountbatten's most outstanding characteristics, his disarming personal magnetism won him enormous respect and admiration.

To the Queen and Prince Philip, 'Dickie' was inordinately valued both as a close friend and mentor, and as an elder member of the royal family councils his opinions and carefully considered advice carried considerable weight. He, too, of course, was possessed of a persuasive tongue and sunshine aura and it was Dickie who put forward the idea for the famous 1969 television film *Royal Family*. At first the Queen didn't care for the sound of something that would give her a 'movie star' image, but Mountbatten's influence won through. He pointed out that, in a modern society, the image of royal family life was an aspect of monarchy that ought to be projected. The ultimate success of the film proved the wisdom of his advice.

To Prince Charles, who was his great-nephew, Lord Mountbatten was a strong guiding light. So great was the Prince's adoration that he referred to the Earl as his 'HGF' – Honorary Grand-Father. Thoughts of this beloved figure were clearly uppermost in the Prince's mind when he was married in 1981; for it was at Mountbatten's estate, Broadlands in Hampshire, that he and his bride began their honeymoon.

Not every member of the royal family adored the Earl,

however, and in fact there are those who stoutly maintain that there was never any love lost between the Queen Mother and Lord Mountbatten. Though for reasons that must be self-evident, it was explained that, 'they were rather too much alike to have been the best of friends'.

With the 'official' celebration over, Queen Elizabeth went on to complete a full schedule of engagements designed to salute her on her eightieth birthday. There was for instance, a special garden party at Buckingham Palace, with some 3,000 guests trampling the sturdy camomile lawn in the hope of being presented; she was the guest-of-honour later in the year at a reception given by the Prime Minister, Margaret Thatcher, at 10 Downing Street, while across the road from Clarence House in St James's Park, a rose avenue planted in her honour duly received a royal visit. Gifts, too, poured into Clarence House, from the smallest posy sent by her youngest 'fan', to the grandest artefacts presented on behalf of the myriad bodies with which she is connected, including her newest appointment as Lord Warden and Admiral of the Cinque Ports, an ancient office to which no female had ever been elected in its entire history.

On 4 August itself, the band of the Welsh Guards marched along Stable Yard Road past Clarence House, playing the customary melody, 'Happy Birthday to You', and later on, Queen Elizabeth stood at the gates to receive the crowd's acclaim. With her were the Queen and Princess Margaret, who helped to collect the flowers and greetings cards showered on her by adults and children alike.

That evening, dressed in a filmy white gown, heavily encrusted with gold, silver and pearl, and wearing a tiara and complementing ear-rings and necklace of diamonds and rubies (which a jovial guest had once likened to sweets, adding 'They look good enough to eat'), Queen Elizabeth attended a gala ballet performance at the Royal Opera House, accompanied by the immediate members of her family. Arranged by Princess Margaret, the birthday gala consisted of a programme of three ballets: *Mam'zelle Angot* (originally choreographed by Léonide Massine), *A Month in the Country*, and *Rhapsody*, Sir Frederick Ashton's new ballet which not only received its world première that night, but was dedicated to Queen Elizabeth by the choreographer.

At the end of the performance thousands of small silver discs were released from the ceiling, and later, back stage – where she was accompanied by Princess Margaret, who is President of the Royal Ballet – the Queen Mother, surrounded by dancers, staff and cameramen, blew out the candles on a surprise birthday cake.

The note of high celebration in royal circles was to be picked up again shortly after the momentous summer of Queen Elizabeth's birthday festivities had subsided. In fact the Queen Mother had been busily working behind the scenes to encourage the Prince of Wales, who is generally regarded to be her favourite grandchild, into a marriage with the young Lady Diana Spencer, granddaughter of Ruth, Lady Fermoy, a close friend as well as a lady-in-waiting to Queen Elizabeth. Fermoys and Spencers were by no means strangers to Court life and, indeed, on the day King George V died in 1936, Queen Mary sent out 'to enquire after Ruth Fermoy's baby'. In 1954 that baby, Frances, married Viscount Althorp, the present Earl Spencer, then an equerry to George VI. In 1961 the youngest of their three daughters, Diana, was born.

At the age of thirty-two Prince Charles was under a certain amount of pressure to take a wife. As Heir to the Throne, his marital horizons were already restricted by the lack of suitable candidates. He had, of course, enjoyed the company of a number of young women more or less his own age. But how many had not already stepped out into the real world? In one or two instances past boyfriends crept out from behind the woodwork to tell their tales, with the obvious result that the unfortunate ladies found themselves struck off the list of potential contenders. There were those, too, who were happy to know the Prince, but who had no desire to find themselves subjected to the rigours a life as a princess would impose.

At nineteen, therefore, the unsullied Lady Diana Spencer was the last in a rapidly dwindling succession, and the Queen Mother, assuming the role of matchmaker (a part Queen Victoria liked to play, incidentally, until her efforts backfired) did much to bring her grandson and the Lady Diana together. At length family hopes came to fruition and, at the end of February 1981, the couple's engagement – by now mooted for some months – was formally announced. There were those, however, both inside and outside royal circles, who wondered if Prince Charles was entirely happy or whether it was more a case of heeding the call of duty.

*191*

Whatever his initial feelings in the matter, the seeds of royal wedding fever were sown and, within twenty-four hours of the Buckingham Palace announcement, the souvenir market had successfully launched its first glossy images of England's presumed future queen. Such icons were rapidly snapped up, along with anything else on offer.

While the phenomenal storm of publicity, not all of it entirely welcome, continued to crack over her head, the bride-to-be was officially staying as a guest of the Queen Mother under the protective roof of Clarence House. In reality it was not long before she slipped away to stay with her sister Lady Jane Fellowes (whose husband Robert is Assistant Private Secretary to the Queen) at her own grace-and-favour residence within the precincts of Kensington Palace.

In what was beginning to look like a permanent break with tradition, the royal wedding was celebrated on 29 July, not at Westminster Abbey as most expected, but at St Paul's Cathedral, chosen once again as the setting for the third major royal occasion in four years. A spectacular pre-wedding night of bonfires – which were lit throughout the country – firework displays, notably that attended by the royal family in Hyde Park, and spontaneous entertainments organized by the crowds, set the tone of jubilation that was to last for another twenty-four hours.

On the morrow the wedding itself was watched on British television by 39 million viewers and around the world, in seventy-four countries, by 750 million; at that date the largest viewing audience in the entire history of television.

Save for coronations, which are in a league of their own, it is safe to assert that the kind of spectacle provided by the royal wedding was without precedent this century. It was Ruritania come to life in fulsomely exaggerated splendour, and in that sense the plaudits were right in proclaiming this 'The Wedding of the Century'. Two thousand men of the armed services and five thousand uniformed police were on duty, twelve military bands deployed along the wedding route entertained the crowds, and the State Trumpeters sounded fanfares from the portico of St Paul's as the glittering carriage processions brought the entire royal family to the door.

Before the time came for her to join the rest of her family on that warm July morning, Queen Elizabeth the Queen Mother was at hand with words of praise and encouragement for the young bride. Dressed by David and Elizabeth Emanuel in a highly theatrical, if somewhat crushable, gown of ivory silk taffeta, finished with frills, bows, lace, and a detachable train twenty-five feet long, over which ten thousand mother-of-pearl sequins had been scattered, the Lady Diana was about to face her biggest test of endurance since rumours linking her with Prince Charles had first plucked her from obscurity nearly a year before.

Inside the Cathedral, the bride's family – her mother, now Mrs Frances Shand-Kydd, her grandmother Ruth, Lady Fermoy, her brother Viscount Althorp and her sisters Sarah and Jane, together with their husbands – sat facing the Queen, the Duke of Edinburgh and Queen Elizabeth the Queen Mother across the specially raised dais where the marriage was to be performed by the Archbishop of Canterbury. The Prince of Wales and his supporters, the Princes Andrew and Edward, took up their places at the steps of the dais as, to the sound of Jeremiah Clarke's *Trumpet Voluntary*, Earl Spencer led his daughter into the cathedral and along a red-carpeted path over 600-feet in length. Behind them, supervised by the senior bridesmaid, Lady Sarah Armstrong-Jones, came the younger bridal attendants: Lord Mountbatten's granddaughter India Hicks, Catherine Cameron, Clementine Hambro and Sarah Jane Gaselee, together with Edward van Cutsem and Lord Nicholas Windsor, younger son of the Duke and Duchess of Kent.

In opening the service Archbishop Runcie spoke of 'this marriage in which are placed so many hopes', and described the scene before him as 'the stuff of which fairytales are made'. In fact the word 'fairytale' seemed to spring readily to everybody's lips, not least to those of nearly every broadcaster, mesmerized by the flamboyance of an occasion it was their task to describe to the world. To be sure, it was not an adjective with which the 600,000 revellers, who packed themselves into every available space along the two-mile route from Buckingham Palace, would have disagreed.

At the close of the ceremony, the Prince and Princess of Wales received the Archbishop's blessing beneath the pillared baldacchino, before retiring from view to a side chapel where, as required by law, they signed the marriage registers. This brief interval, during which the Maori opera singer Kiri Te Kanawa performed

Handel's aria *Let the Bright Seraphim*, also provided a little time for members of the couple's families to greet each other more informally. For the Queen Mother and Ruth Fermoy, the two women who were especially responsible for the start of a new chapter in the nation's history, it was doubtless a moment of profound satisfaction.

It is in the peaceful and secure atmosphere of Royal Lodge, Windsor, with its memories stretching back over more than half a century, that Queen Elizabeth has often reflected on family events, and it was here, as much as anywhere else, that she entertained Prince Charles and his bride in the period which led up to their engagement.

For the Queen Mother Royal Lodge is a beloved weekend retreat and, whenever possible, such as at Easter, somewhere to enjoy a longer break. On a Sunday morning, it is nothing for staff and estate workers to see her walking in the distance with her dogs as they arrive for a service at the Royal Chapel of All Saints.

It is here, too, that the Queen Mother, frequently with the Queen and sometimes with other members of her family, also worships, slipping in just before eleven, having changed her hat and coat what can only have been moments before. It is a surprisingly unpretentious church with white walls, a wooden roof, oak pews and a comparatively simple altar. George IV originally had the chapel built close to Royal Lodge, and Queen Victoria had it altered twice during the 1860s. Queen Elizabeth enters through a separate door which leads directly into the royal pew, and those seated in the body of the chapel wouldn't know she was present were it not for the fact that she leans forward to watch the choir make its entry, smiling at the small boy singers who lead the way.

The order of service is typed out and run off on sheets of paper bearing the royal coat-of-arms and the words, 'The Royal Chapel, Windsor Great Park'. There is no great ceremony here and that is an enormous part of its charm. A psalm will be read, followed by the lessons, three hymns – such as 'God of Mercy, God of Grace', 'Lord of all being, throned afar', and 'Holy, Holy, Holy' – in between which a sermon will be delivered, perhaps by the Dean of Windsor, Dr Michael Mann. Then, following the offertory and a blessing, the congregation files out to be greeted by the Queen and the Queen Mother, who wait outside on the gravel path to chat to anybody who has time to pause – an assured and often unexpected bonus to any guests who might be accompanying members of staff.

It is to the Royal Lodge, too, that Queen Elizabeth invites friends and relations. Princess Margaret, for instance, if she is not spending the weekend further afield is a regular, with her own bedroom (once her father's) on the ground floor. Here, as at all the Queen Mother's houses, the atmosphere is light and relaxed, made more so by what one guest called 'the humour, the banter, the never-ending conversations'. This same guest went on:

> There was an occasion some years ago when Prince Charles with his mother and father were in the Great Saloon, chatting merrily, when the time came for them to leave for lunch at Windsor Castle. The smiles and bows at the leavetaking had not been over a minute when we heard somebody pounding down the corridor, and in ran Prince Charles, who, executing a Renaissance bow with a great flourish, declared 'Your Majesty'.
>
> 'Your Royal Highness,' replied Queen Elizabeth, whereupon her arms flew up over her head as she sank into the most marvellous and funny curtsy. The Prince had simply dashed back to retrieve his mother's gloves, which she had left on the piano. . . . You know Queen Elizabeth has a hearty laugh and whenever she and her family are together it is invariably an occasion of great hilarity.

It is scarcely surprising to know that Queen Elizabeth, whose life has not only been long but remarkably varied and colourful, enjoys reminiscing with surviving contemporaries. In 1982 she said the Falklands conflict was just like 1940 happening all over again. What at first seemed like nothing more than a storm in a teacup, of course erupted into something infinitely more serious, and for the royal family the tension was heightened by Prince Andrew's presence in the front line. The first prince to have seen active service in the armed forces since his father during the Second World War, Prince Andrew was one of the helicopter pilots of 820 Sea King Squadron, aboard HMS *Invincible*, which had been despatched to the South Atlantic as part of Britain's Task Force, when Argentinian troops, under the command of General Galtieri, invaded the almost barren Falkland Islands to 'reclaim' the long-disputed sovereignty for Argentina.

If and when such occasions arise, royal princes are rarely allowed into battle. But this time, having only recently begun a twelve-year commission as a helicopter pilot with the Royal Navy, Prince Andrew made it clear, both to his parents and to the Prime Minister, that should he be prevented from taking part in the campaign, he would have no hesitation in resigning his commission.

In the South Atlantic war-zone Prince Andrew co-piloted a Sea King Mark V anti-submarine helicopter which could carry four torpedoes and four depth charges. When the 'war' was finally over, it was said that, 'One of the most refreshing aspects of Prince Andrew's personality is the candour and honesty which make him unashamed to admit to fear. A hero, most of the time, is an ordinary man who keeps perfectly natural fears under control, accepting risks as part of a sense of duty, but well aware of their nature nevertheless.'

As with his colleagues, the twenty-two-year-old Prince had every reason to sense fear, particularly when his Sea King was used as a decoy for the devastating Exocet missile and when he witnessed the destruction of the *Atlantic Conveyor*.

When HMS *Invincible* returned home to Portsmouth, 166 days after she set sail, it was to a rapturous welcome, and if Sub-Lieutenant HRH The Prince Andrew, RN, had restrained his exuberance on board ship – in the presence of the Lord High Admiral (his mother the Queen) – he was just 'one of the lads' as he set foot on to the quay and, tearing off his cap, leapt into the air. After a slow but informal progress along the quayside with his parents and his sister that morning, Prince Andrew boarded the royal barge at the start of his journey to Balmoral and home to some of the things he had missed: 'the smell of grass, silence . . . milk. I haven't had any real milk for five and a half months,' he said. Prince Andrew declared, 'I am obviously looking forward to going home. But I am not going back to be a prince. I'm a pilot, not a prince.'

Pilot or prince, the news media had no intention of allowing him a month's leave completely free of attention. It was, in fact, at this time that Prince Andrew was enjoying the company of a young American-born 'starlet', Koo Stark, and, as always, in panting anticipation, sections of the Press sniffed what, in journalists' jargon, is generally called a 'sensation'. The sensation, need it be said, was of the media's own making, and when the Prince (who sometimes travelled incognito as 'Mr Johnson' – a name once adopted, it will be remembered, by his grandfather, King George VI) flew out to the Caribbean island of Mustique, made famous by Princess Margaret, for a private holiday rendezvous, Press cameramen went too.

'Let him go,' Queen Elizabeth had advised the Queen when the idea was first raised, 'it will do him good.' Whether it did or not was clearly debatable with long-range lenses continuously searching for a 'scoop' picture with which to titillate the masses at home. Understandably the Queen and the Queen Mother (to say nothing of Prince Andrew and his companion) were angry at this not wholly unexpected turn of events, and the young couple abandoned their hopes for privacy and returned separately to London.

The Falklands crisis during the first half of 1982 had naturally fanned the coals of patriotism so that Britons – and to be fair, Argentinians, too – were solidly united in the interests of their countries. Yet while prime news space was monopolized by developments out in the South Atlantic, at least for much of the time, all but the 'mopping up' was done when the birth of a new Heir Presumptive brought more joyous tidings to the nation's attention.

Born on the longest day of the year, and to his mother, at the end of a thirteen-hour labour, it must have felt like it, Prince William of Wales made his debut at 9.30 p.m. on 21 June. For both the Queen and, indeed, Queen Elizabeth, it was an especially proud moment, celebrated in the usual manner with as much champagne as *bonhomie* in evidence to 'wet the baby's head'. The news of his nephew's birth was relayed that evening to Prince Andrew, still aboard the *Invincible*, while Princess Margaret, attending a charity performance at a London theatre, was cheered by the audience when the news was announced from the stage.

By way of tribute to his great-grandmother, the forty-four-day-old Prince was christened at Buckingham Palace on 4 August, Queen Elizabeth's eighty-second birthday, receiving the names William Arthur Philip Louis, the last in remembrance of the late Lord Mountbatten, whose grandson, Lord Romsey, was among the six godparents.

The following summer Queen Elizabeth was invited to Norway for yet another round of birthday celebrations. In Oslo three days of festivities, over the weekend of 1-3 July, marked the eightieth birthday of King Olav V.

Of her surviving royal contemporaries, the Queen Mother shares with the Norwegian King a deep bond of friendship that has now spanned more than sixty years. Yet friendship is not the King's only tie with the British royal family, for by descent he is part of it. A grandson of Edward VII and Queen Alexandra – his mother Princess Maud was their youngest daughter – King Olav was born at Appleton House, Sandringham, on 2 July 1903. His father, although known as Carl, was Prince Christian of Denmark, second son of King Frederick VIII and, in November 1905, he was elected King of Norway, adopting the style Haakon VII in honour of the country's early Norse rulers.

Through his family connections, therefore, Crown Prince Olav, as he was now known, became particularly firm friends with his first cousin 'Bertie', the future King George VI. In March 1929 when he married Princess Märtha of Sweden, the Crown Prince invited the then Duke and Duchess of York to Oslo, and asked the Duke to act as his best man. During the Second World War Prince Olav and his father, together with the Norwegian government-in-exile, established their base in London. Widowed in 1954, the Crown Prince acted as Regent for his father during the last two years of his life, and finally ascended the throne as Olav V in September 1957. It has been said of the King that, when on duty, he 'is so regal that he appears capable of decapitating with a glance. In private he is like a reassuring Santa Claus . . . a jolly, spirited grandfather whom everyone loves.'

Not only was the warmth of King Olav's rapport with his people reaffirmed over his birthday weekend in July 1983, but so, too, the strength of his personal relationships with the royal families of Britain, Denmark, Sweden and Belgium, all of whom were well represented.

As his principal guest, Queen Elizabeth the Queen Mother was escorted by the King to all the events, private as well as public, that had been arranged to pay tribute to him. The Queen Mother was at his side during an official drive through the city and at the subsequent ceremonial birthday parade; at a gala dinner and concert given by his government at the Akershus Castle, and next to him in the centre of the group when all his royal friends and relations posed for an official commemorative photograph.

During that same summer of 1983, royal rapture in Norway contrasted sharply with the tense situation in Northern Ireland, a country terrorized by marauding Norsemen centuries before the advent of IRA tyranny. Queen Elizabeth was one of the few, however, who had no qualms about her visit to Ballymena in County Antrim to review the Territorial Army's seventy-fifth anniversary parade at St Joseph's Barracks. But with the threat of renewed IRA activity during the visit, security chiefs suggested it should be cancelled. The Queen Mother would have none of it. 'I'll compromise', she said. 'I'll go a few hours earlier than planned.'

From Heathrow she flew to Aldergrove Airport from where, surrounded by tight security, a helicopter ferried her to Hillsborough Castle, the sovereign's official residence in Northern Ireland. Entertained by the then Secretary of State, James Prior and his wife Jane, Queen Elizabeth recalled happy memories of the days when Hillsborough was home to the Earl and Countess Granville, her sister Rose and brother-in-law William, during the Earl's tenure as Governor of the Province.

Among the guests at dinner that evening was one of the Queen Mother's oldest friends, Mary Hamilton, Dowager Duchess of Abercorn, Her Majesty's Mistress of the Robes. The Hamiltons are an old Northern Irish family whose forebears were Lords of Paisley; Abercorn; Strabane; of Hamilton, Mountcastle and Kilpatrick, long before the dukedom of Abercorn was created a century ago. In common with most others who have lived with the prevailing political climate in the Province since trouble began in 1969, the Duchess pointed out to Queen Elizabeth that conditions were not quite as bad as people in mainland Britain were led to believe.

The following day the parade of Territorials went off without incident, save that a thirty-pound device attached to a petrol drum had been intercepted *en route* to Ballymena. The Queen Mother returned safely to London, delighted with the way in which her visit had been effected and the men of the Territorial Army were proud to have had her with them to crown their anniversary celebrations.

Today royalty's more informal approach to their official work means that vast numbers of ordinary people now have a better opportunity of exchanging a few words with the Queen, the Queen Mother and other members of the royal family than ever before. A new kind of informal communication was started by the Queen during her tour of New Zealand in 1970, with the birth of the 'walkabout'. Since then the rewards, on both sides, have been inestimable. This was an example of letting a little daylight filter through the shadows that King George V clung to so tenaciously, with the result that the popular concept of monarchy has been enhanced, not diminished. The Queen and Prince Philip, the Queen Mother, Prince Charles and the Princess of Wales stroll along to the crowd's applause, stopping every so often to talk or, when obliged to do so, to pause as children run forward, sometimes given a helping thrust by eager mothers, to press flowers on to the royal visitors. On a recent visit to the Smithfield Meat Market, porters serenaded the Queen Mother with 'If you were the only girl in the World', while one cockney admirer grasped both her hands in his and pleaded, 'Oh don't go. Can't you stay and talk to us a bit longer?'

In their off duty moments and in less public surroundings members of the royal family have invariably been more informal still, with extra time to stop and talk. Last century, during her long holiday visits to 'this dear Paradise', as she described her Balmoral estates, Queen Victoria was forever popping in unannounced to chat with her tenants and perhaps to take a cup of tea with them. Away from the public gaze, particularly at Sandringham the Queen Mother is frequently to be found in casual clothes stopping to talk with local people. It is also at Sandringham that she visits the local branch of the Women's Institute, sometimes with the Queen and Princess Margaret. Naturally these visits are private; the only noticeable trace of formality observed is that the women curtsey to their royal guest or guests.

Ann Morrow has described one such visit when, upon her arrival, Queen Elizabeth was offered some tea. 'She folded her hands together and, to their surprise, refused. "No," she said with a slight smile, "if you don't mind I'd like to have a drop of whatever that is hiding behind the curtain." She had spotted the bottle of sweet sherry which had been hurriedly stuck on the windowsill behind an inadequate metre of chintz'.

Now in her mid-eighties, Queen Elizabeth the Queen Mother remains as indomitable as ever, something she so ably demonstrated during her first visit to Venice at the end of October 1984. Britain's contribution to the Venice in Peril salvation enterprise, both in terms of hard cash and craftsmen supremely skilled in the art of restoration, has been considerable. It was in this connection that Queen Elizabeth spent four days in the city.

On the morning of her arrival the Royal Yacht *Britannia* slowly emerged through the mists to anchor off St Mark's Square and the Queen Mother, as eager as any visitor to catch her first glimpse of Venice, was already out on deck and waving to the small boats manned by local people who came out to meet her. As one writer put it at the time, 'Venice in autumn is particularly magical.' Queen Elizabeth apparently agreed. From a window in the Doge's Palace, looking across the Grand Canal and the island of Giorgio Maggiore with its splendid Palladian church, she turned to say, 'How lovely, and the mist makes Venice look even more romantic, doesn't it?'

Carefully negotiating her steps, the Queen Mother, dressed most often in blue, was helped on and off the royal barge and in and out of water taxis with comparative ease. This aspect of her visit had caused its organizers some anxious moments of anticipation, but the royal visitor was not perturbed.

She walked leisurely through the streets – followed by hordes of cameramen and journalists, tourists and local people – inspecting St Mark's Basilica and this church and that palace; captivated by the decaying magnificence of a city originally built on the mud flats of the Venetian lagoon in the sixth century, and once called *La Serenissima*, the Most Serene Republic. It is, of course, impossible not to be moved by Venice, as witness the works or reminiscences of Byron, Goethe, Henry James, Thomas Mann and countless others; and Queen Elizabeth the Queen Mother was no exception.

Lady Clarke, the wife of former British ambassador Sir Ashley Clarke, told journalists that the Queen Mother had said she hadn't had so much fun for a long time. The 'fun' so clearly included slipping in to Florian's for a cup of tea, while the attendant *papparazzi* squabbled to get yet more pictures, and the traditional, ten-minute gondola ride she took along the busy canals. 'It would have been such a pity to have come here without being able to take a ride on a gondola,' she said afterwards.

As a grandfather King George VI had only known Prince Charles and Princess Anne, and then but briefly. During the intervening years his consort has watched six grandchildren grow up and develop into very distinctive individuals. Moreover she has, to the present day, welcomed the births of four great-grandchildren; Princess Anne's son Peter and daughter Zara, born on 15 May 1981; and Prince Charles' sons William and Henry, or 'Harry' as his parents say he will be known.

For the Prince of Wales, as he wrote in his foreword to Godfrey Talbot's adoringly effusive study of Queen Elizabeth, his grand-mother 'has always been one of those extraordinarily rare people whose touch can turn everything to gold – whether it be putting people at their ease, turning something dull into something amusing, bringing happiness and comfort by her presence or making any house she lives in a unique haven of cosiness and character.'

Princess Anne, who remained a tomboy until her early teens, and who has since managed to retain a refreshing streak of independence, has admitted that in her formative years she didn't go along 'with the family bit', and wasn't quite so close to Queen Elizabeth as her brothers. 'Grandmothers have a feeling for grandsons that is unique', the Princess says, but adds, 'Nobody can refuse her anything so she recruits most of us at some time or another.' Thus far neither Prince Andrew nor his younger brother Prince Edward, have publicly discussed their lives as members of the royal family, so have given no indication of their affection or feelings for their closest relations. All the same, if appearances tell us anything, then they, too, are deeply attached to their indulgent 'Granny'. A small, almost imperceptible indication of their close-ness was glimpsed in 1977, as they carefully escorted her down the steps of St Paul's Cathedral to their waiting carriage, after the Silver Jubilee thanksgiving service.

Princess Margaret's children, David, Viscount Linley and Lady Sarah Armstrong-Jones, have naturally caused Queen Elizabeth some surprise. Infinitely less conservative both in outlook and action than any before them, they represent a new strain of royal progeny. They are what might even be called free spirits. Certainly, with few responsibilities of which to speak, David and Sarah will enjoy most of the privileges, but will ever be free of the constraints that royal rank and the obligations of duty impose on their cousins. For while they are placed in the royal line of succession they are not, strictly speaking, members of the royal family. This means that while each benefits from a private trust fund set up by their parents, neither will be eligible for allowances under the aegis of the Civil List.

Like their contemporaries, the sons and daughters of the Duke of Kent and Princess Alexandra and, in time, the offspring of Princess Anne, the Duke of Gloucester and Prince Michael of Kent, Viscount Linley and Lady Sarah will have no public roles to play in the life of the monarchy. It will therefore fall to them to follow careers of their own choosing. To that end Lord Linley – though seen as an exuberant young man with a definite taste for the high-life – has already revealed himself capable of earning a living as a carpenter. A graduate of the John Makepiece School for Craftsmen in Parnham, Dorset, his wedding present to the Prince and Princess of Wales, for example, was a full-length, light wood dining-table, with frosted glass panels let into the top.

For her part, the lively, immensely likeable Lady Sarah, blessed with natural good looks and a warm, friendly personality, graduated from Camberwell Art College in 1984, intent on finding work to utilize her talents to the full. Indeed she, perhaps more than her brother, is seen to be following in the footsteps of her father and her great-uncle, the late Oliver Messel.

As children both Viscount Linley and Lady Sarah Armstrong-Jones became especially attached to the Queen Mother, and the relationship established in those early days, naturally continues to be reciprocated with no less affection today. One small facet of their lives, however, has irked their grandmother from time to time – the way in which they choose to dress. David Linley's tweed overcoat, at least one size too large, looked amusing and was perhaps worn for effect, but his appearance at a wedding – attended by most of the royal family – with closely-cut hair, dyed blond, definitely did not amuse.

Modern, even bizarre, trends do not appeal to Queen Elizabeth who understandably prefers a more soigné appearance. 'Granny doesn't understand about students' clothes', Sarah reputedly protested when discussing the type of everyday wear widely favoured by most of her generation. Some time later during a lull she reported with a sigh of relief, 'I think Granny has at last stopped going on at me.'

At the beginning of the present Queen's reign it was still customary for members of the royal family to spend Christmas together at Sandringham. By the late 1960s, however, the 'Big House' was no longer quite big enough and the much-multiplied ranks of the Queen's family had to gather at Windsor Castle instead. Christmas is, in fact, the one occasion in the year on which the entire royal family regularly meets *en masse*, and like any other family, there are those who enjoy the close proximity of their relations more than others. There have been times, too, when one member of the family has seen his or her opportunity to air a grievance, while others simply like to doze off after lunch – having first watched the Queen's Christmas Day message to the Commonwealth, it should be said – or take themselves out for a walk.

In 1981 the Christmas gathering had something more to celebrate; the eightieth birthday of Queen Elizabeth's sister-in-law, Princess Alice, Duchess of Gloucester, mother of the present Duke and the widow of Prince Henry, George VI's younger brother 'Harry'. Three years later, on 21 December 1984, the holiday season was opened at Windsor on yet another high note, this time the christening of a new Prince Harry, the fourth of Queen Elizabeth's great-grandchildren. Like his elder brother, the Prince was born at St Mary's Hospital, Paddington at 4.20 p.m. on 15 September. Fourteen weeks later, the christening service, a private affair as royal christenings always are, took place in St George's Chapel. The scene of many a royal wedding during the reigns of Queen Victoria and King Edward VII and, of course, the resting-place of kings and queens, the last recorded royal christening there was that of Prince Leopold of Battenberg, in 1889.

Turning from the youngest prince, let us take one final look at the most senior member of the royal family. For more than sixty years Queen Elizabeth the Queen Mother has fulfilled three quite separate, albeit inter-related roles in the service of the Crown.

Her first appearance as a member of the royal family was as Duchess of York. When she married 'Bertie' in 1923, she and her husband naturally envisaged a full life ahead of them, but one in which the obligations of public service would be carefully balanced against the quiet pleasures of a jealously guarded home life. For thirteen years the Duke and Duchess of York were able to maintain that balance. Then the events in 1936, when the Duke was catapulted from second in succession to King of England, not only violated their personal world, but the system of which they were an integral part. Save for this trauma the Yorks' well-ordered existence may have seen them safely and comfortably into old age. Who can say?

The aim of King George VI and Queen Elizabeth, once they had faced the gim realities of the Abdication, was 'to make amends' for so violent a convulsion in the life of the nation. In the event they did much more. As Prince of Wales, King Edward VIII had indisputably proved himself the 'People's Prince', but George VI for all his apparent disadvantages became the 'People's King', his consort very much the 'People's Queen'.

In retrospect there is an almost pioneering spirit about their reign: for while King George and Queen Elizabeth re-established the stability of the monarchy and helped free it from fierce reactionary influences, so they invested it with human qualities recognizable to the ordinary man. Indeed, it has been suggested that the image of the King and Queen skipping hand in hand down a Buckingham Palace corridor enshrines the essential humanness not only of their reign, but of their story.

With the King's death in February 1952, his widow assumed her third and final role, that of Queen Dowager, or as she preferred, Queen Mother.

In much the same way that the allure of the monarchy itself defies positive identification, so the full extent of Queen Elizabeth's personal contribution to its survival remains an intangible quantity, contemptuous of close analysis.

Nevertheless the Queen Mother's professionalism and her indisputable artistry as a diplomat have ensured her a popularity that has always been impervious to criticism and exempt from the caprices of public opinion. Indeed never before has so prominent a royal figure been held in such high esteem as the woman whom the nation knows as the 'Queen Mum'.

# Select Bibliography

The author and publishers gratefully acknowledge permission to quote from certain specific books listed below: *King George VI: His Life and Reign* by Sir John Wheeler-Bennett; *Queen Mary* by James Pope Hennessy; *Queen Elizabeth the Queen Mother* by Dorothy Laird; *The Queen Mother* by Elizabeth Longford; *King George V* by Kenneth Rose; and *A King's Story* by His Royal Highness The Duke of Windsor.

The following publications have been particularly useful in the writing of this book:

Theo Aronson *Royal Family: Years of Transition* (John Murray, 1983)

John W. Wheeler-Bennett *King George VI: His Life and Reign* (Macmillan, 1958)

Aubrey Buxton *The King and His Country* (Longmans, Green & Co, 1955)

Helen Cathcart *The Queen Mother Herself* (Hamlyn, 1980)

Frances Donaldson *King George VI and Queen Elizabeth* (Weidenfeld & Nicolson, 1977)

H.C. Dent (Ed) *Milestones to The Silver Jubilee* (Halcyon Book Company, 1935)

Andrew Duncan *The Reality of Monarchy* (William Heinemann, 1970)

James Pope Hennessy *Queen Mary* (George Allen and Unwin, 1959)

Robert Rhodes James (Ed) *Chips: The Diaries of Sir Henry Channon*

(Penguin, 1984)

Dorothy Laird *Queen Elizabeth the Queen Mother* (Hodder & Stoughton, 1966)

Elizabeth Longford *Victoria R.I.* (Weidenfeld & Nicolson, 1964)

Elizabeth Longford *The Queen Mother* (Weidenfeld & Nicolson, 1981)

Elizabeth Longford *Elizabeth R* (Weidenfeld & Nicolson, 1983)

Ann Morrow *The Queen Mother* (Granada, 1984)

Diana Mosley *The Duchess of Windsor* (Sidgwick & Jackson, 1980)

Stanley Olson (Ed) *Harold Nicolson Diaries and Letters 1930-1964* (Penguin, 1980)

Graham Payn and Sheridan Morley *The Noel Coward Diaries* (Weidenfeld & Nicolson, 1982)

Kenneth Rose *King George V* (Papermac/Macmillan, 1983)

Meryle Secrest *Kenneth Clark* (Weidenfeld & Nicolson, 1984)

David Sinclair *Snowdon* (Proteus, 1982)

Christopher Warwick *Two Centuries of Royal Weddings* (Arthur Barker, 1980)

Christopher Warwick *Princess Margaret* (Weidenfeld & Nicolson, 1983)

HRH The Duke of Windsor *A King's Story* (Cassell & Company, 1951)

Philip Ziegler *Mountbatten* (Collins, 1985)

*The Times*

*The Daily Telegraph*

The Illustrated London News

Majesty – The Monthly Royal Review

# Table I

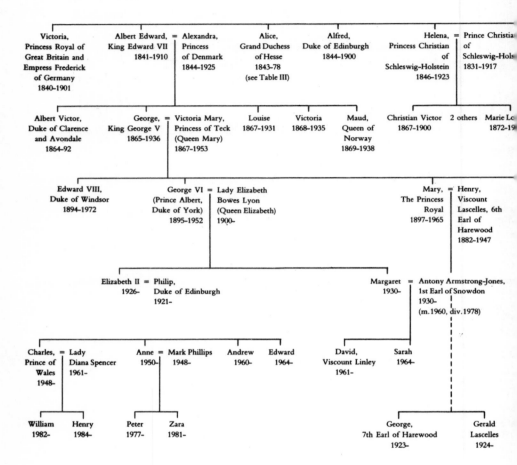

Queen Victoria
1819-190

Victoria,
Princess Royal of
Great Britain and
Empress Frederick
of Germany
1840-1901

Albert Edward, = Alexandra,
King Edward VII      Princess
1841-1910             of Denmark
                      1844-1925

Alice,
Grand Duchess
of Hesse
1843-78
(see Table III)

Alfred,
Duke of Edinburgh
1844-1900

Helena, = Prince Christia
Princess Christian   of
of                   Schleswig-Hols
Schleswig-Holstein   1831-1917
1846-1923

Albert Victor,
Duke of Clarence
and Avondale
1864-92

George, = Victoria Mary,
King George V   Princess of Teck
1865-1936      (Queen Mary)
               1867-1953

Louise
1867-1931

Victoria
1868-1935

Maud,
Queen of
Norway
1869-1938

Christian Victor
1867-1900

2 others

Marie Lo
1872-19

Edward VIII,
Duke of Windsor
1894-1972

George VI = Lady Elizabeth
(Prince Albert,   Bowes Lyon
Duke of York)    (Queen Elizabeth)
1895-1952        1900-

Mary, = Henry,
The Princess   Viscount
Royal          Lascelles, 6th
1897-1965      Earl of
               Harewood
               1882-1947

Elizabeth II = Philip,
1926-          Duke of Edinburgh
               1921-

Margaret = Antony Armstrong-Jones,
1930-        1st Earl of Snowdon
             1930-
             (m.1960, div.1978)

Charles, = Lady
Prince of   Diana Spencer
Wales       1961-
1948-

Anne = Mark Phillips
1950-   1948-

Andrew
1960-

Edward
1964-

David,
Viscount Linley
1961-

Sarah
1964-

William
1982-

Henry
1984-

Peter
1977-

Zara
1981-

George,
7th Earl of Harewood
1923-

Gerald
Lascelles
1924-

Prince Albert of Saxe-Coburg-Gotha
1819-61

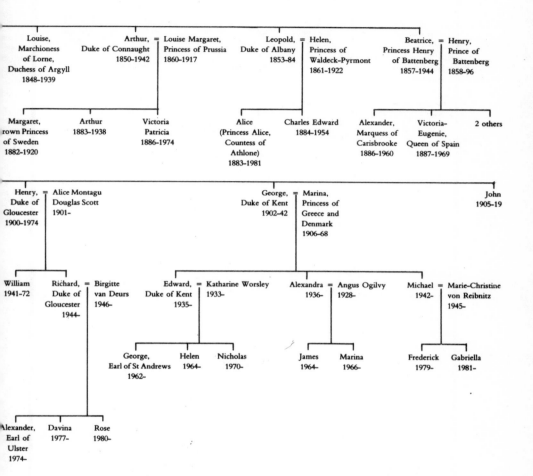

Louise,
Marchioness
of Lorne,
Duchess of Argyll
1848-1939

Arthur,
Duke of Connaught
1850-1942

= Louise Margaret,
Princess of Prussia
1860-1917

Leopold, = Helen,
Duke of Albany
1853-84

Princess of
Waldeck-Pyrmont
1861-1922

Beatrice, = Henry,
Princess Henry
of Battenberg
1857-1944

Prince of
Battenberg
1858-96

Margaret,
Crown Princess
of Sweden
1882-1920

Arthur
1883-1938

Victoria
Patricia
1886-1974

Alice
(Princess Alice,
Countess of
Athlone)
1883-1981

Charles Edward
1884-1954

Alexander,
Marquess of
Carisbrooke
1886-1960

Victoria-
Eugenie,
Queen of Spain
1887-1969

2 others

Henry, = Alice Montagu
Duke of
Gloucester
1900-1974

Douglas Scott
1901-

George, = Marina,
Duke of Kent
1902-42

Princess of
Greece and
Denmark
1906-68

John
1905-19

William
1941-72

Richard, = Birgitte
Duke of
Gloucester
1944-

van Deurs
1946-

Edward, = Katharine Worsley
Duke of Kent
1935-

1933-

Alexandra = Angus Ogilvy
1936-

1928-

Michael = Marie-Christine
1942-

von Reibnitz
1945-

George,
Earl of St Andrews
1962-

Helen
1964-

Nicholas
1970-

James
1964-

Marina
1966-

Frederick
1979-

Gabriella
1981-

Alexander,
Earl of
Ulster
1974-

Davina
1977-

Rose
1980-

# Table II

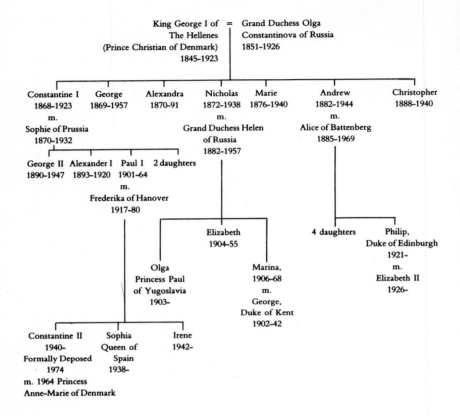

King George I of = Grand Duchess Olga
The Hellenes    Constantinova of Russia
(Prince Christian of Denmark)    1851–1926
1845–1923

| Constantine I | George | Alexandra | Nicholas | Marie | Andrew | Christopher |
|---|---|---|---|---|---|---|
| 1868–1923 | 1869–1957 | 1870–91 | 1872–1938 | 1876–1940 | 1882–1944 | 1888–1940 |
| m. | | | m. | | m. | |
| Sophie of Prussia | | | Grand Duchess Helen | | Alice of Battenberg | |
| 1870–1932 | | | of Russia | | 1885–1969 | |
| | | | 1882–1957 | | | |

George II   Alexander I   Paul I   2 daughters
1890–1947   1893–1920   1901–64
m.
Frederika of Hanover
1917–80

Elizabeth
1904–55

4 daughters        Philip,
Duke of Edinburgh
1921–
m.
Elizabeth II
1926–

Olga
Princess Paul
of Yugoslavia
1903–

Marina,
1906–68
m.
George,
Duke of Kent
1902–42

Constantine II   Sophia   Irene
1940–   Queen of   1942–
Formally Deposed   Spain
1974   1938–
m. 1964 Princess
Anne-Marie of Denmark

# Table III

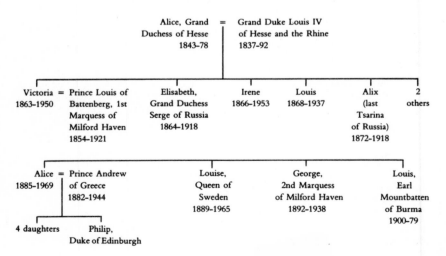

Alice, Grand = Grand Duke Louis IV
Duchess of Hesse   of Hesse and the Rhine
1843–78   1837–92

| Victoria = Prince Louis of | Elisabeth, | Irene | Louis | Alix | 2 |
|---|---|---|---|---|---|
| 1863–1950 Battenberg, 1st | Grand Duchess | 1866–1953 | 1868–1937 | (last | others |
| Marquess of | Serge of Russia | | | Tsarina | |
| Milford Haven | 1864–1918 | | | of Russia) | |
| 1854–1921 | | | | 1872–1918 | |

Alice = Prince Andrew
1885–1969   of Greece
1882–1944

Louise,
Queen of
Sweden
1889–1965

George,
2nd Marquess
of Milford Haven
1892–1938

Louis,
Earl
Mountbatten
of Burma
1900–79

4 daughters        Philip,
Duke of Edinburgh

# Index

211